ONE CUP at a TIME

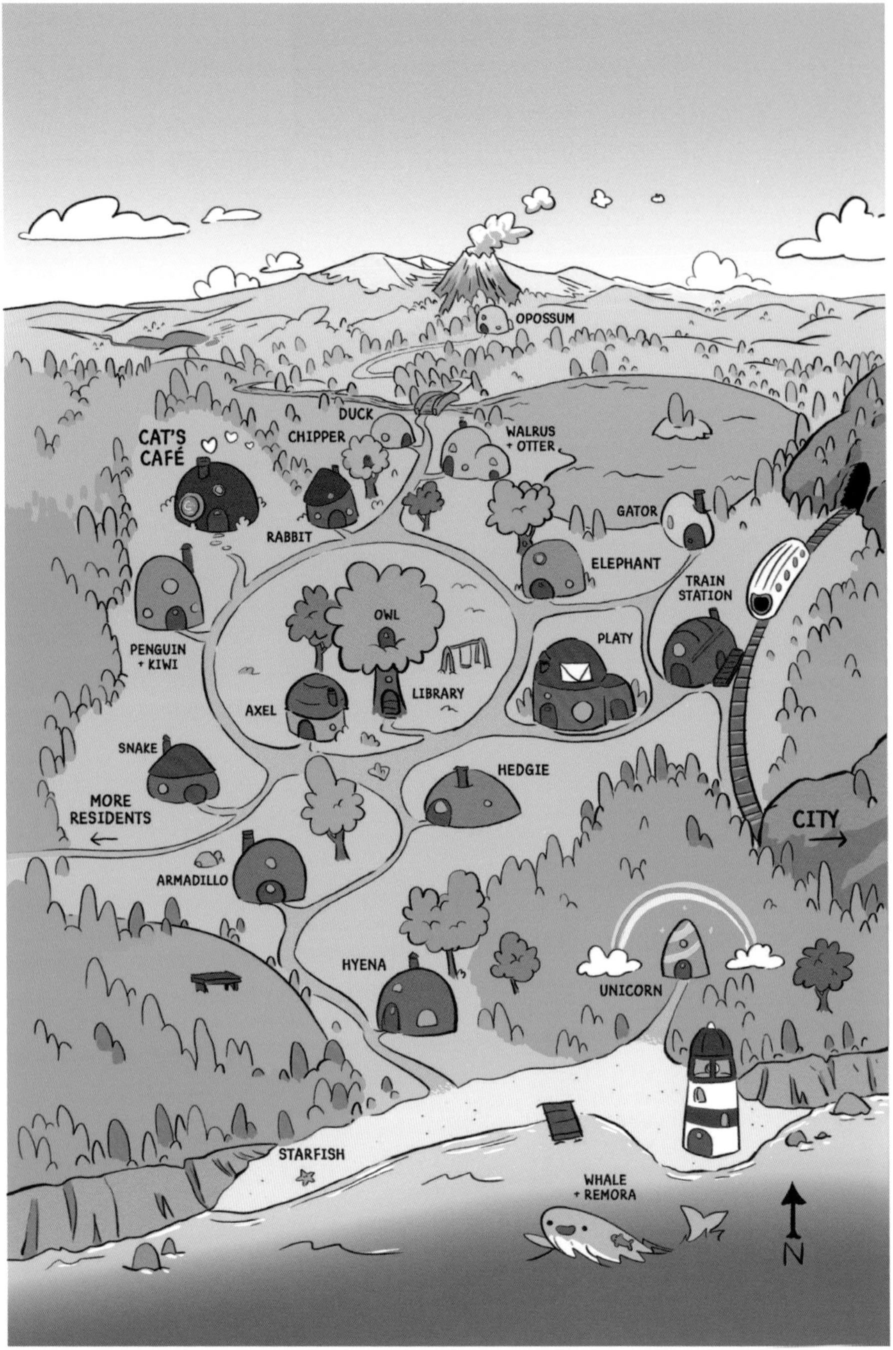
OPOSSUM
DUCK
CHIPPER
CAT'S CAFÉ
WALRUS + OTTER
GATOR
RABBIT
ELEPHANT
TRAIN STATION
OWL
PLATY
PENGUIN + KIWI
LIBRARY
AXEL
SNAKE
HEDGIE
MORE RESIDENTS
CITY
ARMADILLO
HYENA
UNICORN
STARFISH
WHALE + REMORA
N

ONE CUP at a TIME

a Cat's Café collection

MATT TARPLEY

Andrews McMeel
PUBLISHING®

FOR YOU

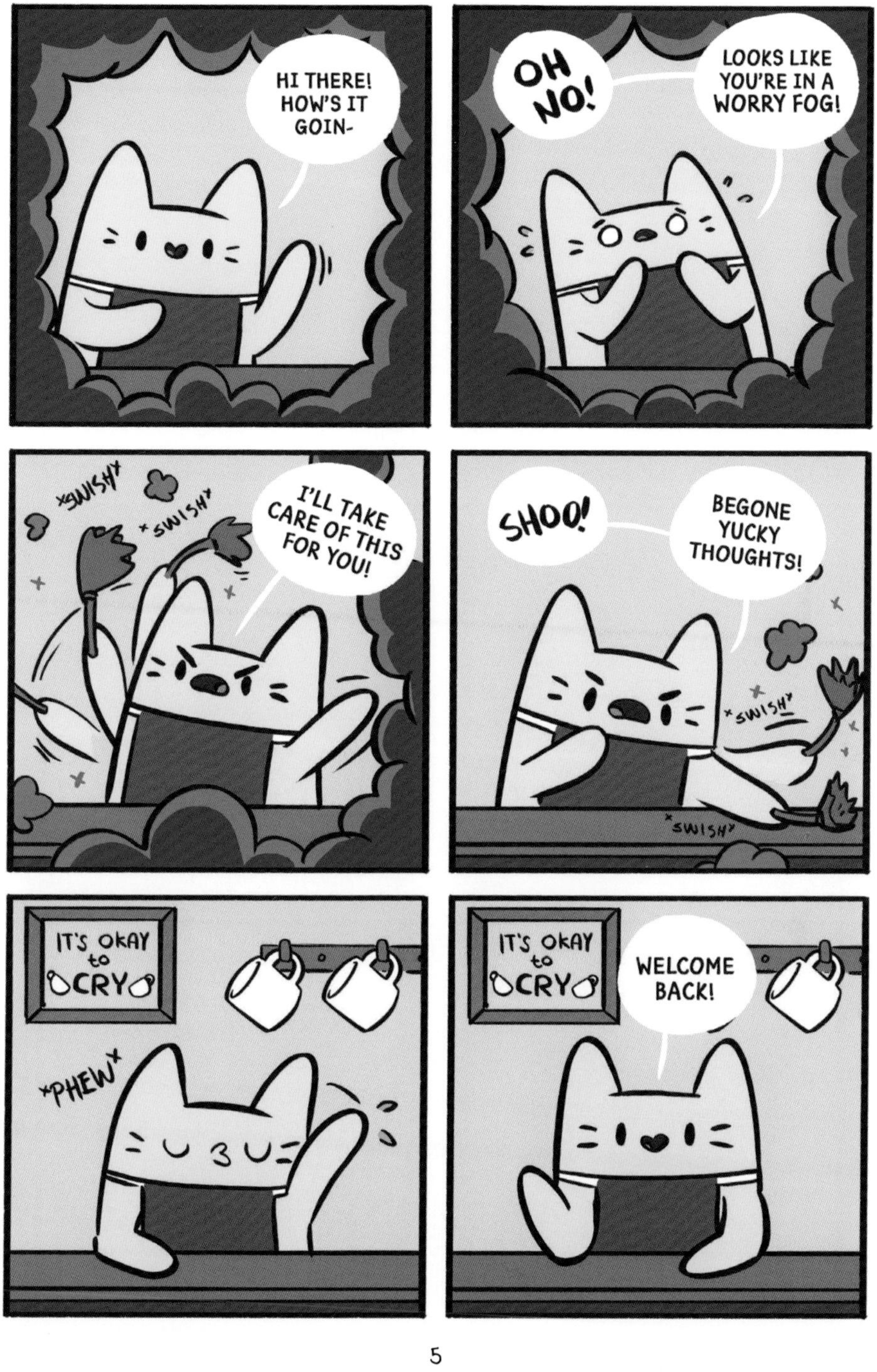
HI THERE! HOW'S IT GOIN-
OH NO!
LOOKS LIKE YOU'RE IN A WORRY FOG!
SWISH
SWISH
I'LL TAKE CARE OF THIS FOR YOU!
SHOO!
BEGONE YUCKY THOUGHTS!
SWISH
SWISH
IT'S OKAY to CRY
PHEW
IT'S OKAY to CRY
WELCOME BACK!

CELEBRATE YOUR WINS!

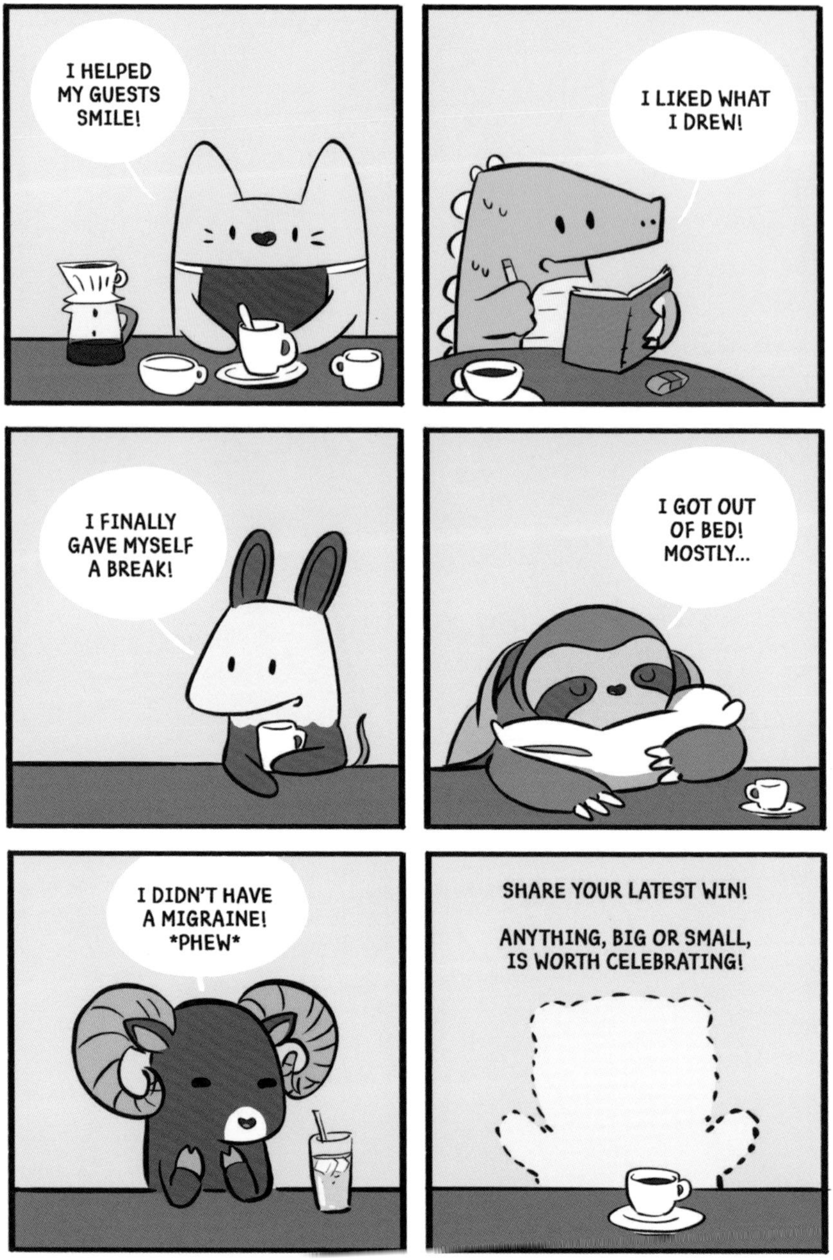
I HELPED MY GUESTS SMILE!
I LIKED WHAT I DREW!
I FINALLY GAVE MYSELF A BREAK!
I GOT OUT OF BED! MOSTLY...
I DIDN'T HAVE A MIGRAINE! *PHEW*
SHARE YOUR LATEST WIN!
ANYTHING, BIG OR SMALL, IS WORTH CELEBRATING!

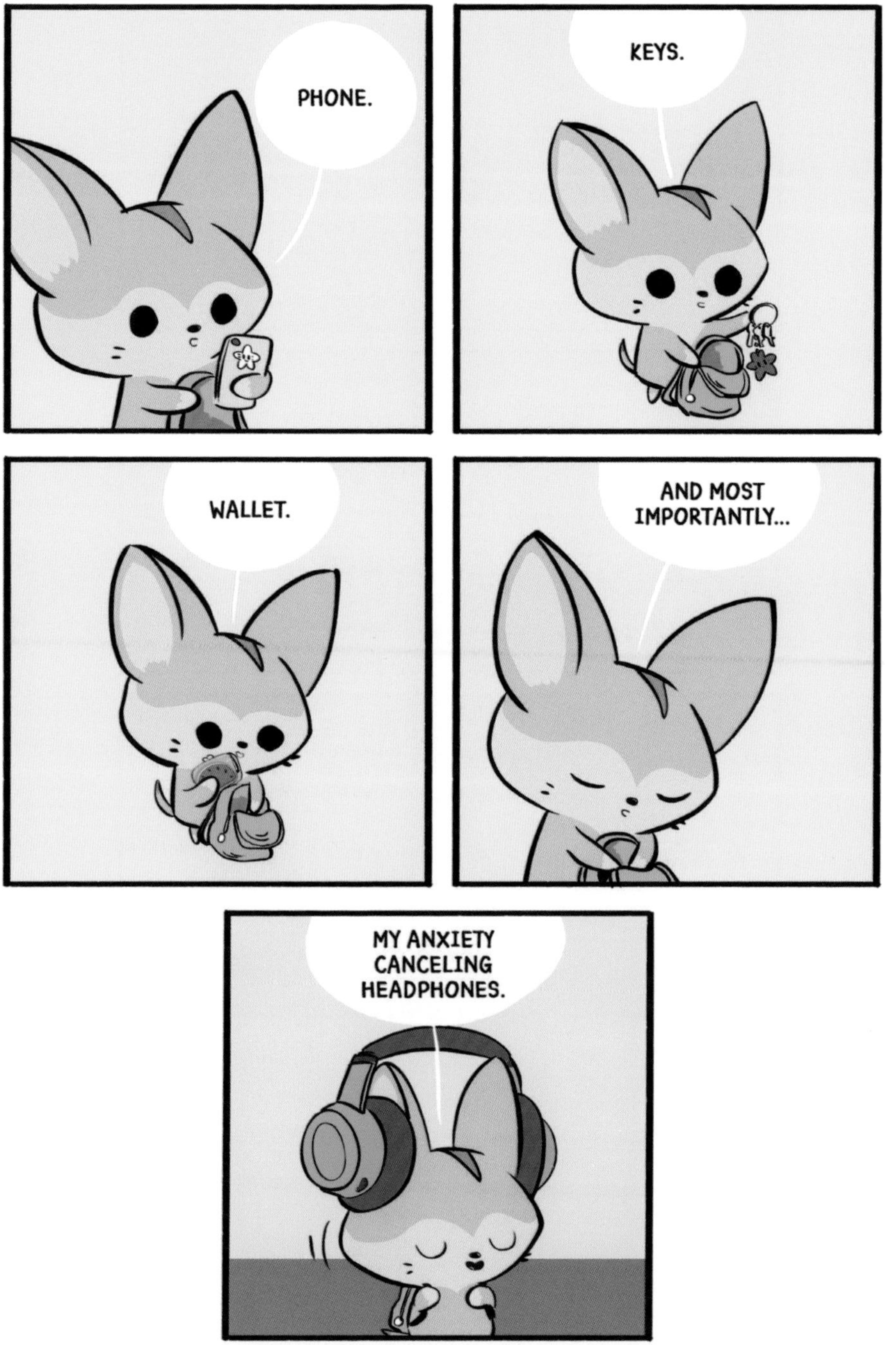
PHONE.
KEYS.
WALLET.
AND MOST IMPORTANTLY...
MY ANXIETY CANCELING HEADPHONES.

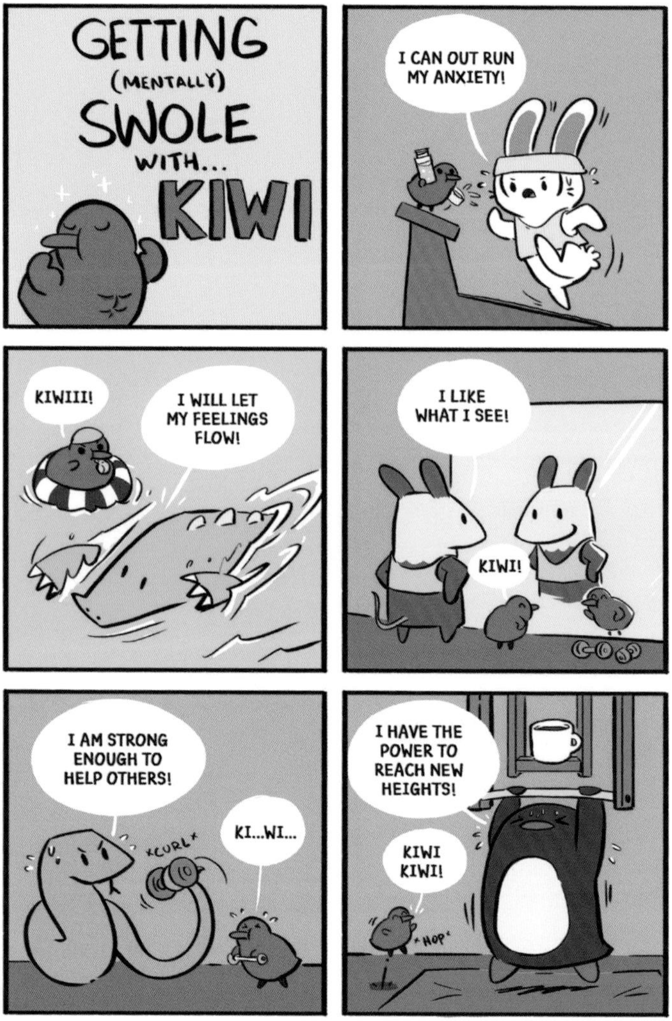
GETTING (MENTALLY) SWOLE WITH... KIWI
I CAN OUT RUN MY ANXIETY!
KIWIII!
I WILL LET MY FEELINGS FLOW!
I LIKE WHAT I SEE!
KIWI!
I AM STRONG ENOUGH TO HELP OTHERS!
CURL
KI...WI...
I HAVE THE POWER TO REACH NEW HEIGHTS!
KIWI KIWI!
HOP

KIWI KIWI!

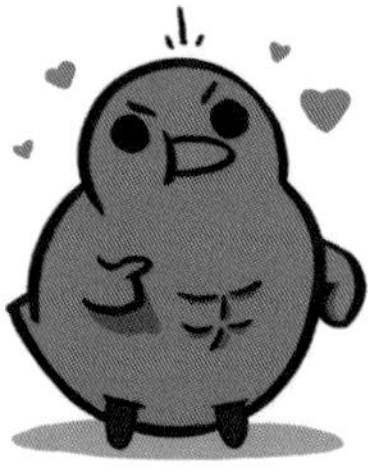

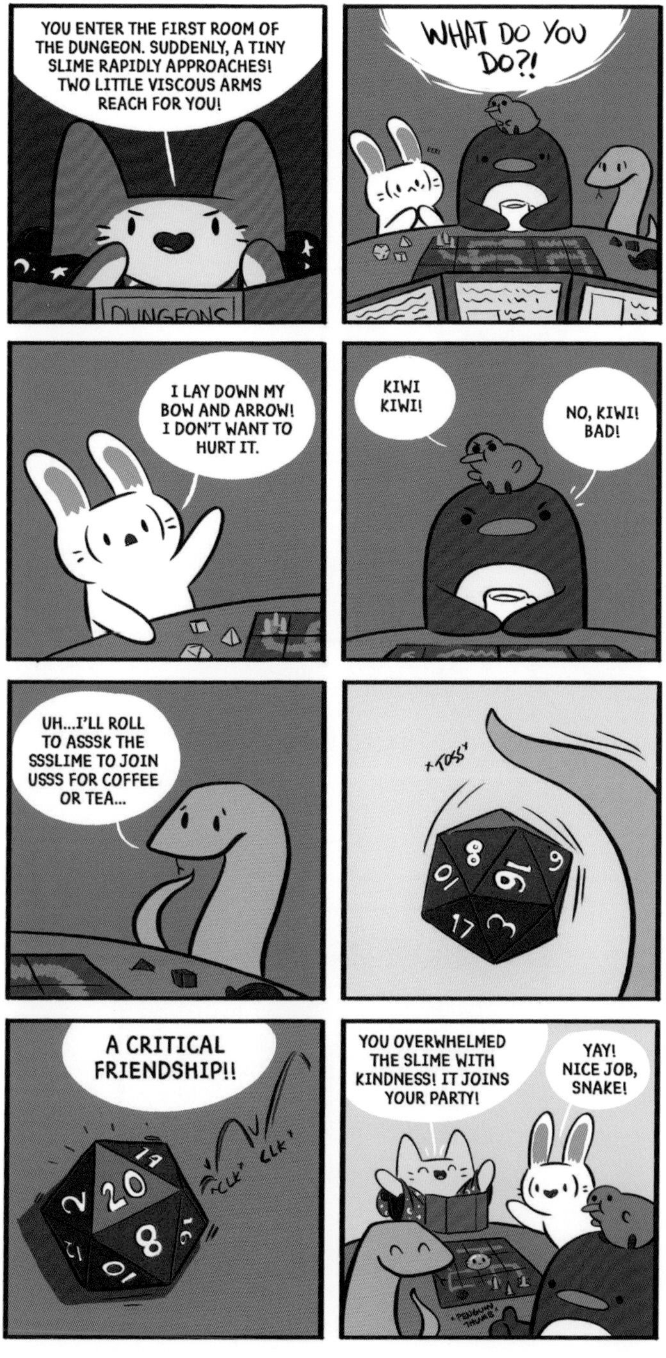

YOU ENTER THE FIRST ROOM OF THE DUNGEON. SUDDENLY, A TINY SLIME RAPIDLY APPROACHES! TWO LITTLE VISCOUS ARMS REACH FOR YOU!
DUNGEONS
WHAT DO YOU DO?!
I LAY DOWN MY BOW AND ARROW! I DON'T WANT TO HURT IT.
KIWI KIWI!
NO, KIWI! BAD!
UH...I'LL ROLL TO ASSSK THE SSSLIME TO JOIN USSS FOR COFFEE OR TEA...
TOSS
A CRITICAL FRIENDSHIP!!
CLK CLK*
YOU OVERWHELMED THE SLIME WITH KINDNESS! IT JOINS YOUR PARTY!
YAY! NICE JOB, SNAKE!
PENGUIN THUMB

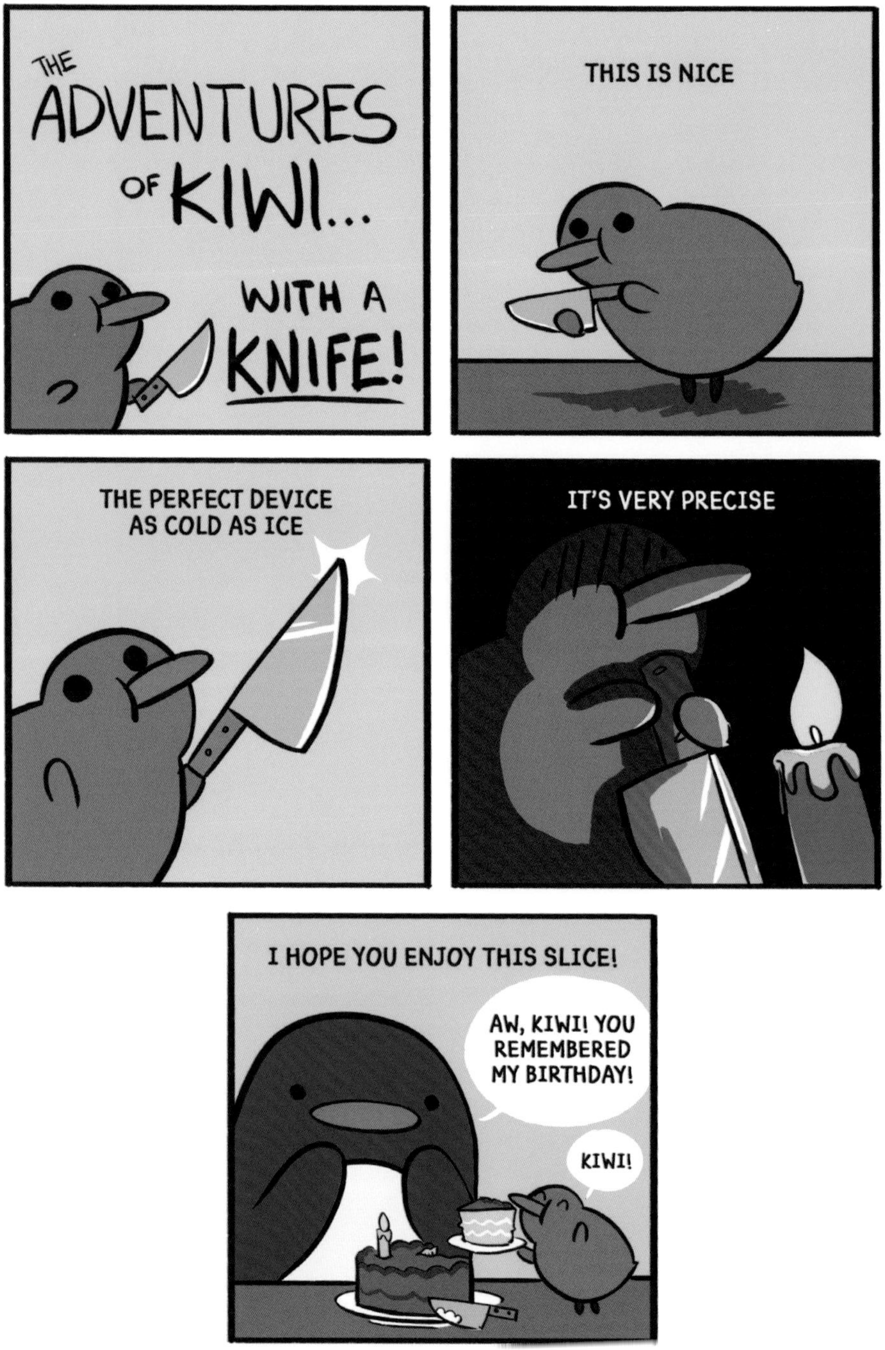
THE ADVENTURES OF KIWI...
WITH A KNIFE!
THIS IS NICE
THE PERFECT DEVICE AS COLD AS ICE
IT'S VERY PRECISE
I HOPE YOU ENJOY THIS SLICE!
AW, KIWI! YOU REMEMBERED MY BIRTHDAY!
KIWI!

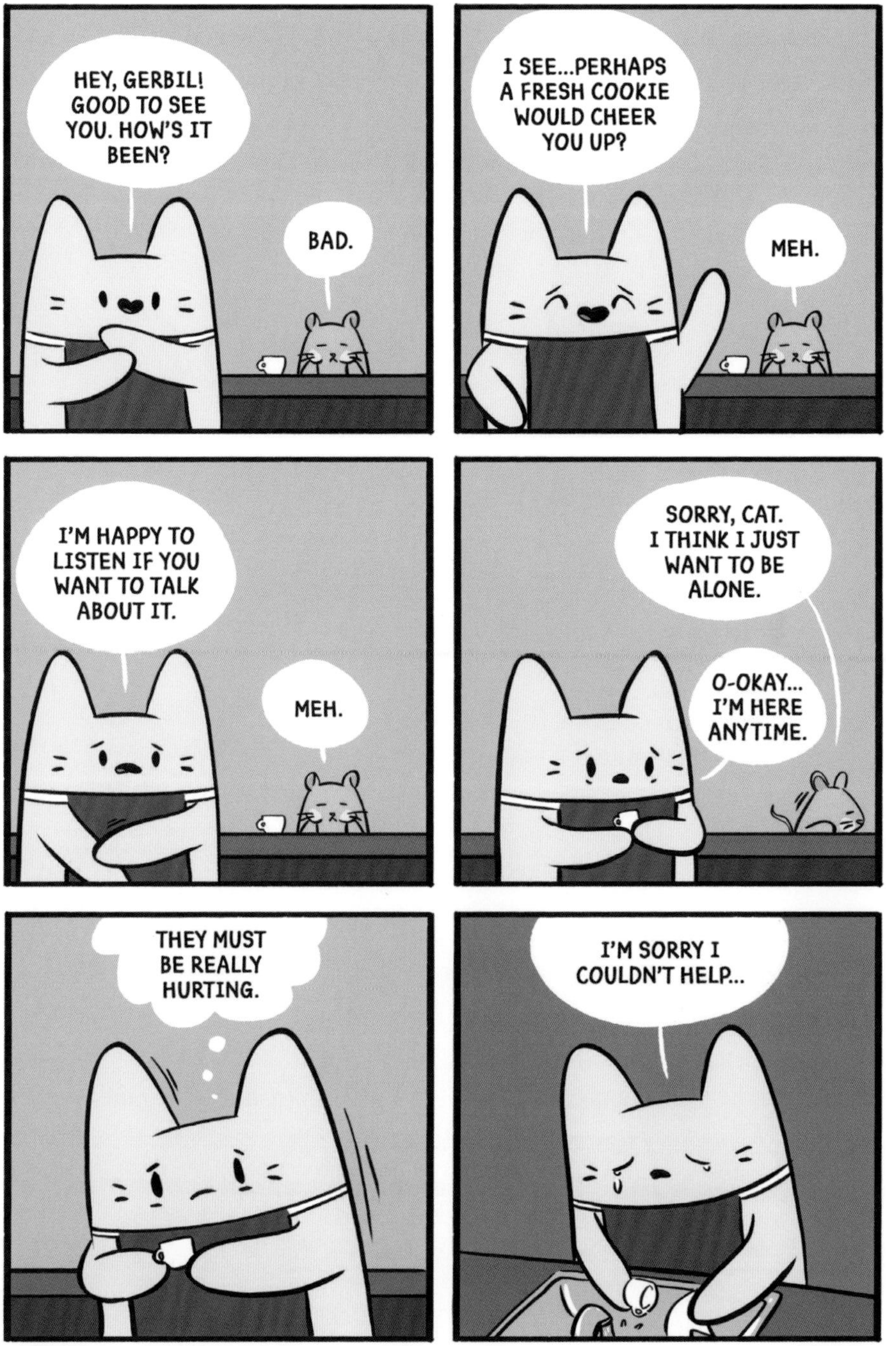
HEY, GERBIL! GOOD TO SEE YOU. HOW'S IT BEEN?
BAD.
I SEE...PERHAPS A FRESH COOKIE WOULD CHEER YOU UP?
MEH.
I'M HAPPY TO LISTEN IF YOU WANT TO TALK ABOUT IT.
MEH.
SORRY, CAT. I THINK I JUST WANT TO BE ALONE.
O-OKAY... I'M HERE ANYTIME.
THEY MUST BE REALLY HURTING.
I'M SORRY I COULDN'T HELP...

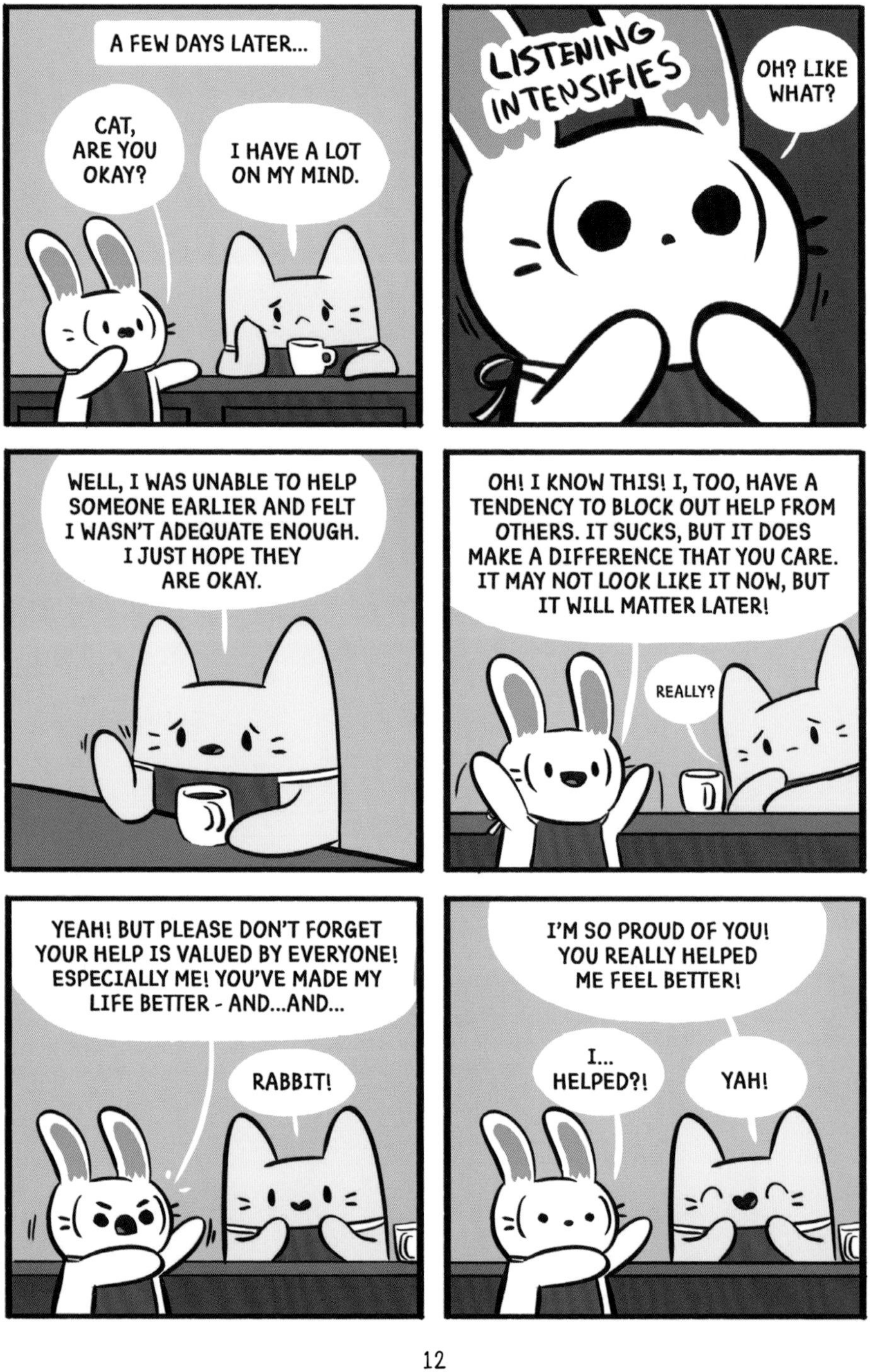
A FEW DAYS LATER...
CAT, ARE YOU OKAY?
I HAVE A LOT ON MY MIND.
LISTENING INTENSIFIES
OH? LIKE WHAT?
WELL, I WAS UNABLE TO HELP SOMEONE EARLIER AND FELT I WASN'T ADEQUATE ENOUGH. I JUST HOPE THEY ARE OKAY.
OH! I KNOW THIS! I, TOO, HAVE A TENDENCY TO BLOCK OUT HELP FROM OTHERS. IT SUCKS, BUT IT DOES MAKE A DIFFERENCE THAT YOU CARE. IT MAY NOT LOOK LIKE IT NOW, BUT IT WILL MATTER LATER!
REALLY?
YEAH! BUT PLEASE DON'T FORGET YOUR HELP IS VALUED BY EVERYONE! ESPECIALLY ME! YOU'VE MADE MY LIFE BETTER - AND...AND...
RABBIT!
I'M SO PROUD OF YOU! YOU REALLY HELPED ME FEEL BETTER!
I... HELPED?!
YAH!

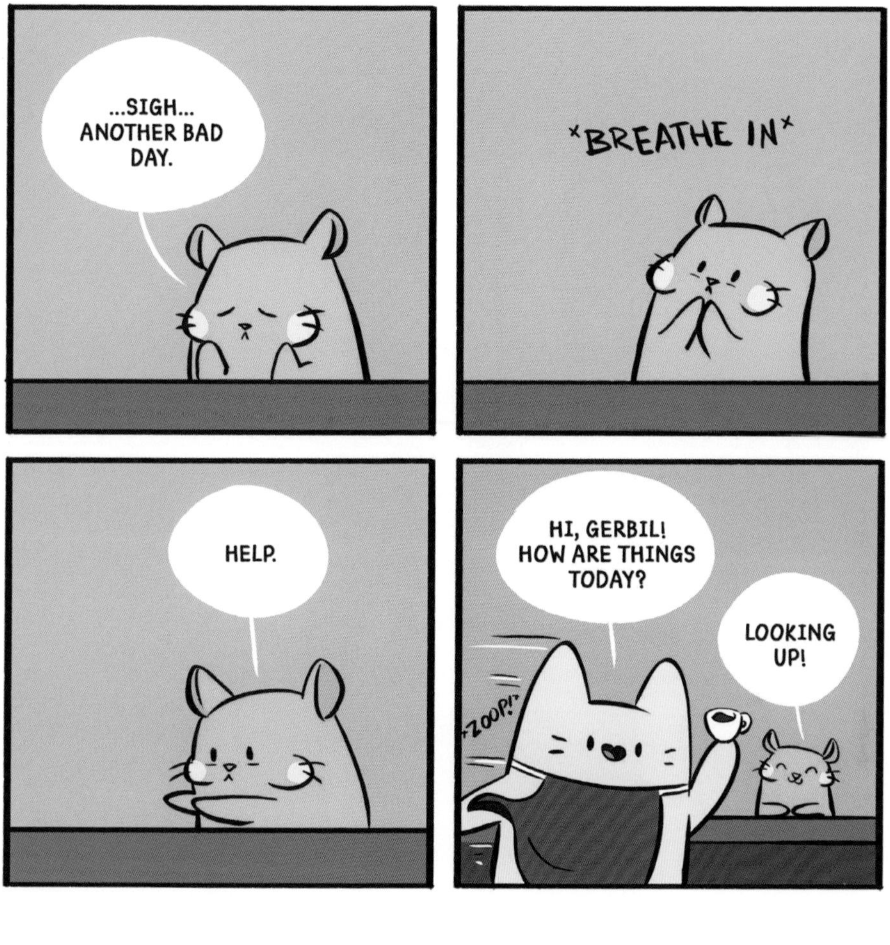
...SIGH... ANOTHER BAD DAY.
BREATHE IN
HELP.
HI, GERBIL! HOW ARE THINGS TODAY?
ZOOP!
LOOKING UP!

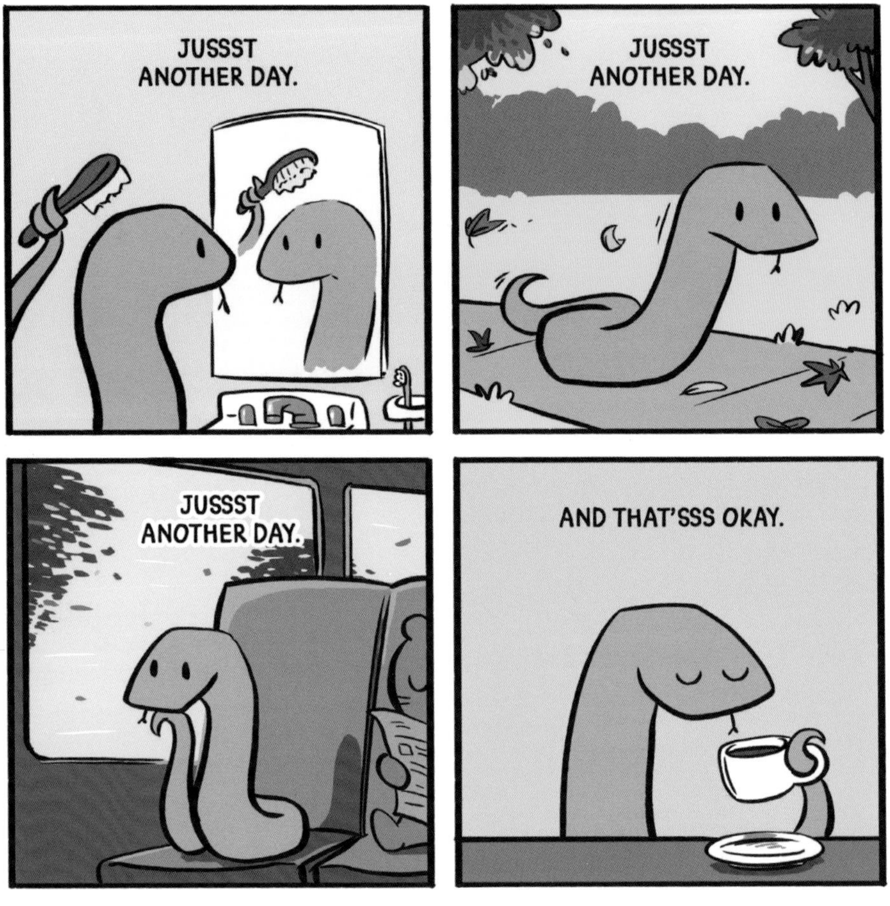
JUSSST ANOTHER DAY.
JUSSST ANOTHER DAY.
JUSSST ANOTHER DAY.
AND THAT'SSS OKAY.

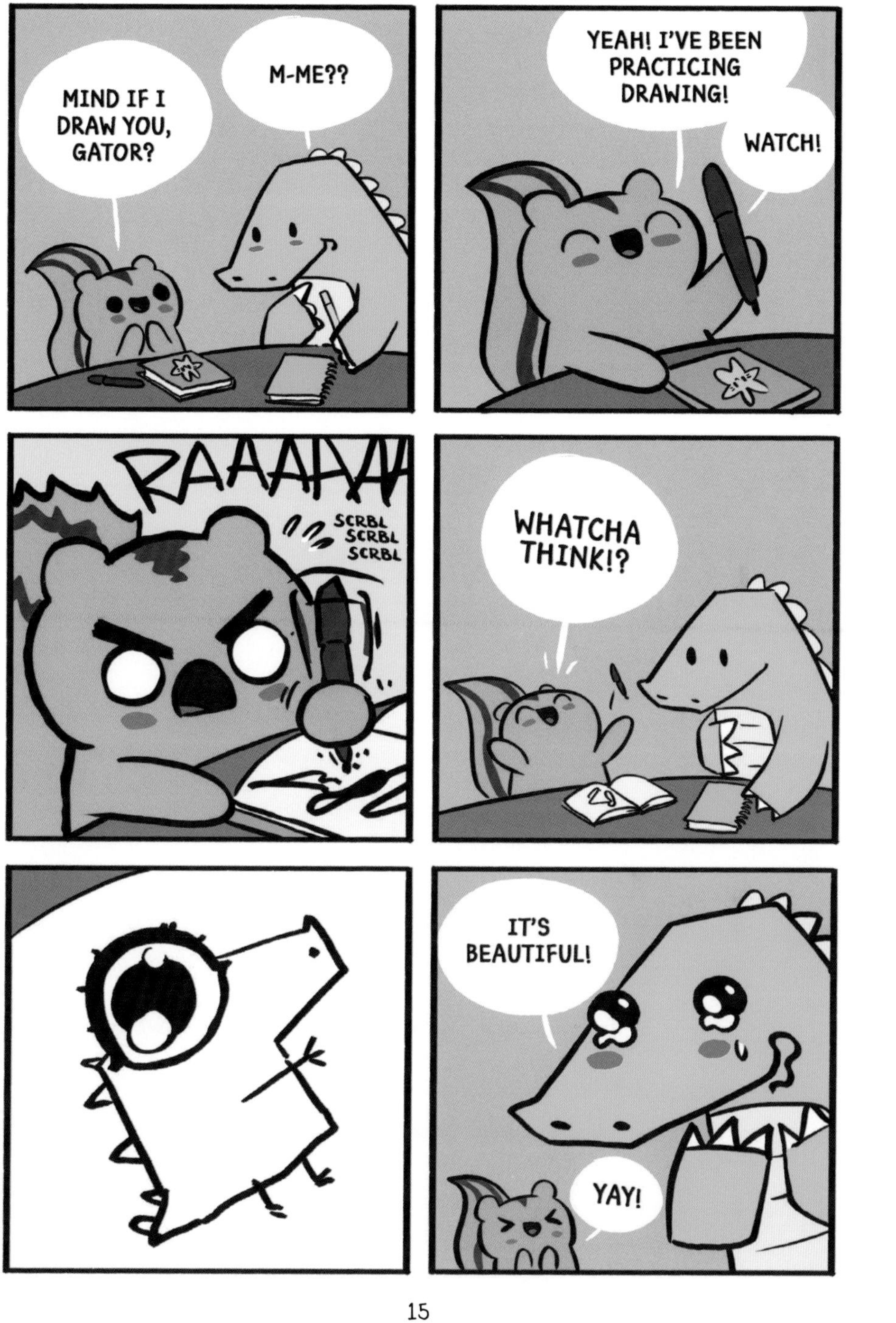
MIND IF I DRAW YOU, GATOR?
M-ME??
YEAH! I'VE BEEN PRACTICING DRAWING!
WATCH!
RAAAH
SCRBL SCRBL SCRBL
WHATCHA THINK!?
IT'S BEAUTIFUL!
YAY!

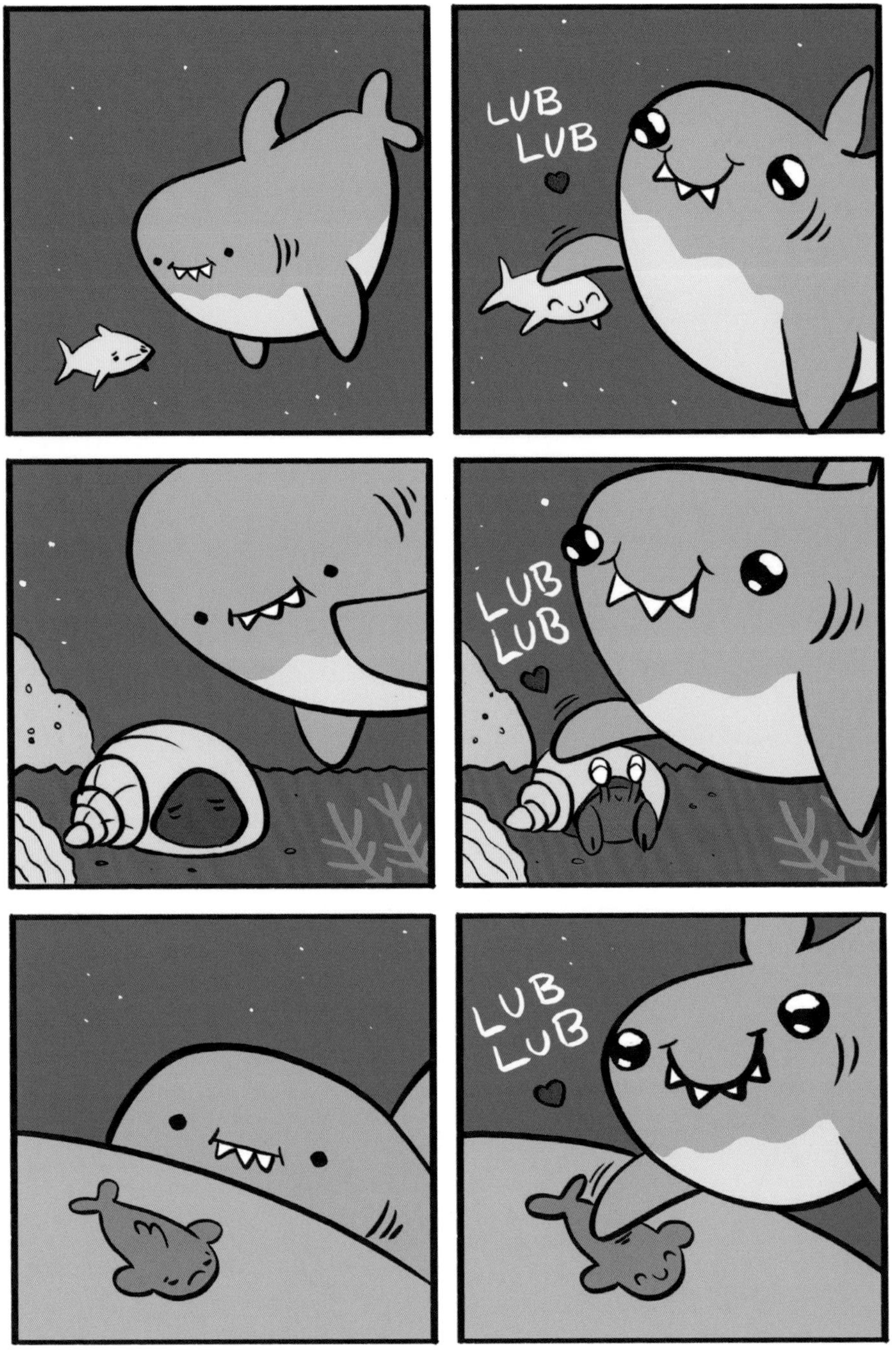
LUB LUB
LUB LUB
LUB LUB

THE TYPES OF RAIN

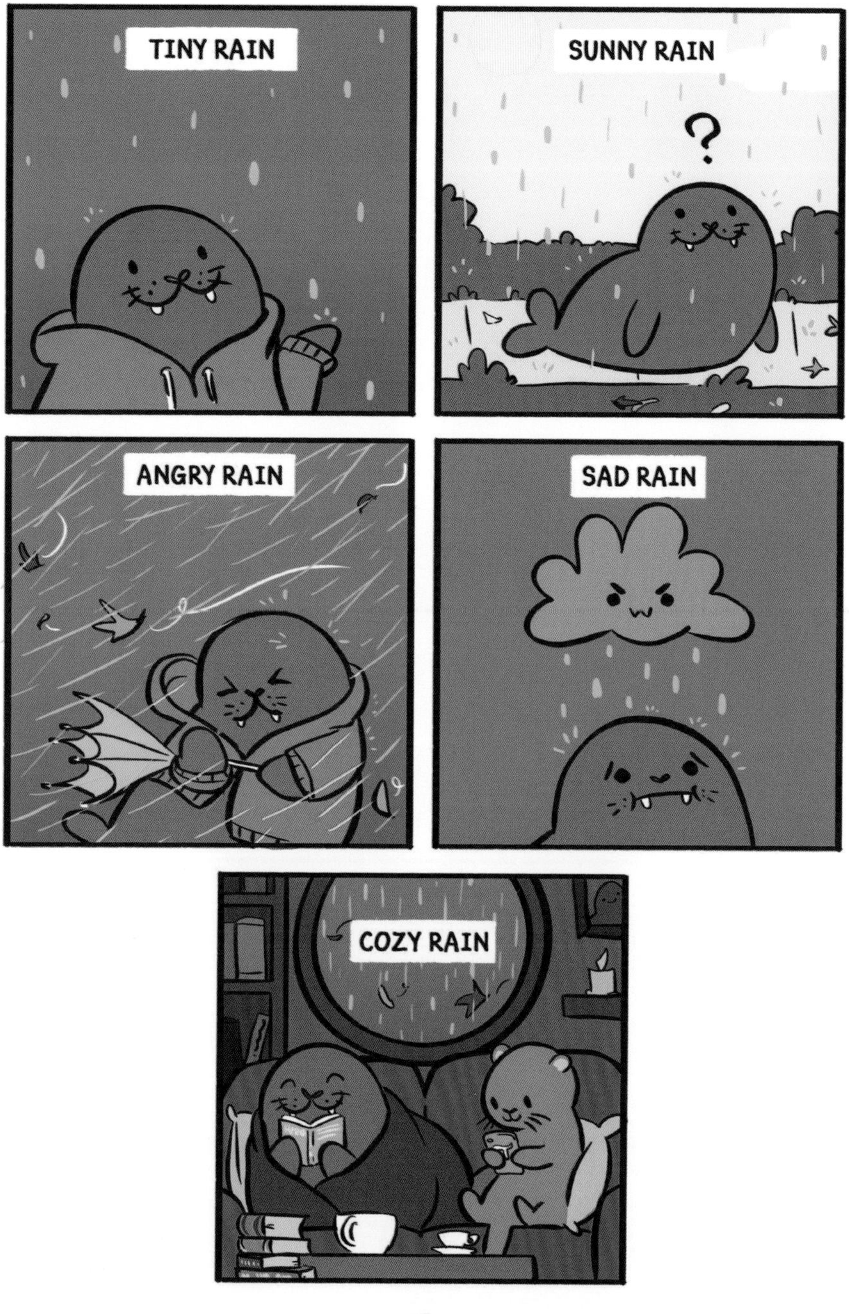

TINY RAIN
SUNNY RAIN
?
ANGRY RAIN
SAD RAIN
COZY RAIN

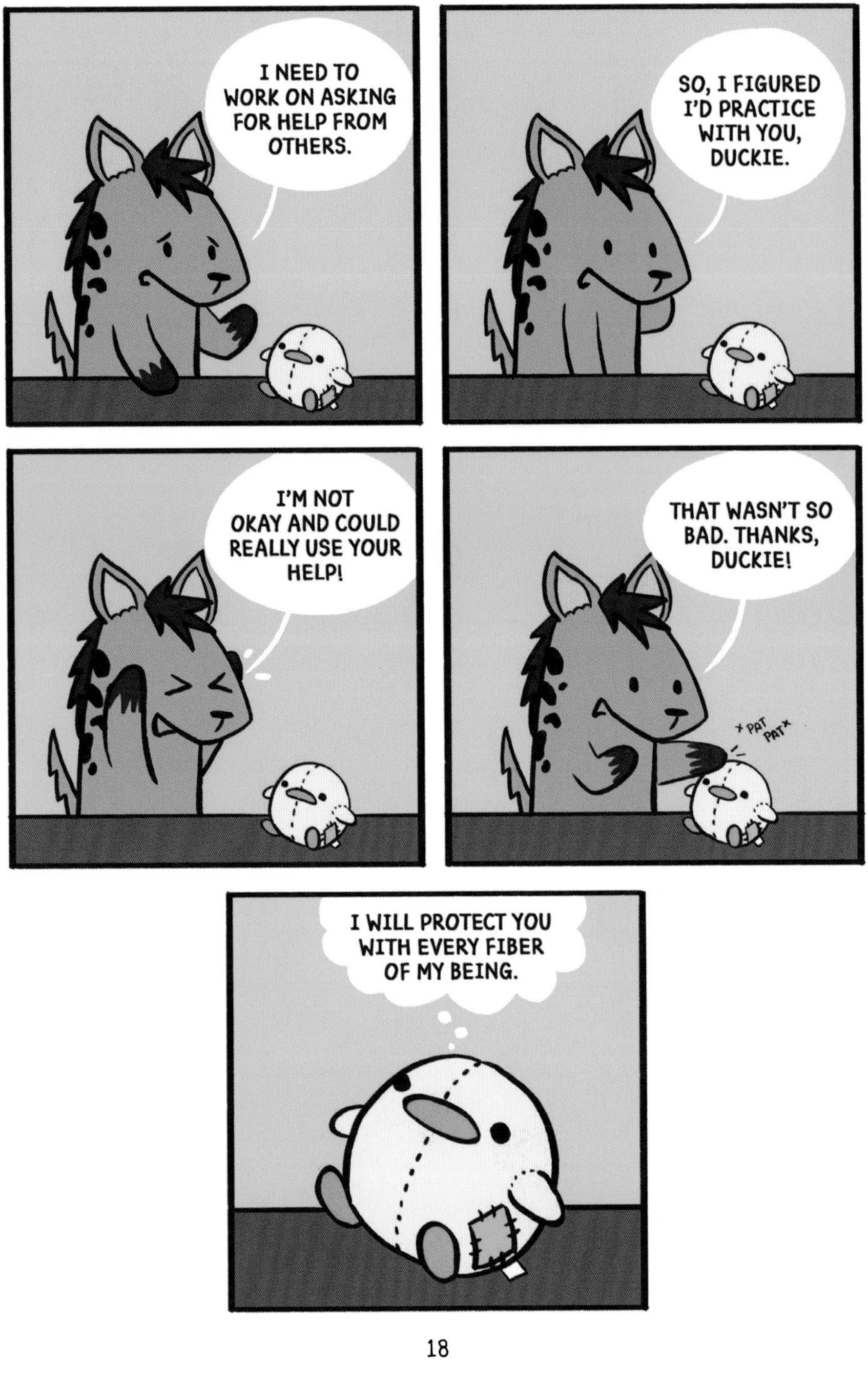
I NEED TO WORK ON ASKING FOR HELP FROM OTHERS.
SO, I FIGURED I'D PRACTICE WITH YOU, DUCKIE.
I'M NOT OKAY AND COULD REALLY USE YOUR HELP!
THAT WASN'T SO BAD. THANKS, DUCKIE!
PAT PAT
I WILL PROTECT YOU WITH EVERY FIBER OF MY BEING.

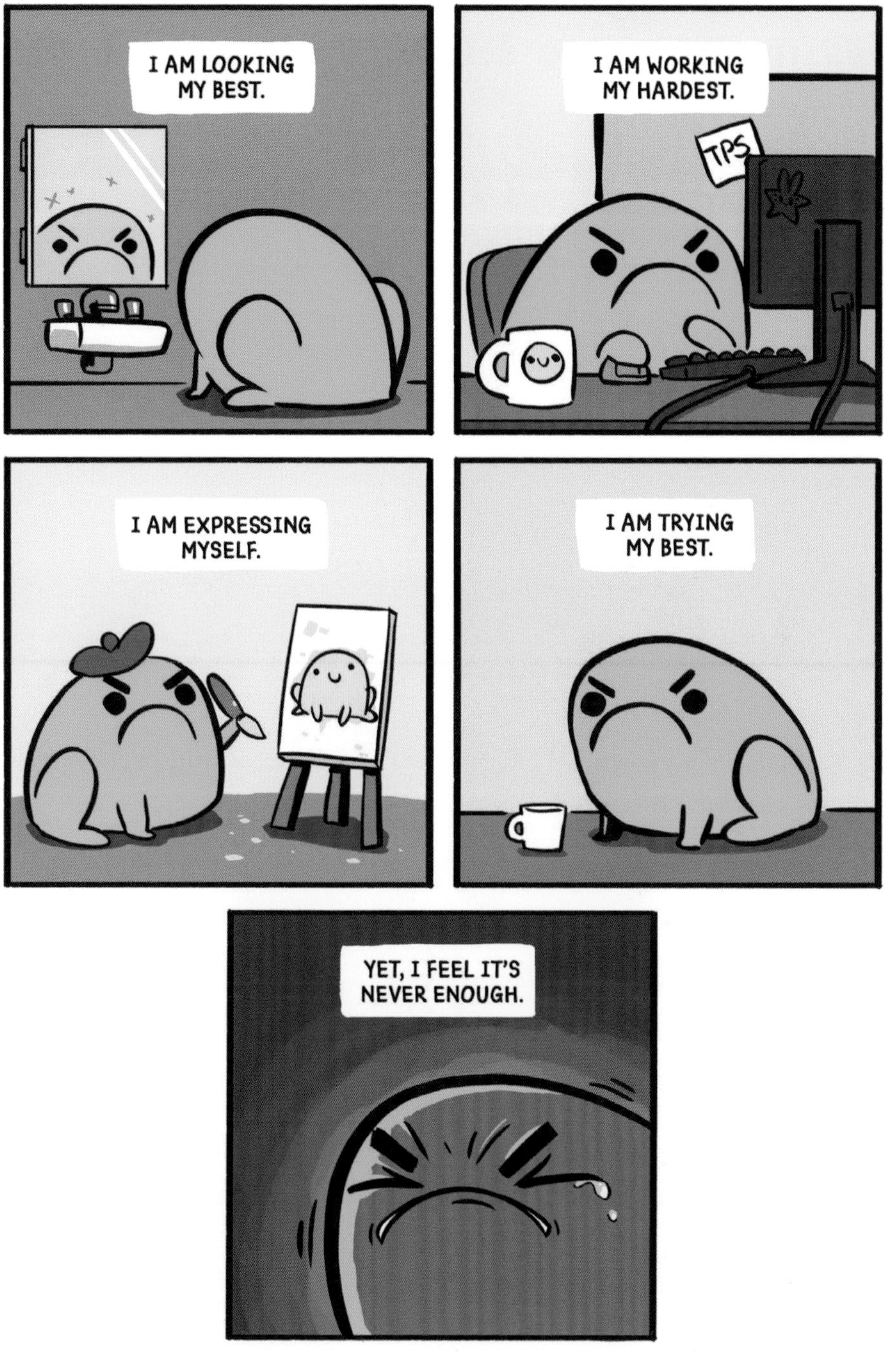
I AM LOOKING MY BEST.
I AM WORKING MY HARDEST.
TPS
I AM EXPRESSING MYSELF.
I AM TRYING MY BEST.
YET, I FEEL IT'S NEVER ENOUGH.

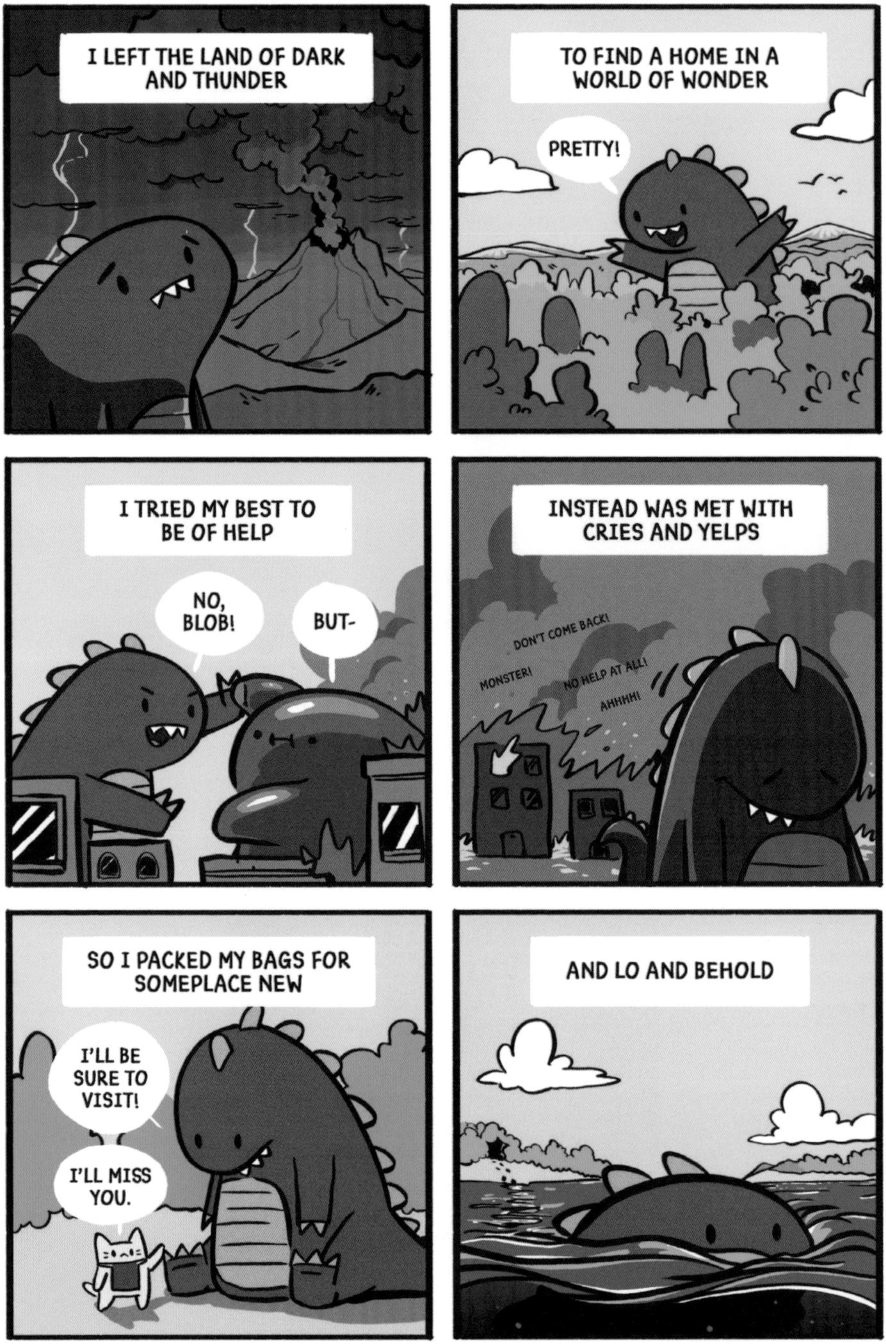
I LEFT THE LAND OF DARK AND THUNDER
TO FIND A HOME IN A WORLD OF WONDER
PRETTY!
I TRIED MY BEST TO BE OF HELP
NO, BLOB!
BUT-
INSTEAD WAS MET WITH CRIES AND YELPS
DON'T COME BACK!
MONSTER!
NO HELP AT ALL!
AHHHH!
SO I PACKED MY BAGS FOR SOMEPLACE NEW
I'LL BE SURE TO VISIT!
I'LL MISS YOU.
AND LO AND BEHOLD

YEESSSH! WHAT A DAY...
I SSSHOULD GO CURL UP.
SSSSSSIGH
FUMP
ROLL
ROLL
ROLL

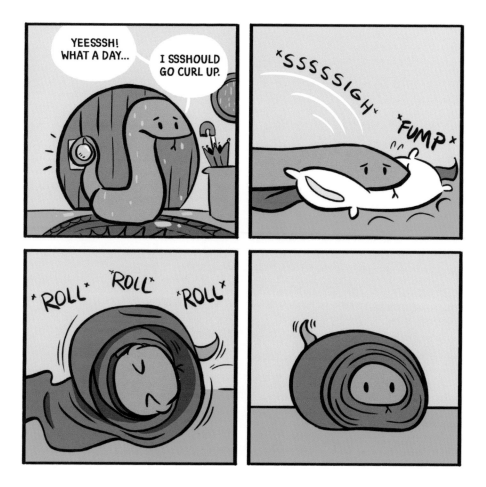

FIND THE 13 STAR BUNNIES!

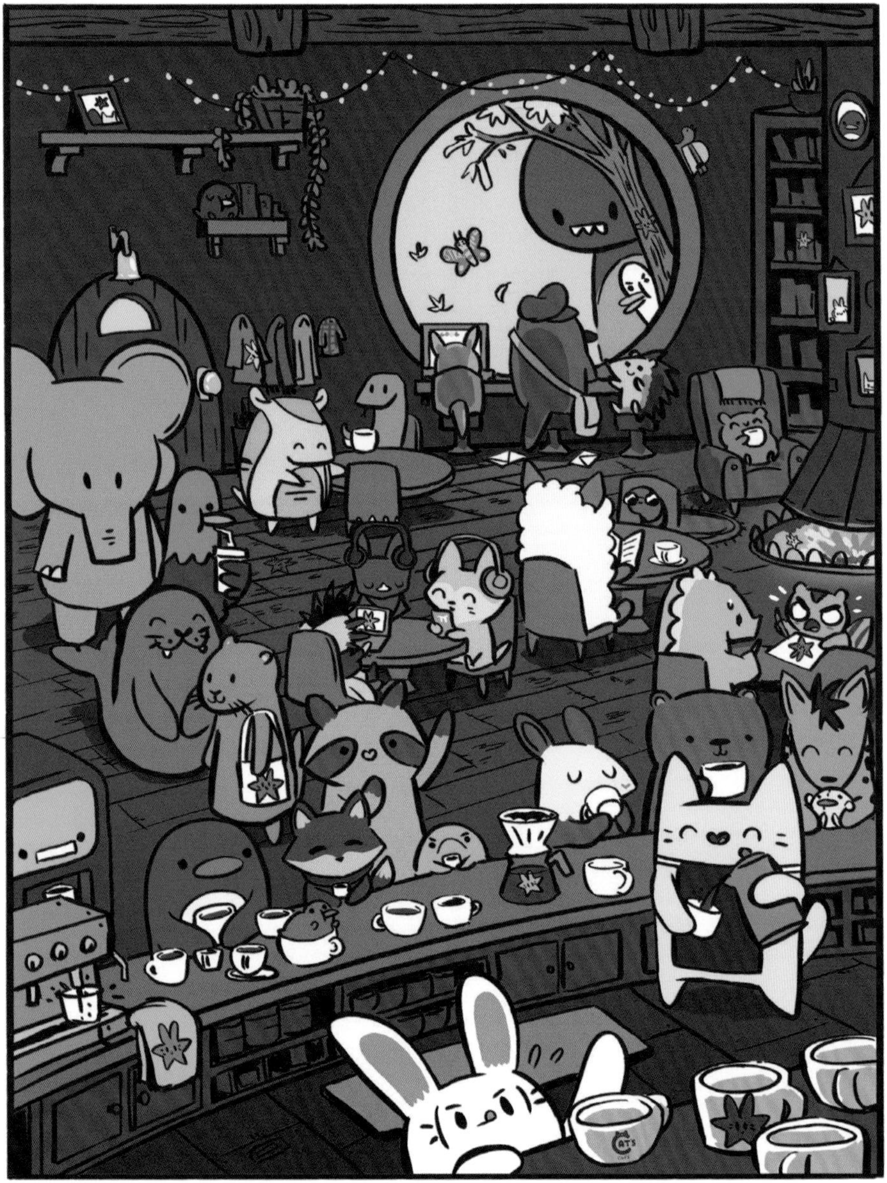

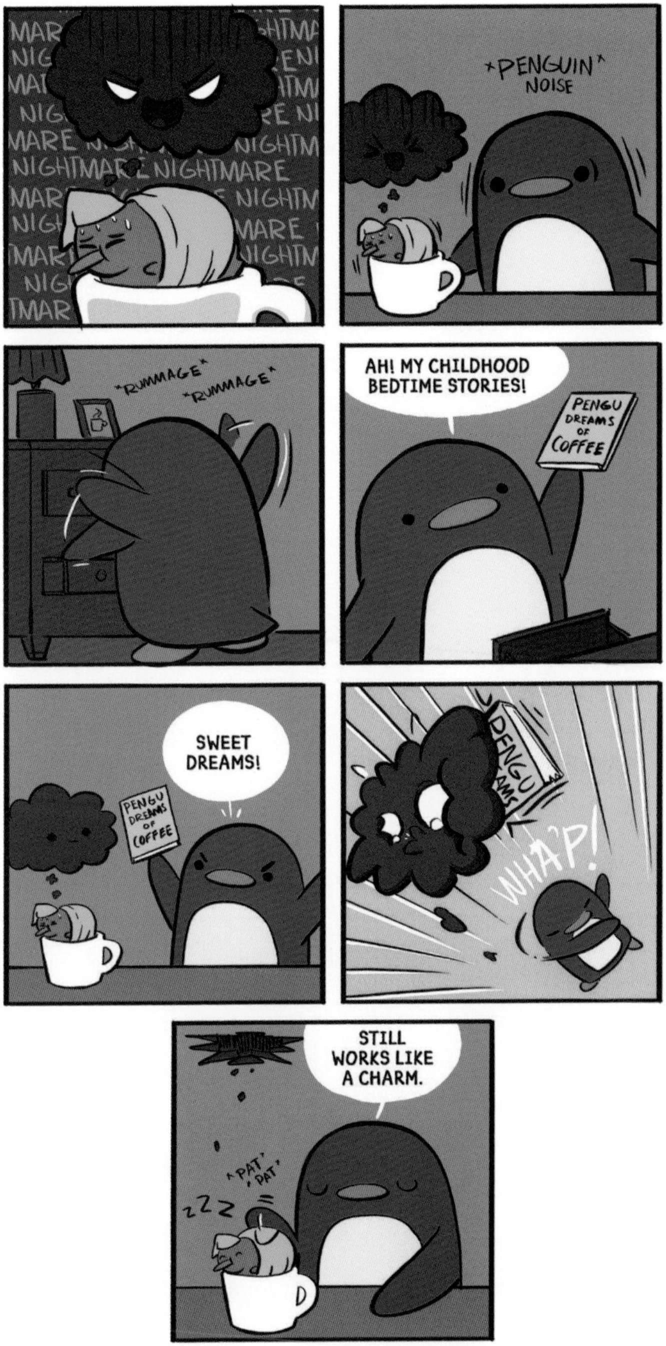
NIGHTMARE NIGHTMARE
PENGUIN NOISE
RUMMAGE *RUMMAGE*
AH! MY CHILDHOOD BEDTIME STORIES!
PENGU DREAMS OF COFFEE
SWEET DREAMS!
PENGU DREAMS OF COFFEE
WHAP!
STILL WORKS LIKE A CHARM.
PAT *PAT*
ZZZ

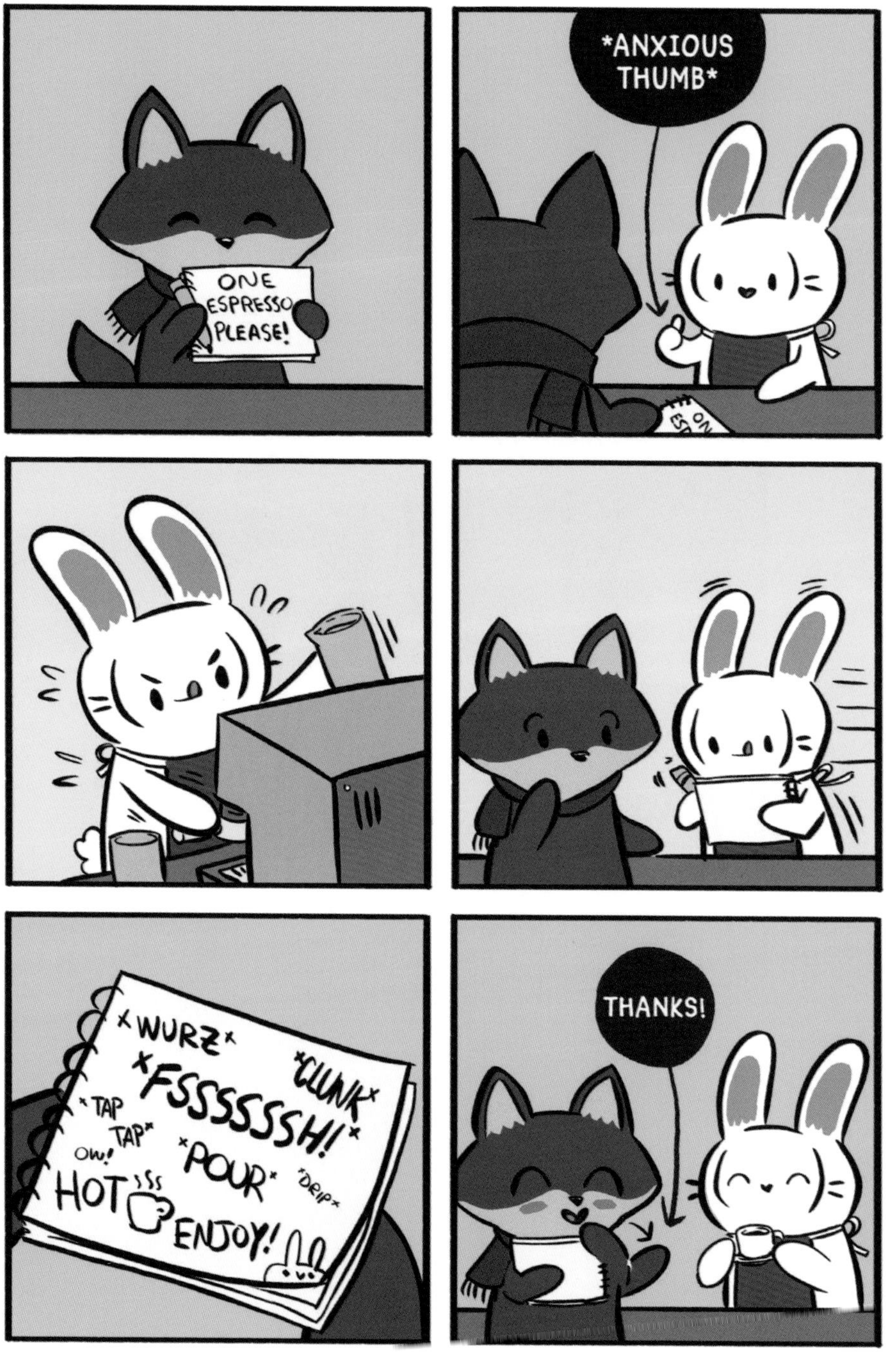
ONE ESPRESSO PLEASE!
ANXIOUS THUMB
WURZ
FSSSSSSSH!
CLUNK
TAP TAP
OW!
POUR
DRIP
HOT
ENJOY!
THANKS!

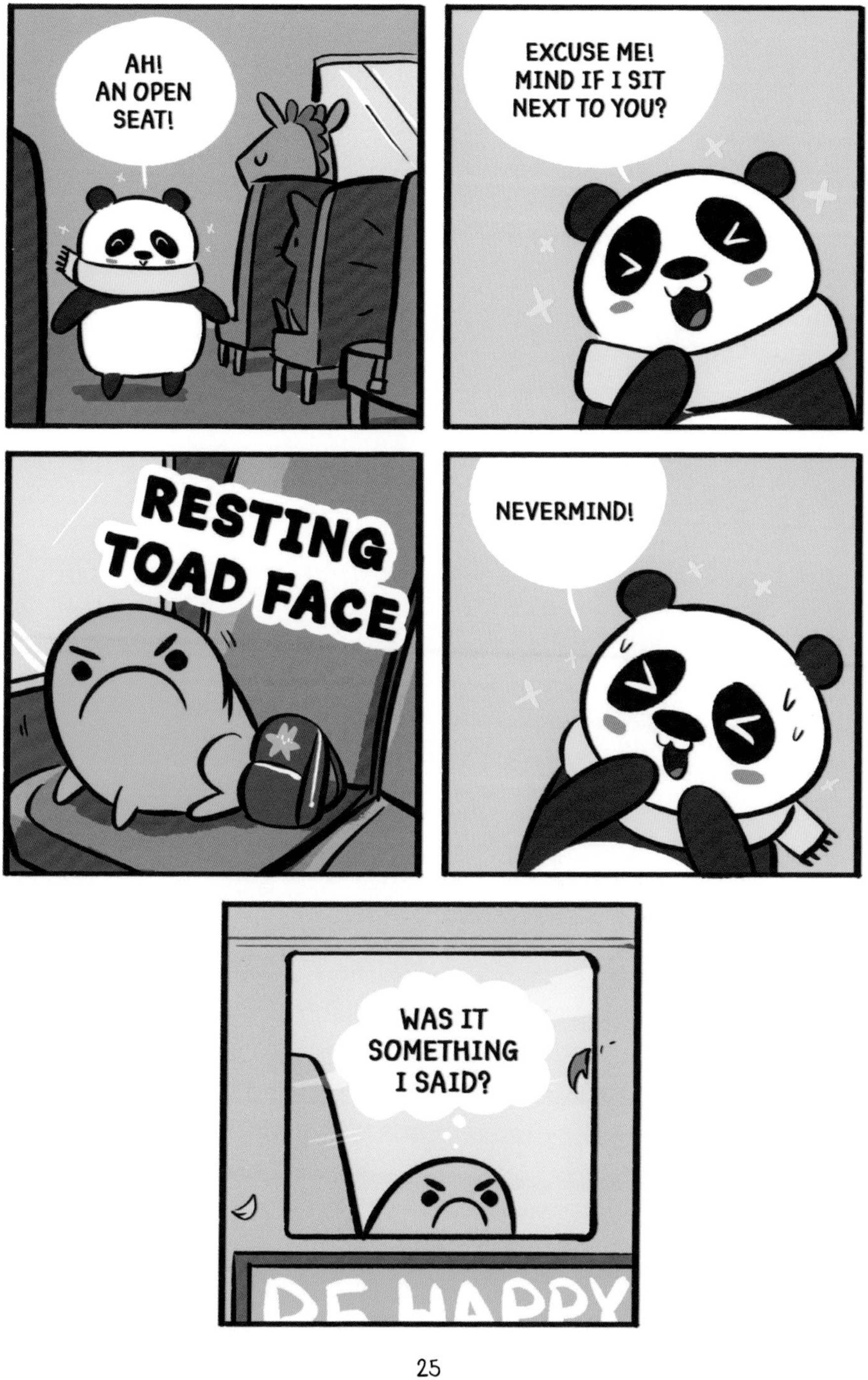
AH! AN OPEN SEAT!
EXCUSE ME! MIND IF I SIT NEXT TO YOU?
RESTING TOAD FACE
NEVERMIND!
WAS IT SOMETHING I SAID?

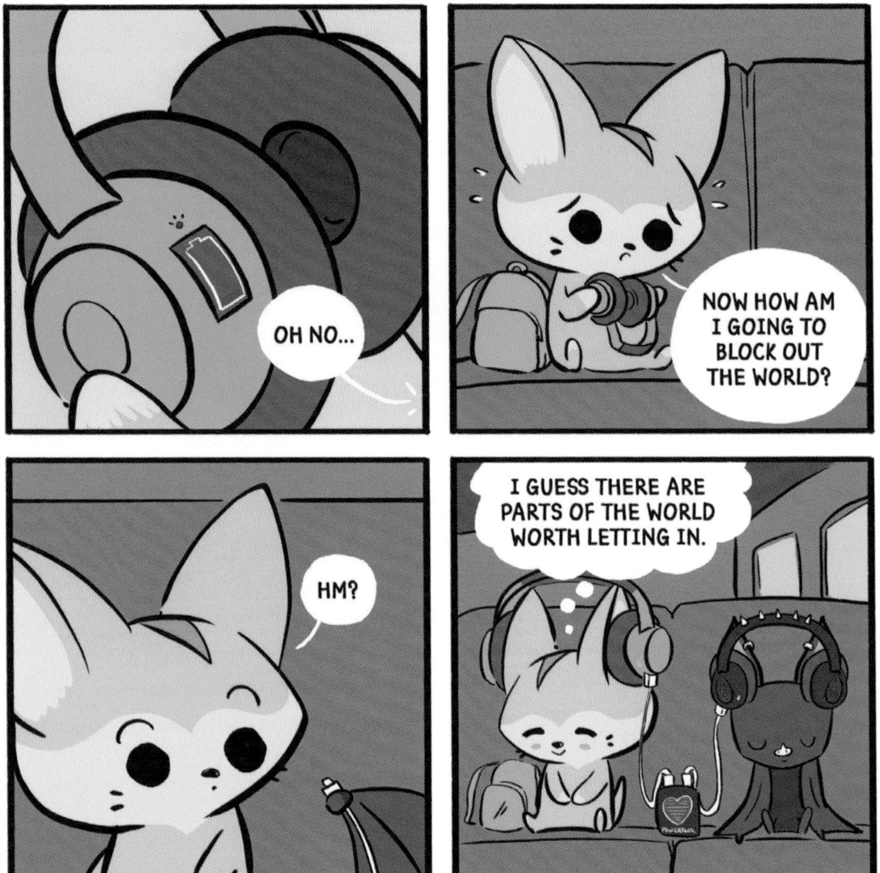
OH NO...
NOW HOW AM I GOING TO BLOCK OUT THE WORLD?
HM?
I GUESS THERE ARE PARTS OF THE WORLD WORTH LETTING IN.

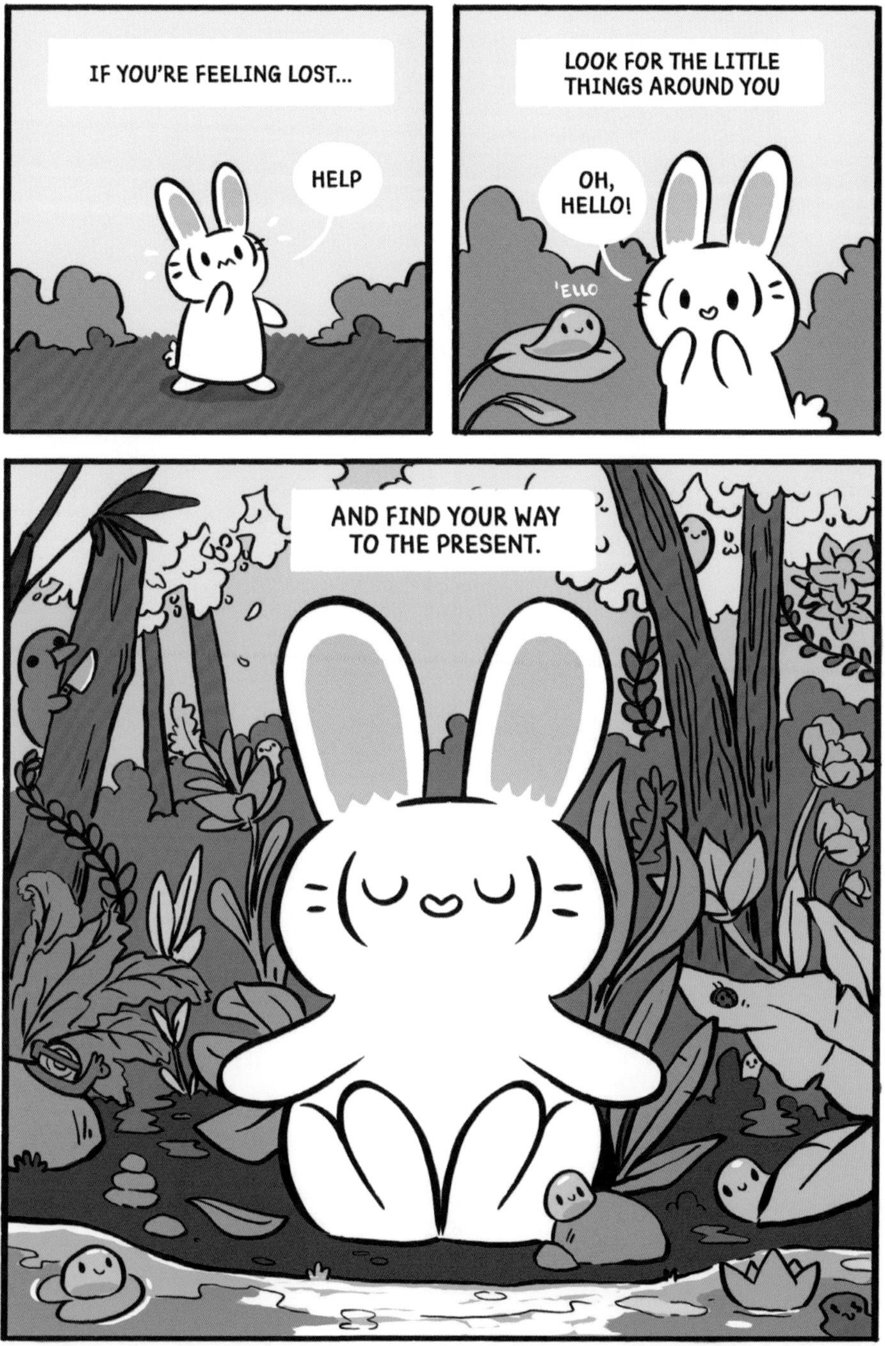
IF YOU'RE FEELING LOST...
HELP
LOOK FOR THE LITTLE THINGS AROUND YOU
OH, HELLO!
'ELLO
AND FIND YOUR WAY TO THE PRESENT.

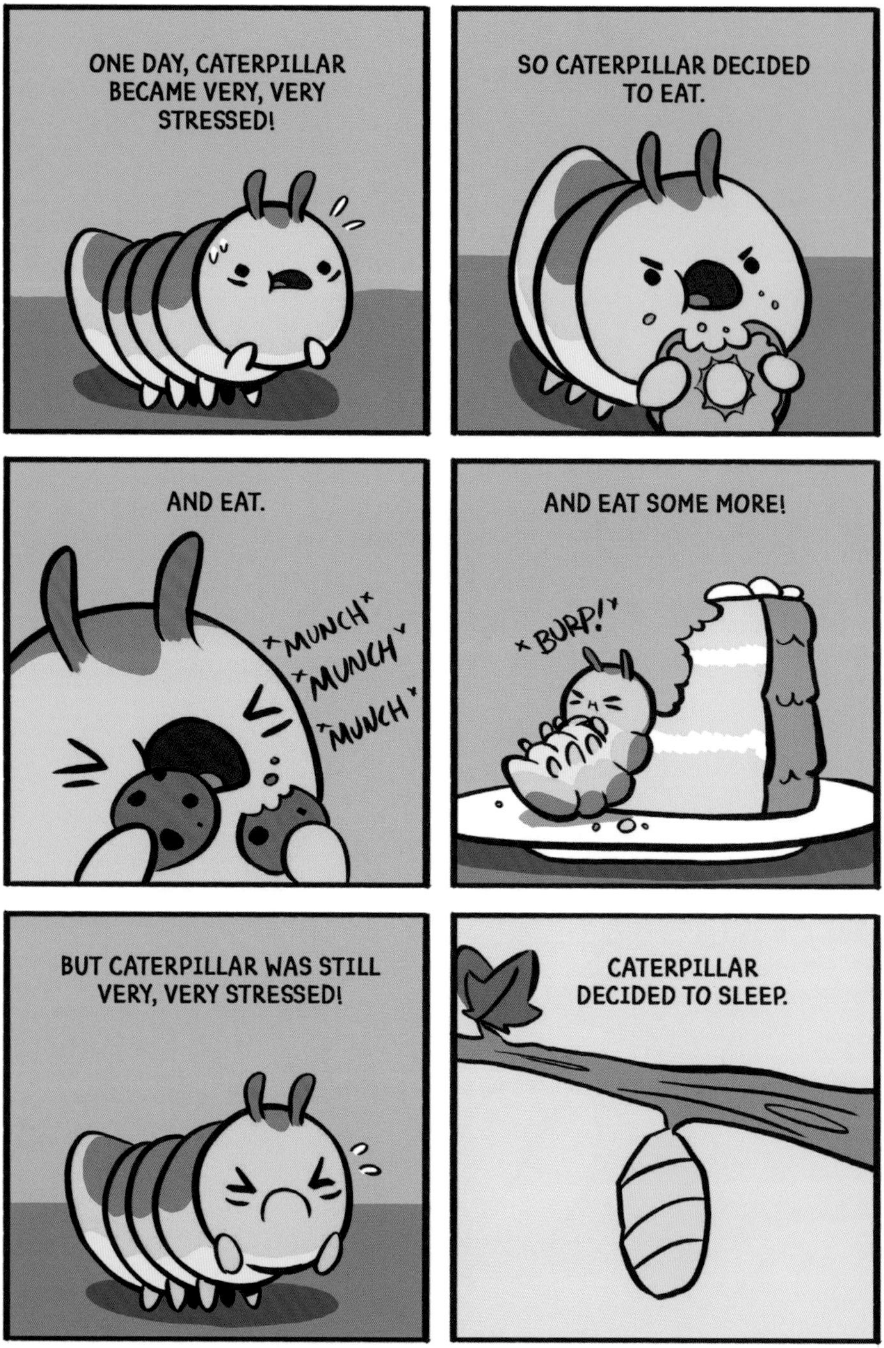
ONE DAY, CATERPILLAR BECAME VERY, VERY STRESSED!
SO CATERPILLAR DECIDED TO EAT.
AND EAT.
MUNCH
MUNCH
MUNCH
AND EAT SOME MORE!
BURP!
BUT CATERPILLAR WAS STILL VERY, VERY STRESSED!
CATERPILLAR DECIDED TO SLEEP.

AND SLEEP.
UNTIL ONE DAY...
AHH...
POK
OH, COME ON!
STRESS
STRESS

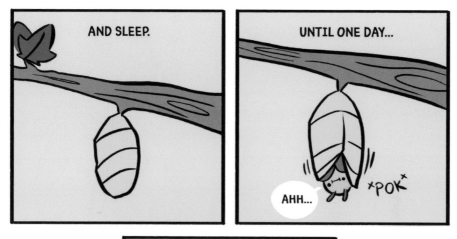

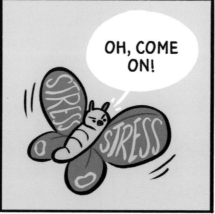

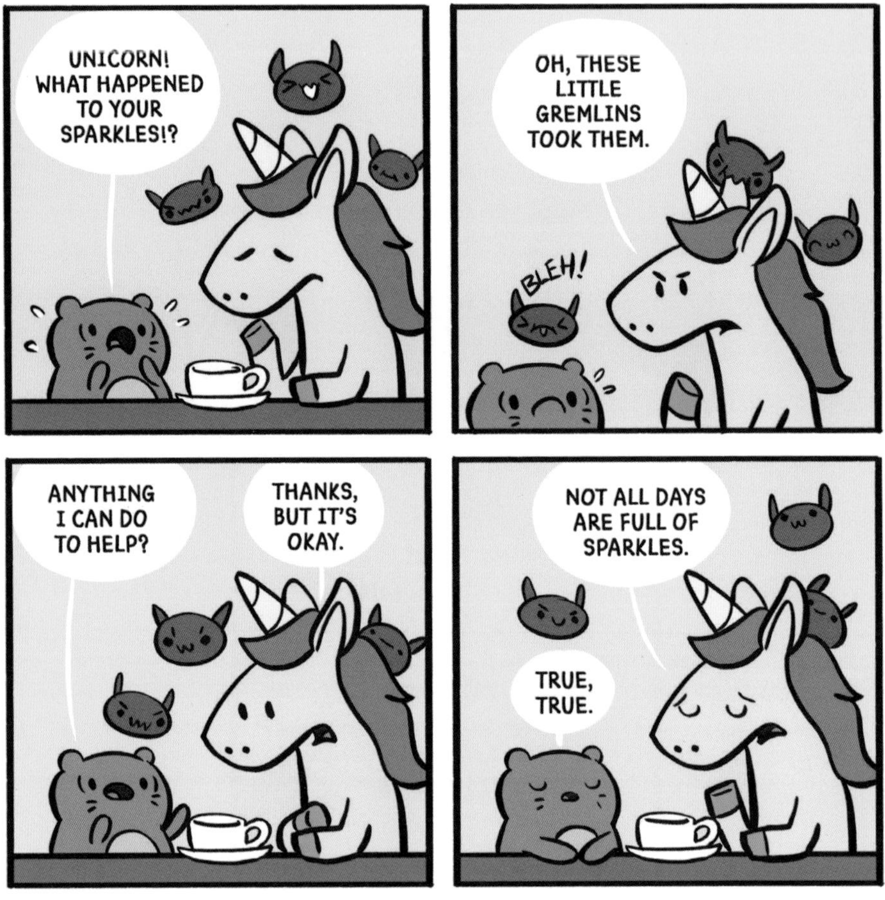
UNICORN! WHAT HAPPENED TO YOUR SPARKLES!?
OH, THESE LITTLE GREMLINS TOOK THEM.
BLEH!
ANYTHING I CAN DO TO HELP?
THANKS, BUT IT'S OKAY.
NOT ALL DAYS ARE FULL OF SPARKLES.
TRUE, TRUE.

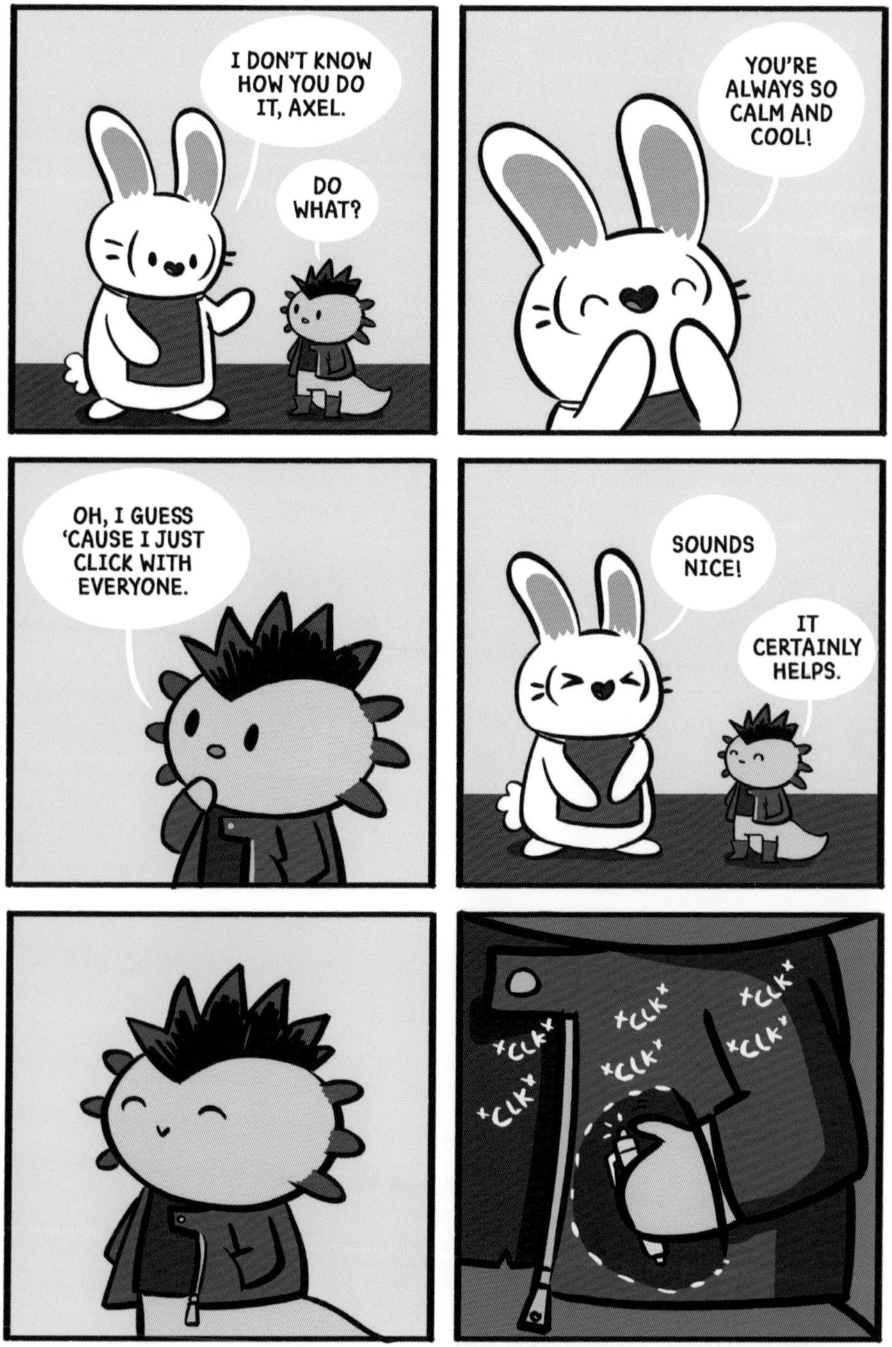
I DON'T KNOW HOW YOU DO IT, AXEL.
DO WHAT?
YOU'RE ALWAYS SO CALM AND COOL!
OH, I GUESS 'CAUSE I JUST CLICK WITH EVERYONE.
SOUNDS NICE!
IT CERTAINLY HELPS.
CLK CLK CLK CLK CLK CLK CLK

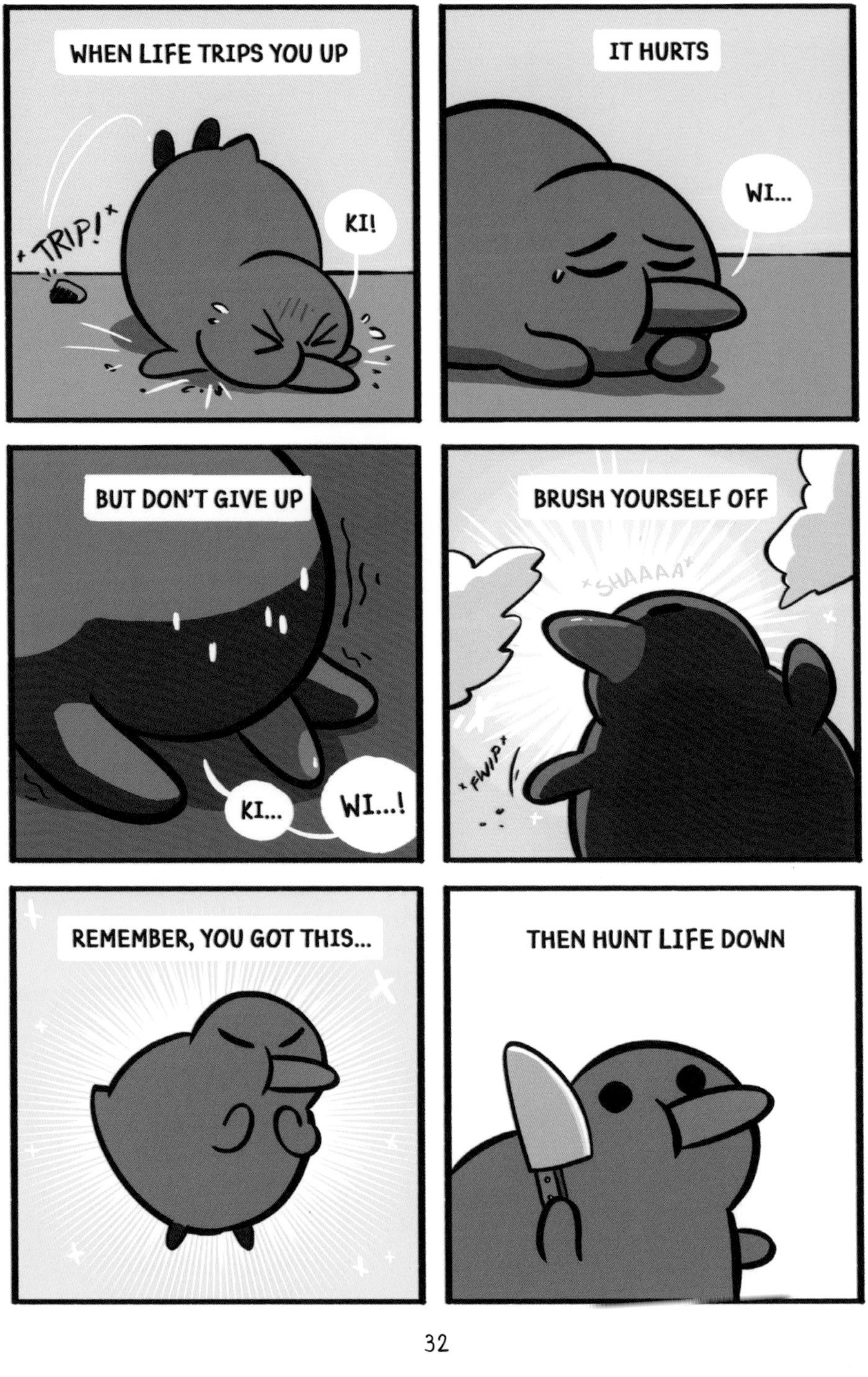
WHEN LIFE TRIPS YOU UP
TRIP!
KI!
IT HURTS
WI...
BUT DON'T GIVE UP
KI...
WI...!
BRUSH YOURSELF OFF
SHAAAA
FWIP
REMEMBER, YOU GOT THIS...
THEN HUNT LIFE DOWN

HI!
WANNA GET
COFFEE?
SORRY,
IT'S HAMMER
TIME.
WOW, YOU
ARE GOOD
AT THAT!
THANKS!
BYE!
GOT ROOM
FOR ONE
MORE?
SORRY,
WE'RE FULL
UP.
WHY IS THIS
SO HARD...

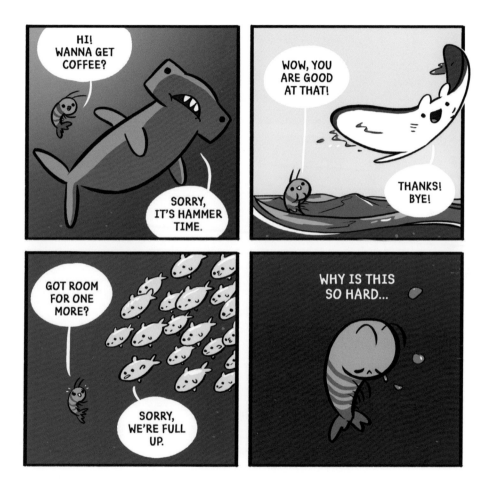

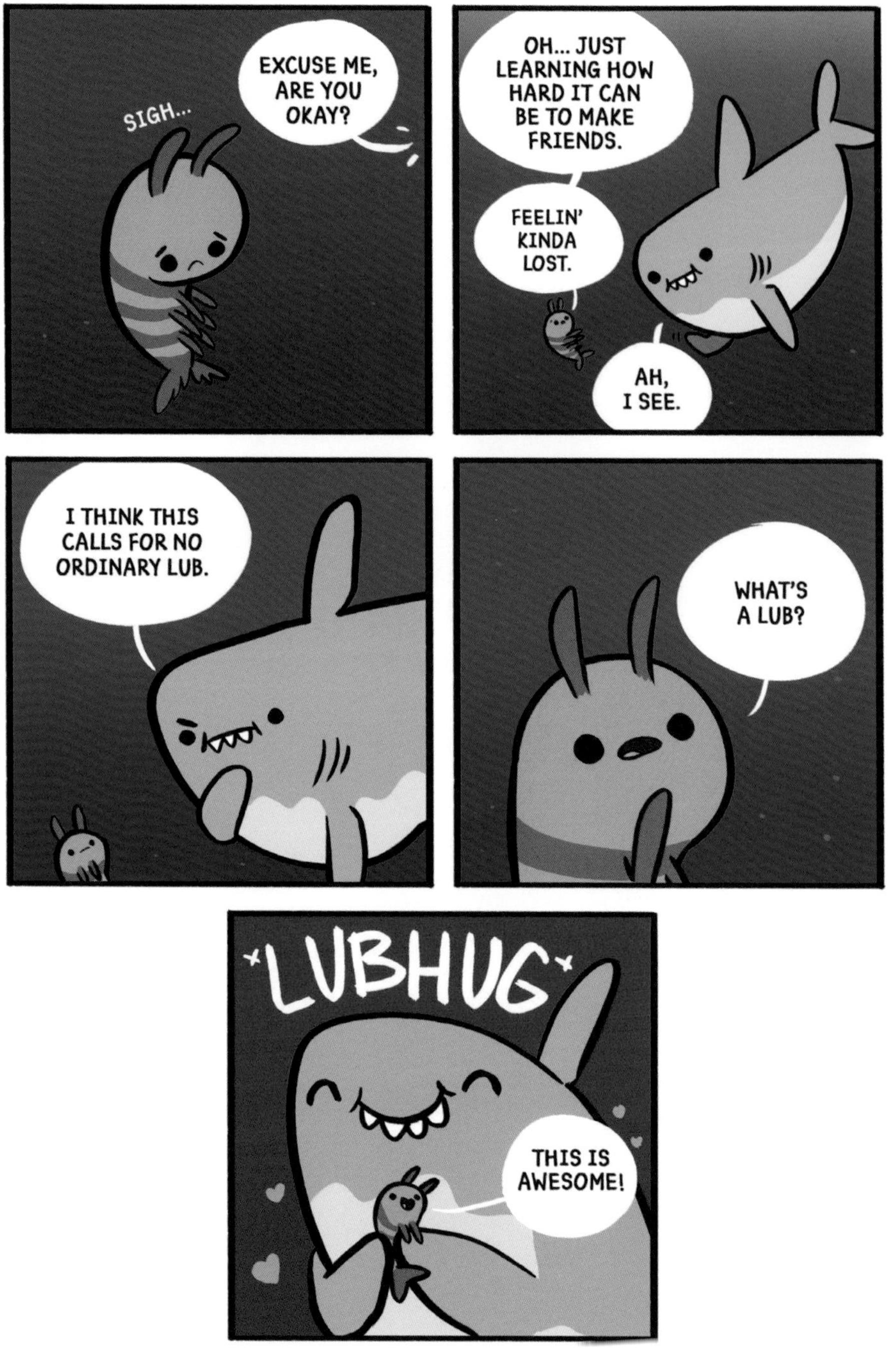
SIGH...
EXCUSE ME, ARE YOU OKAY?
OH... JUST LEARNING HOW HARD IT CAN BE TO MAKE FRIENDS.
FEELIN' KINDA LOST.
AH, I SEE.
I THINK THIS CALLS FOR NO ORDINARY LUB.
WHAT'S A LUB?
LUBHUG
THIS IS AWESOME!

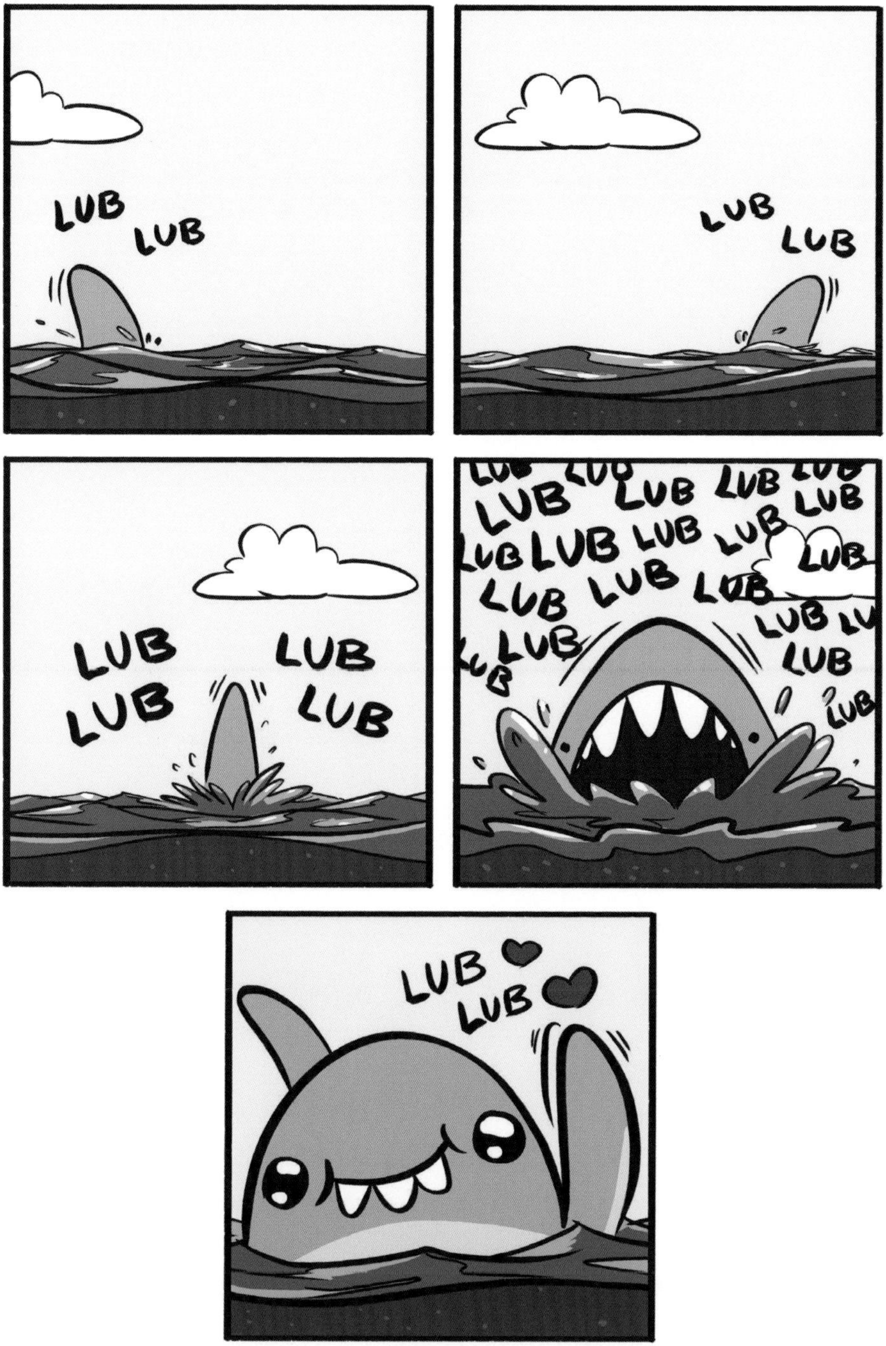
LUB
LUB
LUB
LUB
LUB
LUB
LUB
LUB
LUB LUB LUB
LUB LUB
LUB LUB LUB
LUB LUB LUB
LUB
LUB
LUB
LUB
LUB
LUB
LUB
LUB

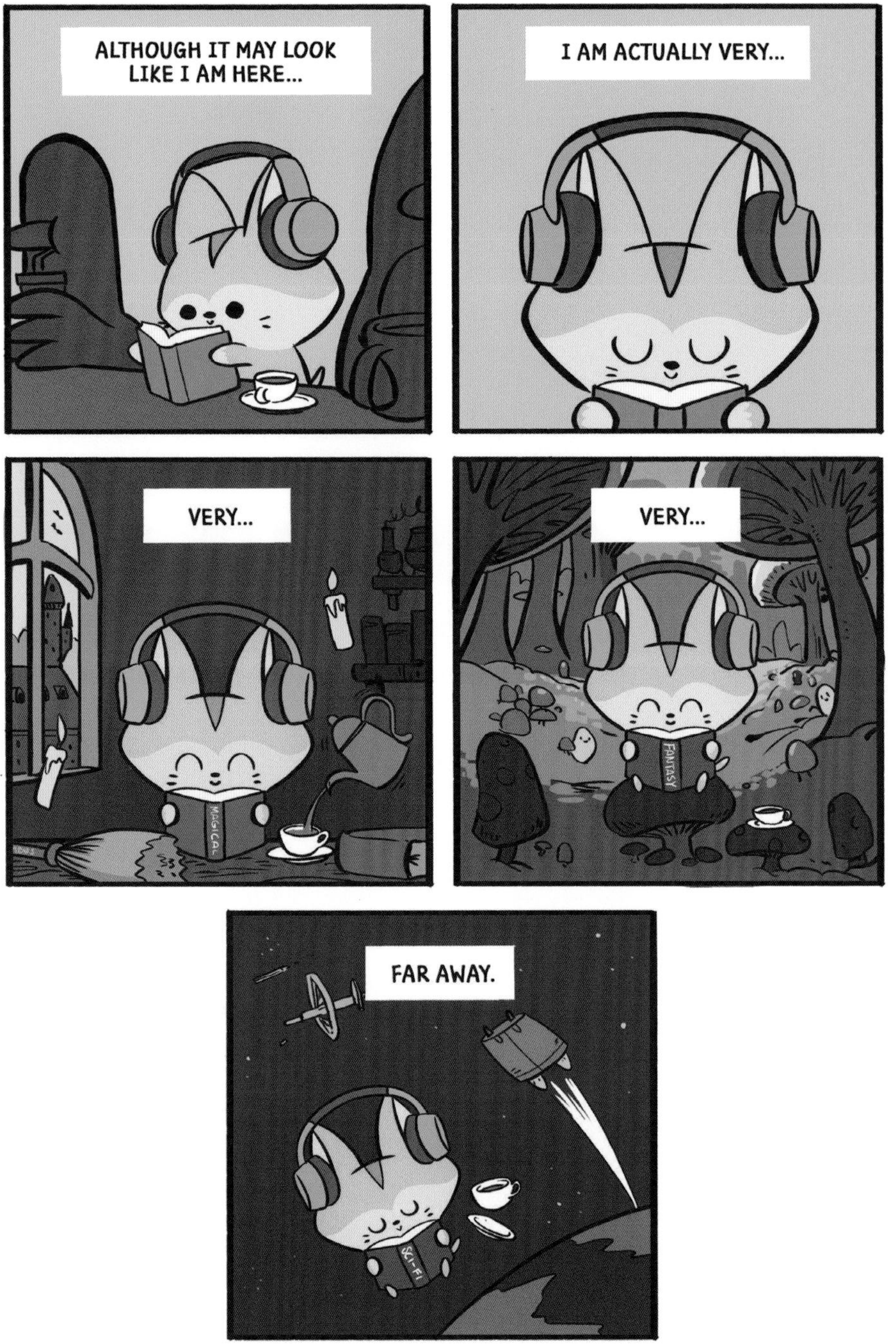
ALTHOUGH IT MAY LOOK LIKE I AM HERE...
I AM ACTUALLY VERY...
VERY...
MAGICAL
VERY...
FANTASY
FAR AWAY.
SCI-FI

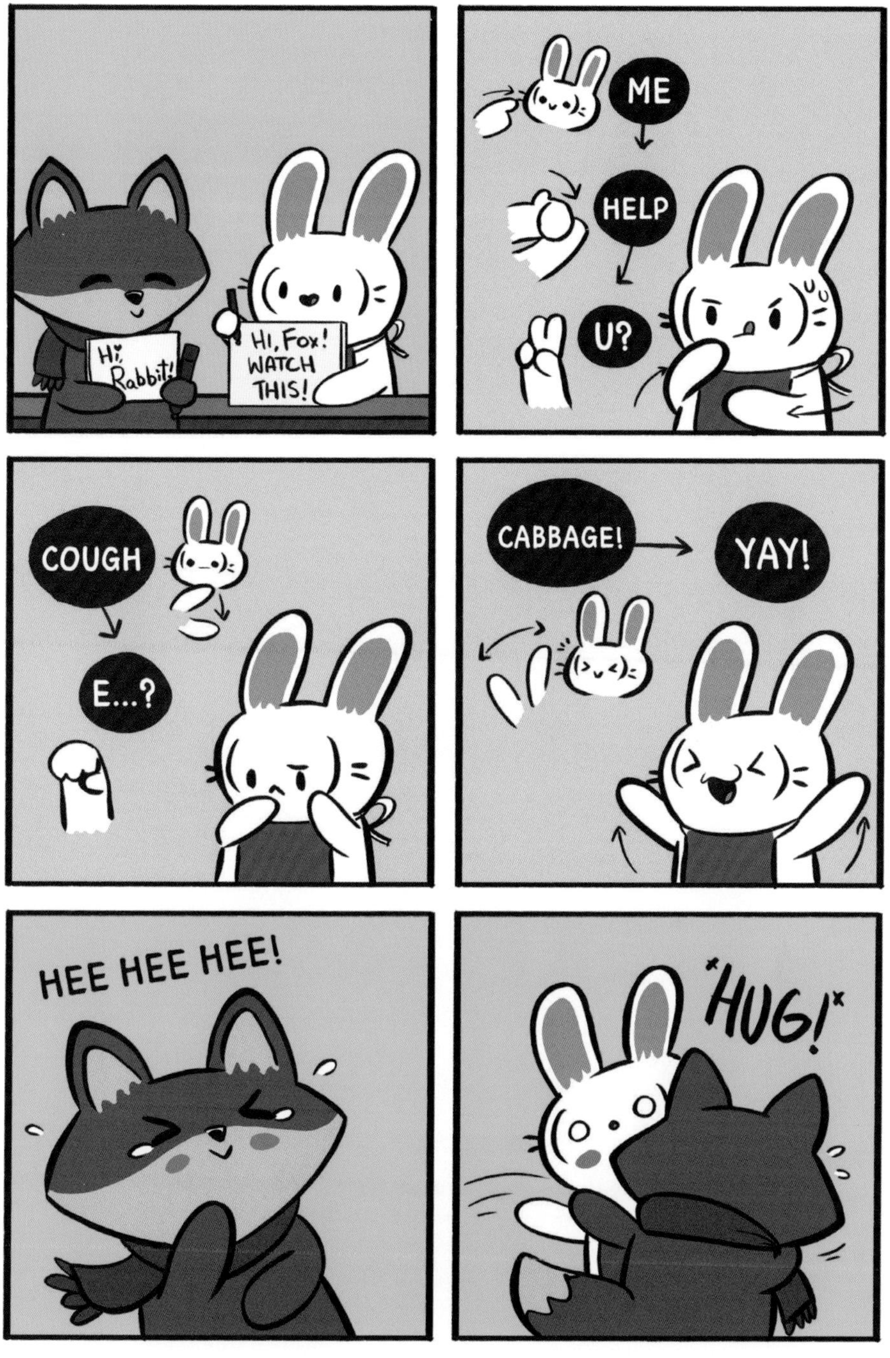
Hi, Rabbit!
HI, Fox! WATCH THIS!
ME
HELP
U?
COUGH
E...?
CABBAGE!
YAY!
HEE HEE HEE!
HUG!

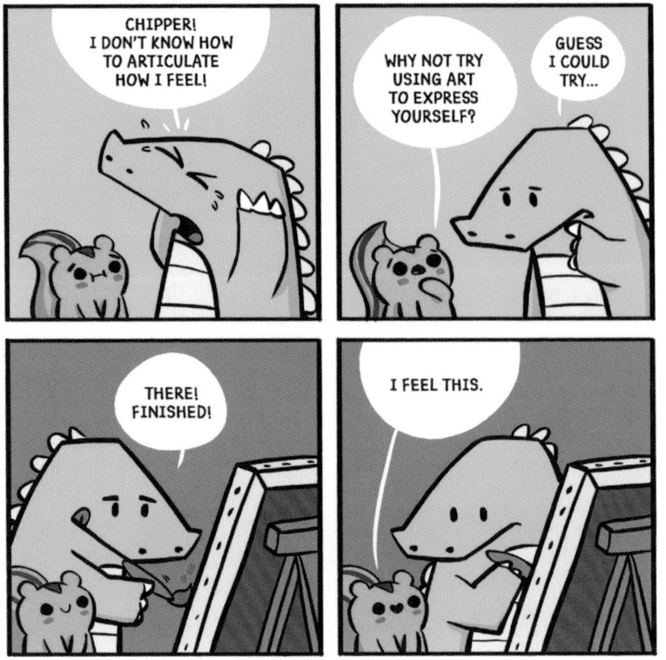
CHIPPER! I DON'T KNOW HOW TO ARTICULATE HOW I FEEL!
WHY NOT TRY USING ART TO EXPRESS YOURSELF?
GUESS I COULD TRY...
THERE! FINISHED!
I FEEL THIS.

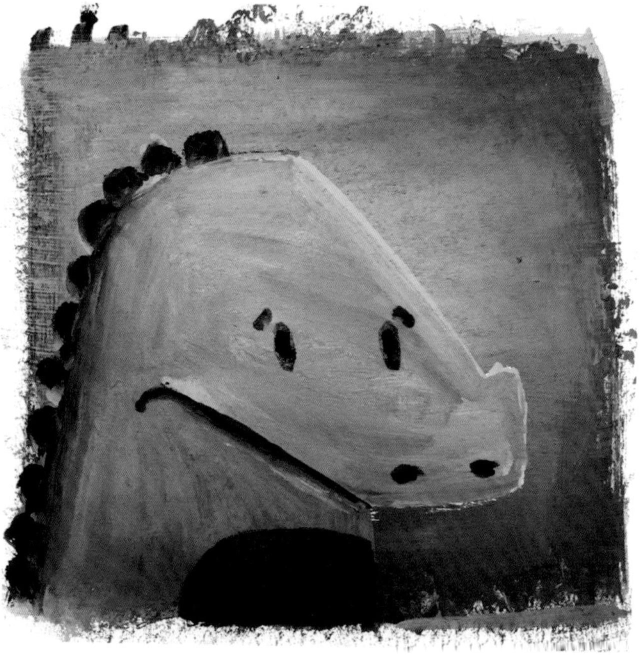

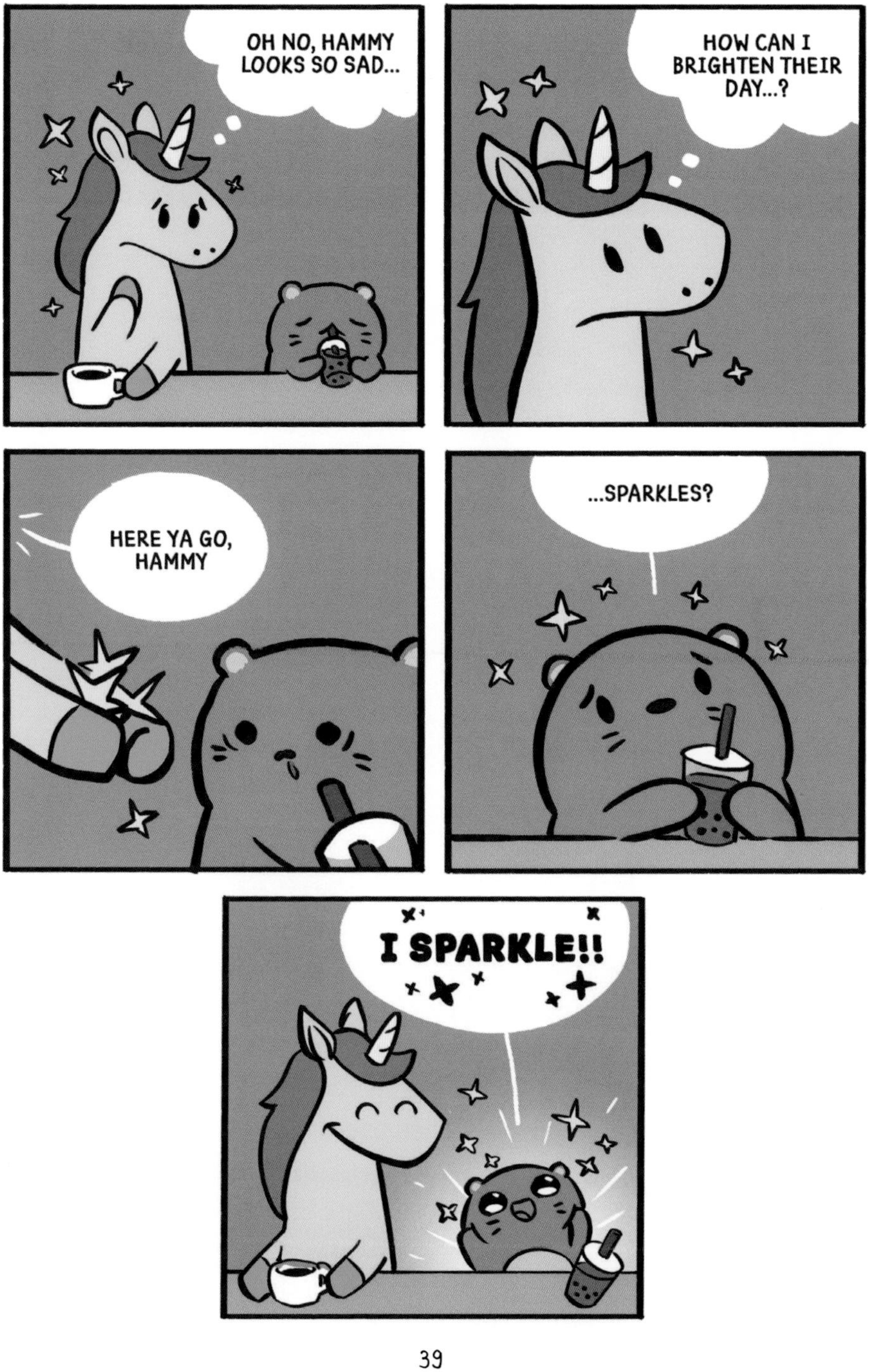
OH NO, HAMMY LOOKS SO SAD...
HOW CAN I BRIGHTEN THEIR DAY...?
HERE YA GO, HAMMY
...SPARKLES?
I SPARKLE!!

A BREW TO REMEMBER

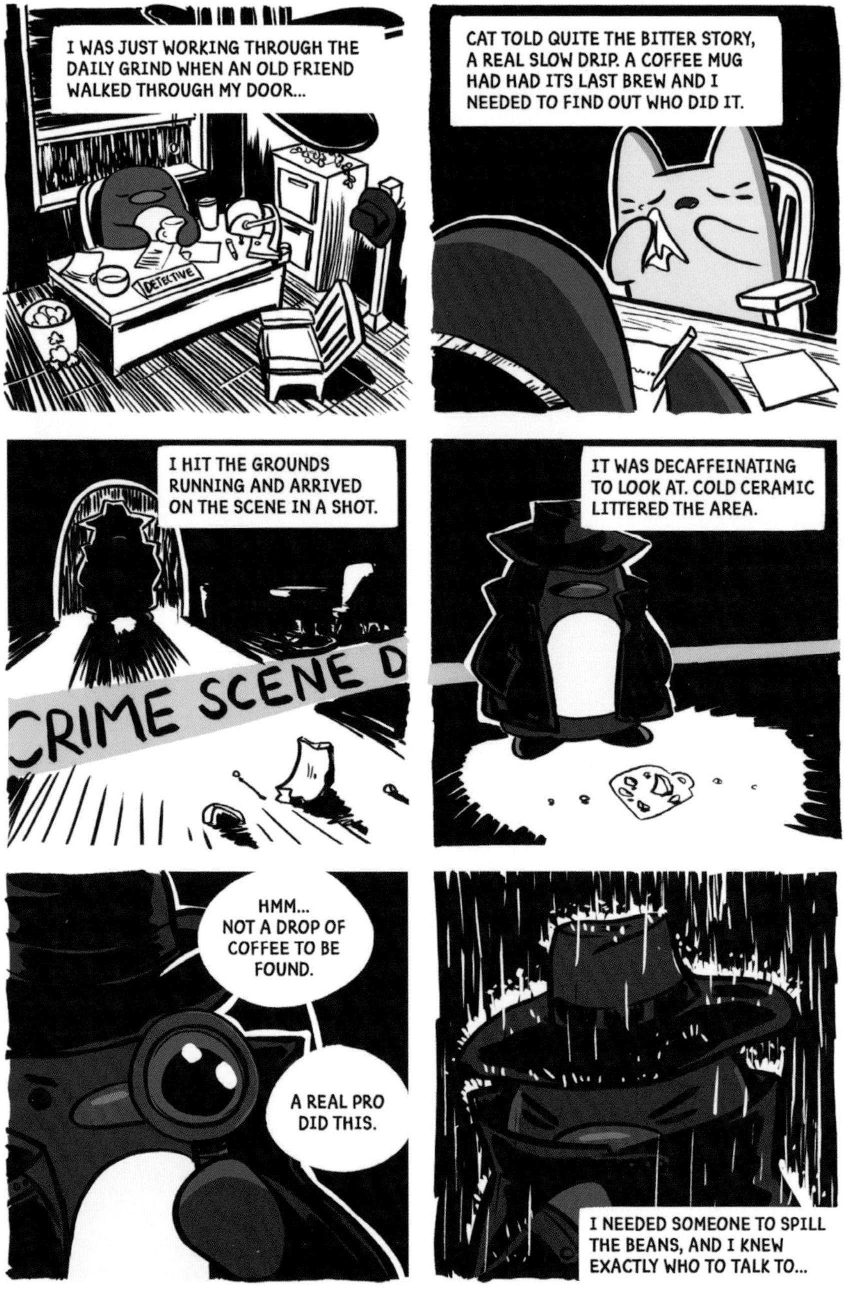

I WAS JUST WORKING THROUGH THE DAILY GRIND WHEN AN OLD FRIEND WALKED THROUGH MY DOOR...
DETECTIVE
CAT TOLD QUITE THE BITTER STORY, A REAL SLOW DRIP. A COFFEE MUG HAD HAD ITS LAST BREW AND I NEEDED TO FIND OUT WHO DID IT.
I HIT THE GROUNDS RUNNING AND ARRIVED ON THE SCENE IN A SHOT.
CRIME SCENE D
IT WAS DECAFFEINATING TO LOOK AT. COLD CERAMIC LITTERED THE AREA.
HMM... NOT A DROP OF COFFEE TO BE FOUND.
A REAL PRO DID THIS.
I NEEDED SOMEONE TO SPILL THE BEANS, AND I KNEW EXACTLY WHO TO TALK TO...

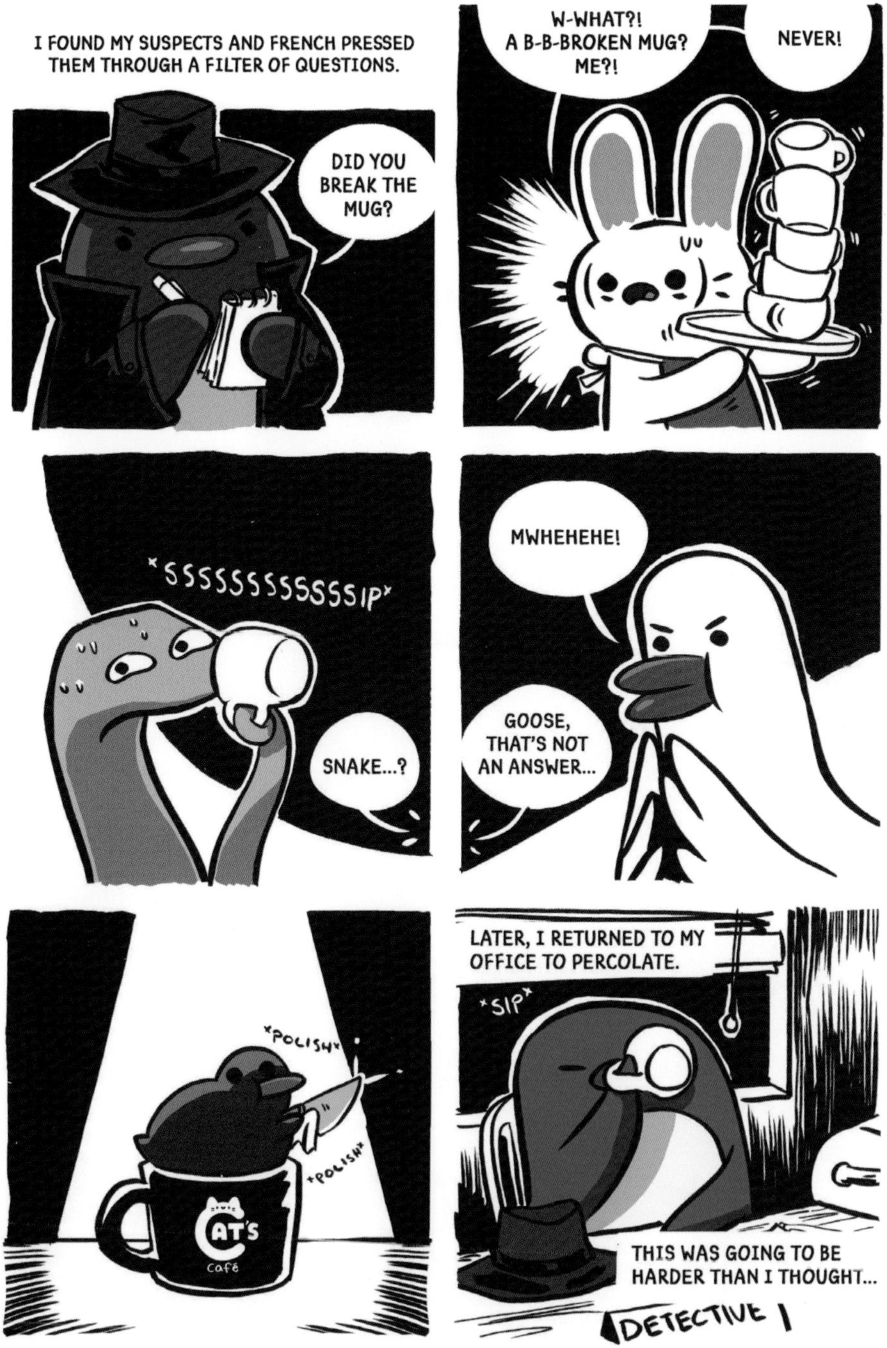
I FOUND MY SUSPECTS AND FRENCH PRESSED THEM THROUGH A FILTER OF QUESTIONS.
DID YOU BREAK THE MUG?
W-WHAT?! A B-B-BROKEN MUG? ME?!
NEVER!
SSSSSSSSSSSSSIP
SNAKE...?
MWHEHEHE!
GOOSE, THAT'S NOT AN ANSWER...
POLISH
POLISH
CAT'S Café
LATER, I RETURNED TO MY OFFICE TO PERCOLATE.
SIP
THIS WAS GOING TO BE HARDER THAN I THOUGHT...
DETECTIVE

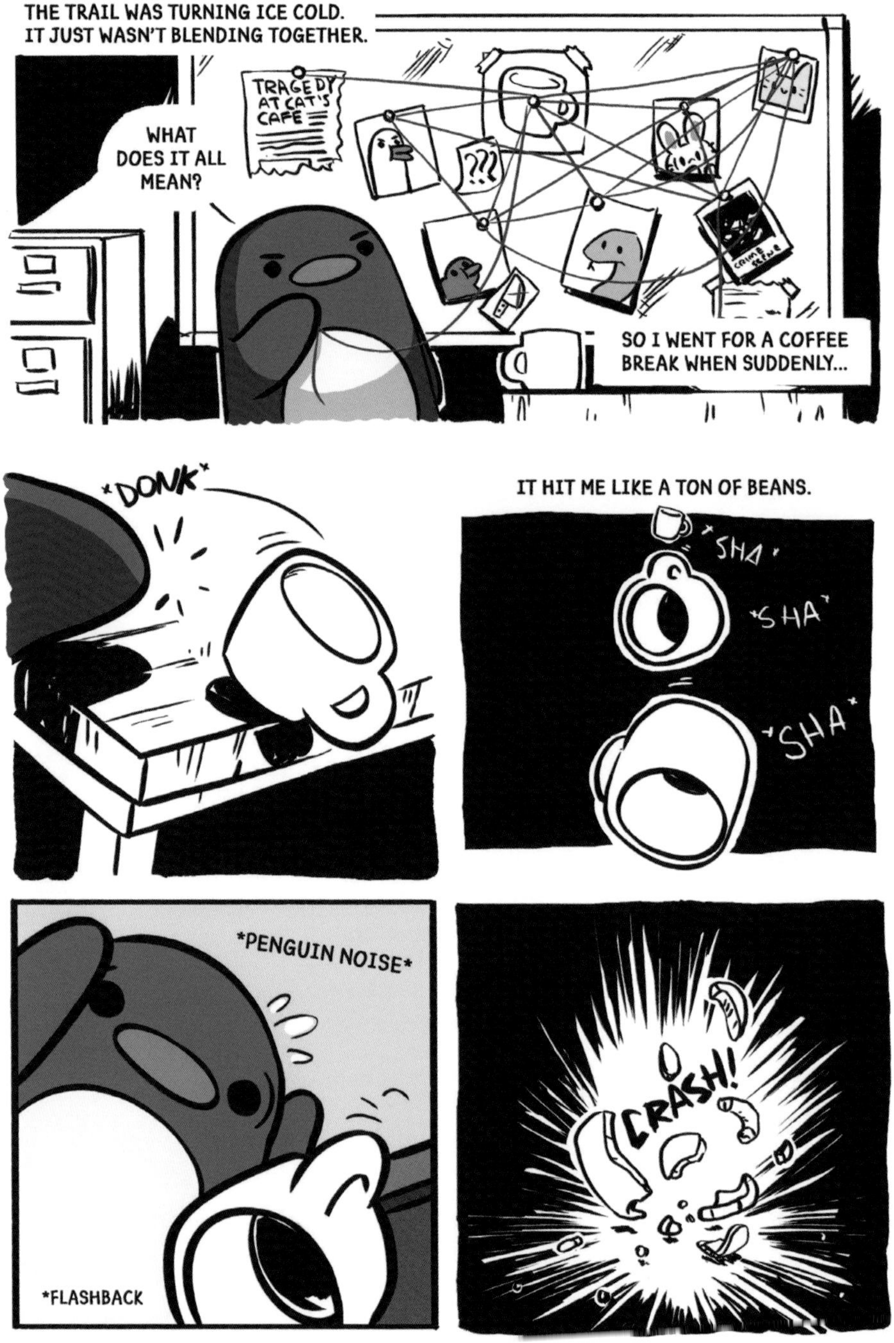
THE TRAIL WAS TURNING ICE COLD.
IT JUST WASN'T BLENDING TOGETHER.
TRAGEDY AT CAT'S CAFE
???
CRIME SCENE
WHAT DOES IT ALL MEAN?
SO I WENT FOR A COFFEE BREAK WHEN SUDDENLY...
DONK
IT HIT ME LIKE A TON OF BEANS.
SHA
SHA
SHA
PENGUIN NOISE
*FLASHBACK
CRASH!

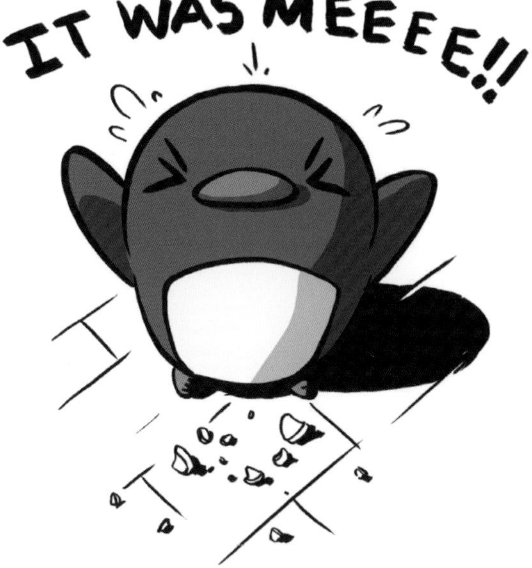
IT WAS MEEEEE!!

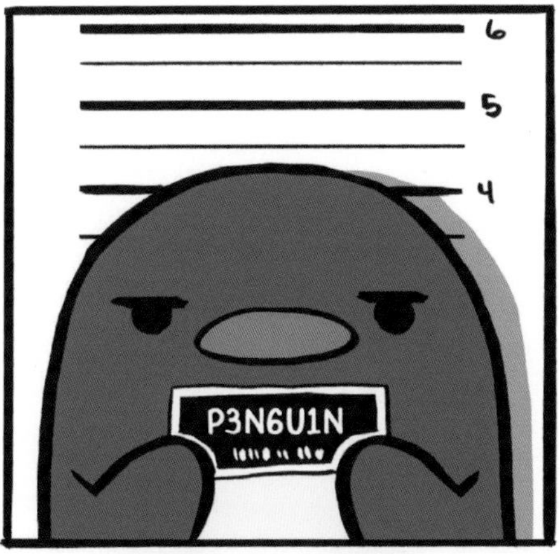
6
5
4
P3N6U1N

CASE CLOSED!

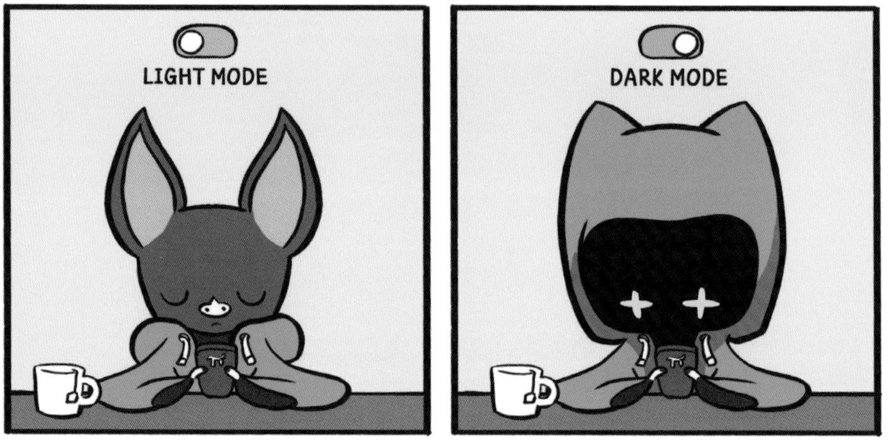
LIGHT MODE
DARK MODE

CAPTAIN!
FAST APPROACHING OBJECT!
GIVE ME VISUAL!
GAH!
IT'S RIGHT UPON US! PREPARE FOR EVASIVE MANEUVERS!
LIFE
BAM!
DISENGAGE!
RETREAT!
CAT:
YOU OK, OPOSSUM?
I'M HERE IF YOU NEED.
RABBIT:
WANNA HANG OUT?
AXEL:
MISS U!
SNAKE:
SSSUP

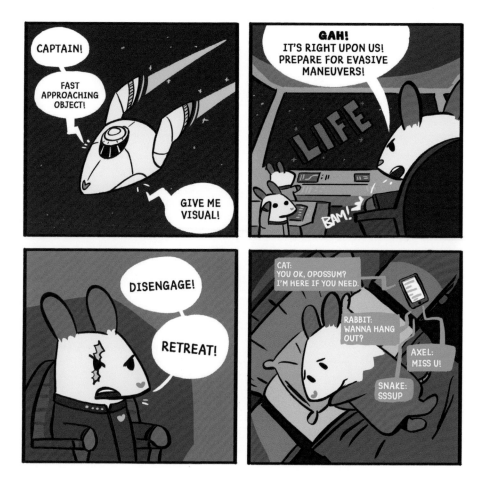

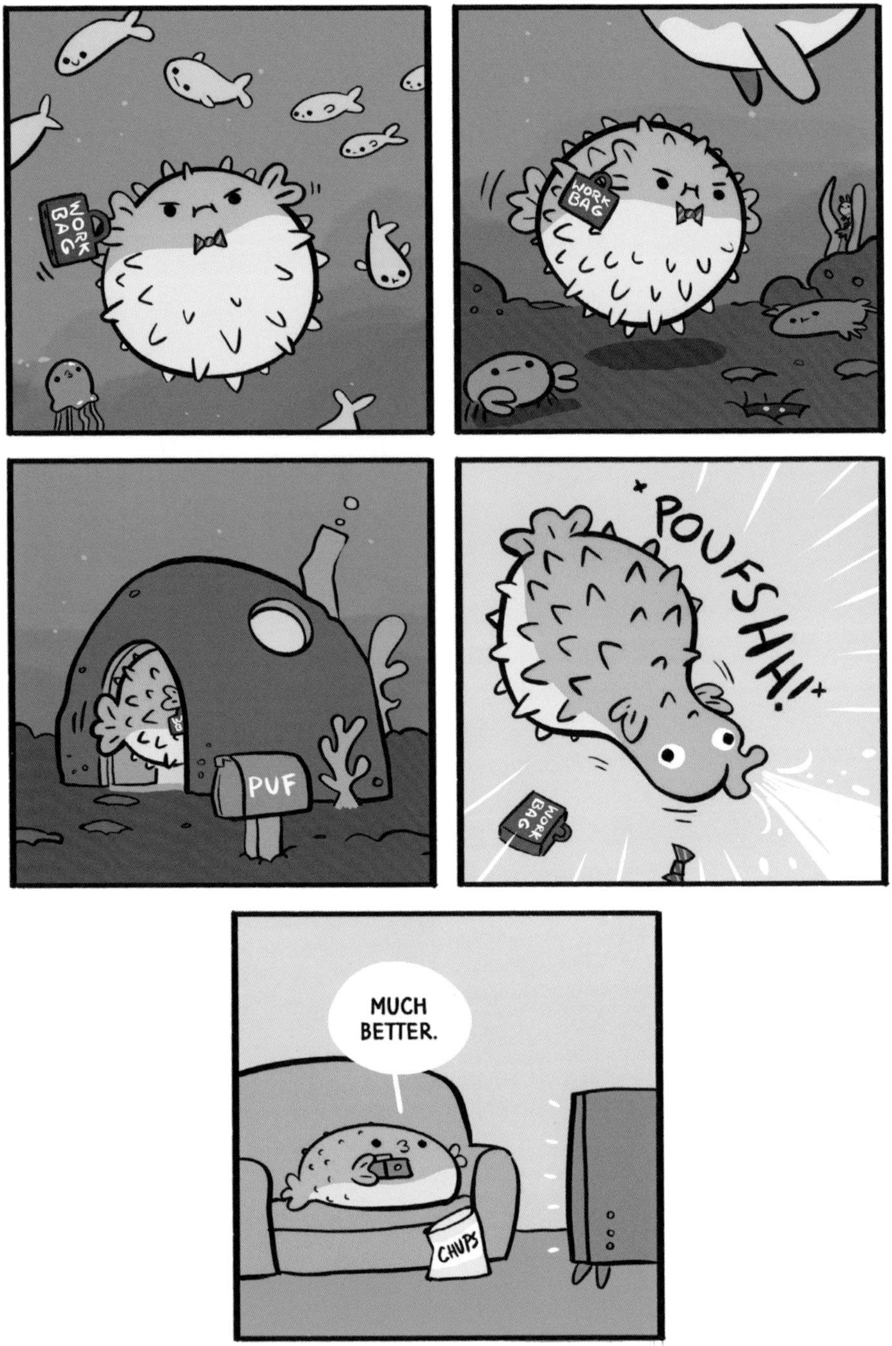
WORK BAG
WORK BAG
PUF
POUFSHH!
WORK BAG
MUCH BETTER.
CHIPS

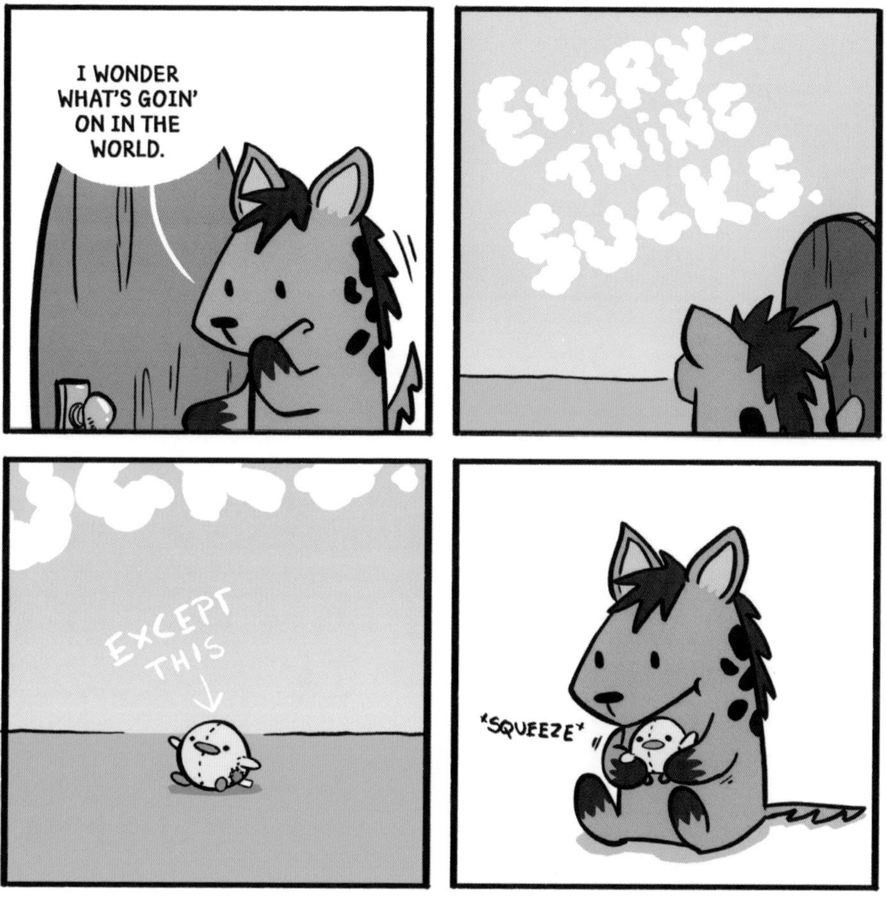
I WONDER WHAT'S GOIN' ON IN THE WORLD.
EVERY-THING SUCKS.
EXCEPT THIS
SQUEEZE

SELF-LOVE IS...

MAKING A
HOME-COOKED MEAL

SEEING A GOOD
FRIEND

HI, OPOSSUM!

ENJOYING A HOBBY

NICE ATTACK,
KIWI!

ASKING FOR HELP

DR. PIGEON
THERAPIST

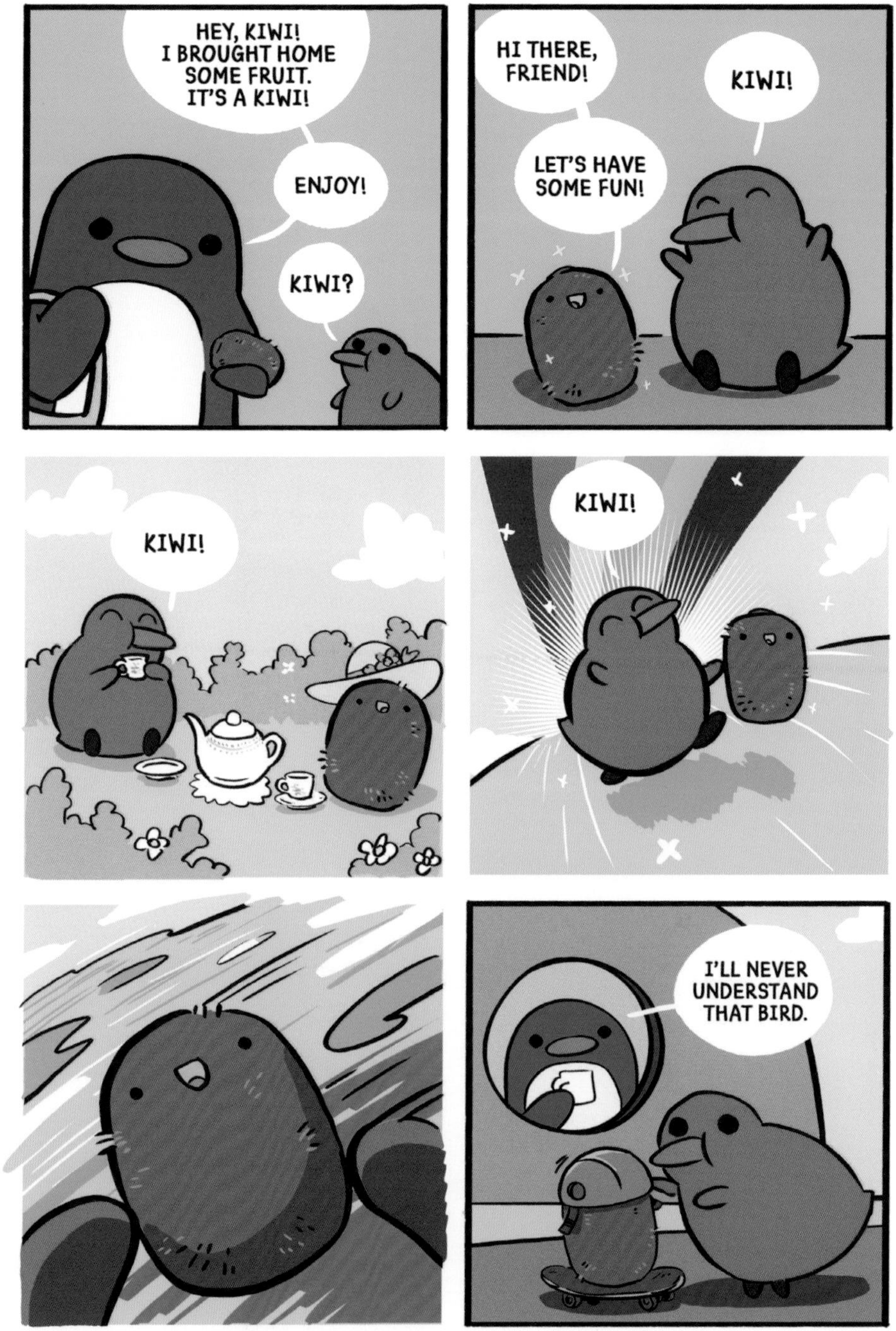
HEY, KIWI! I BROUGHT HOME SOME FRUIT. IT'S A KIWI!
ENJOY!
KIWI?
HI THERE, FRIEND!
LET'S HAVE SOME FUN!
KIWI!
KIWI!
KIWI!
I'LL NEVER UNDERSTAND THAT BIRD.

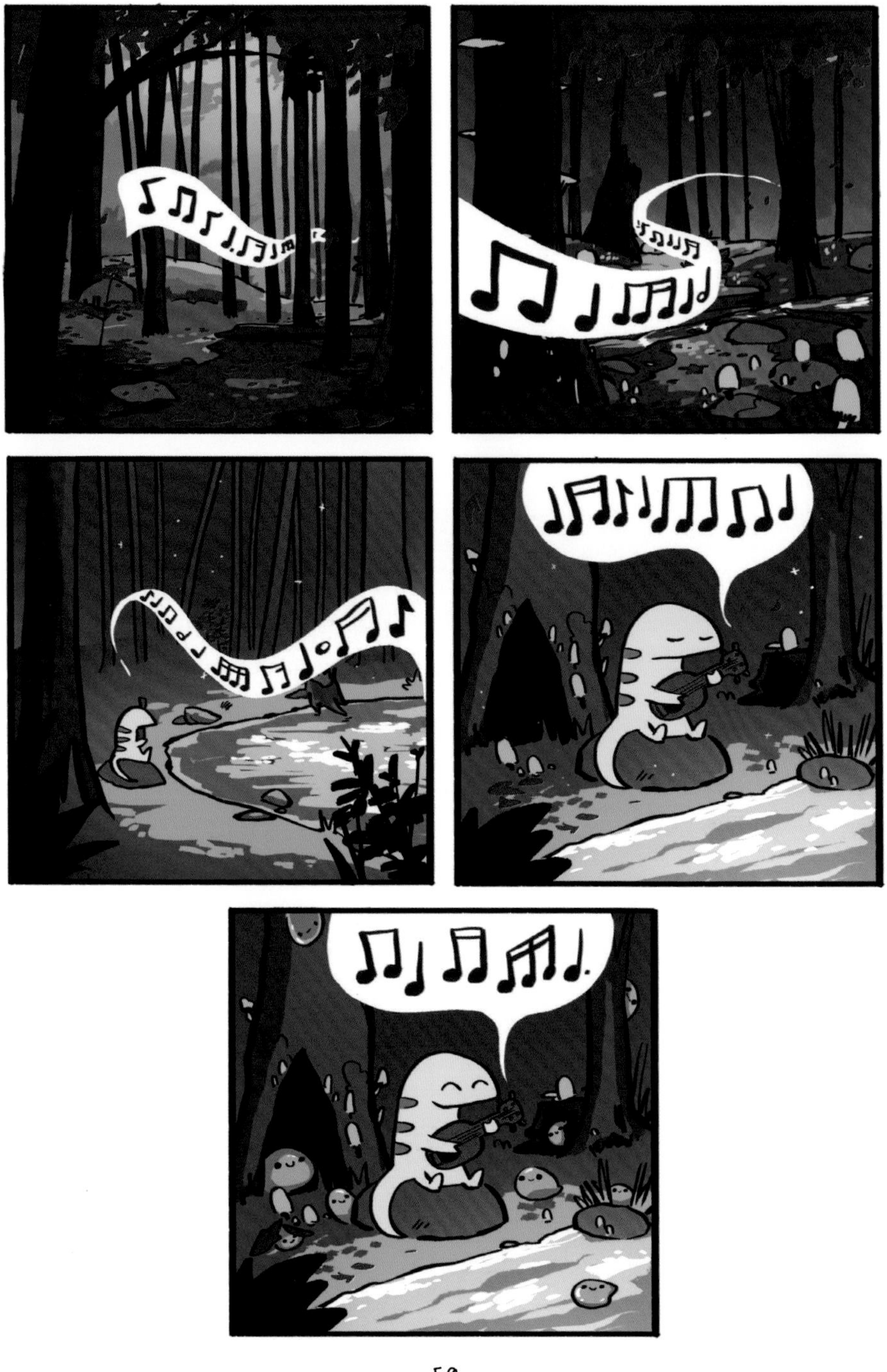

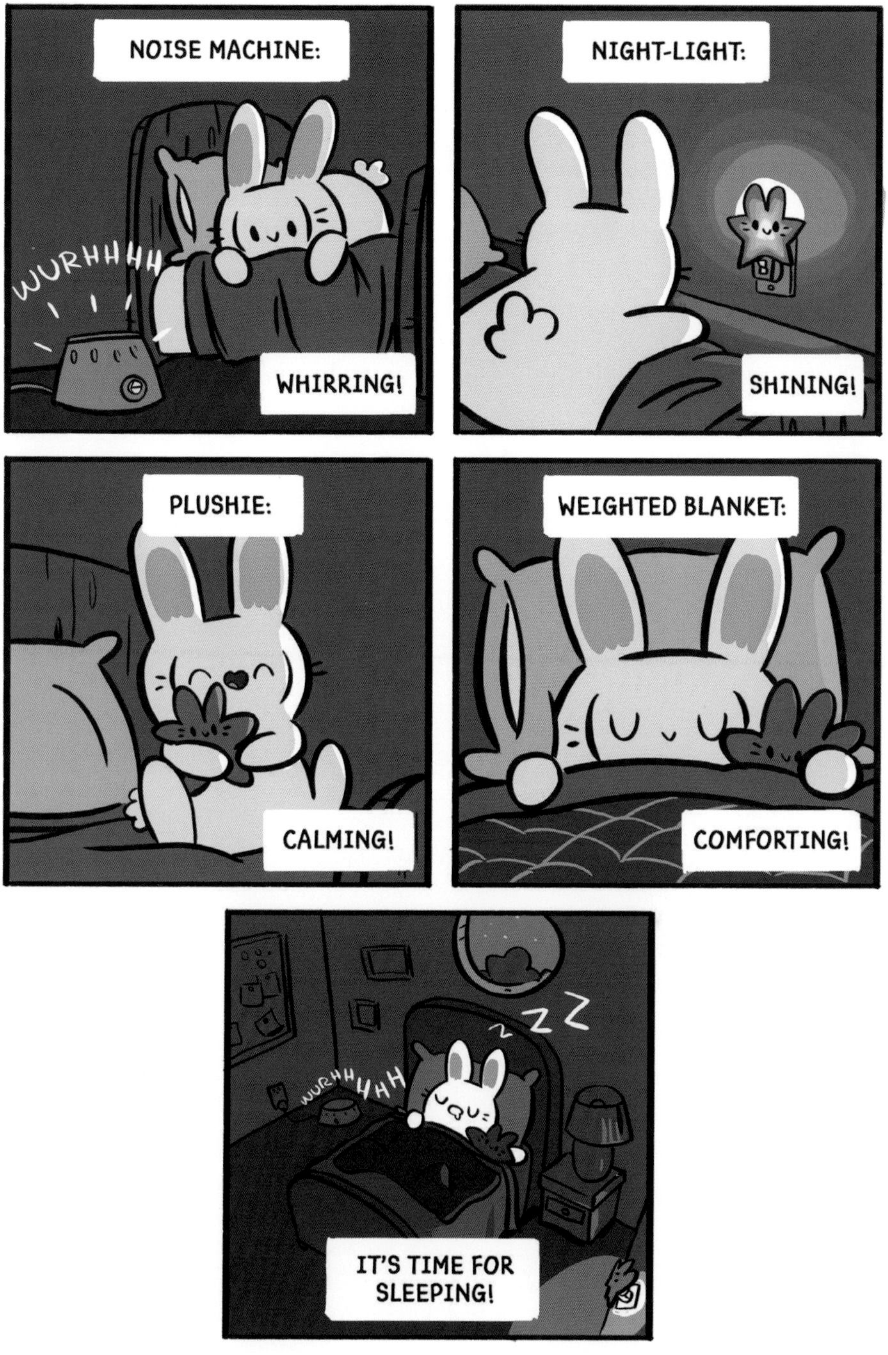
NOISE MACHINE:
WURHHHHH
WHIRRING!
NIGHT-LIGHT:
SHINING!
PLUSHIE:
CALMING!
WEIGHTED BLANKET:
COMFORTING!
Z Z Z
WURHHHHH
IT'S TIME FOR SLEEPING!

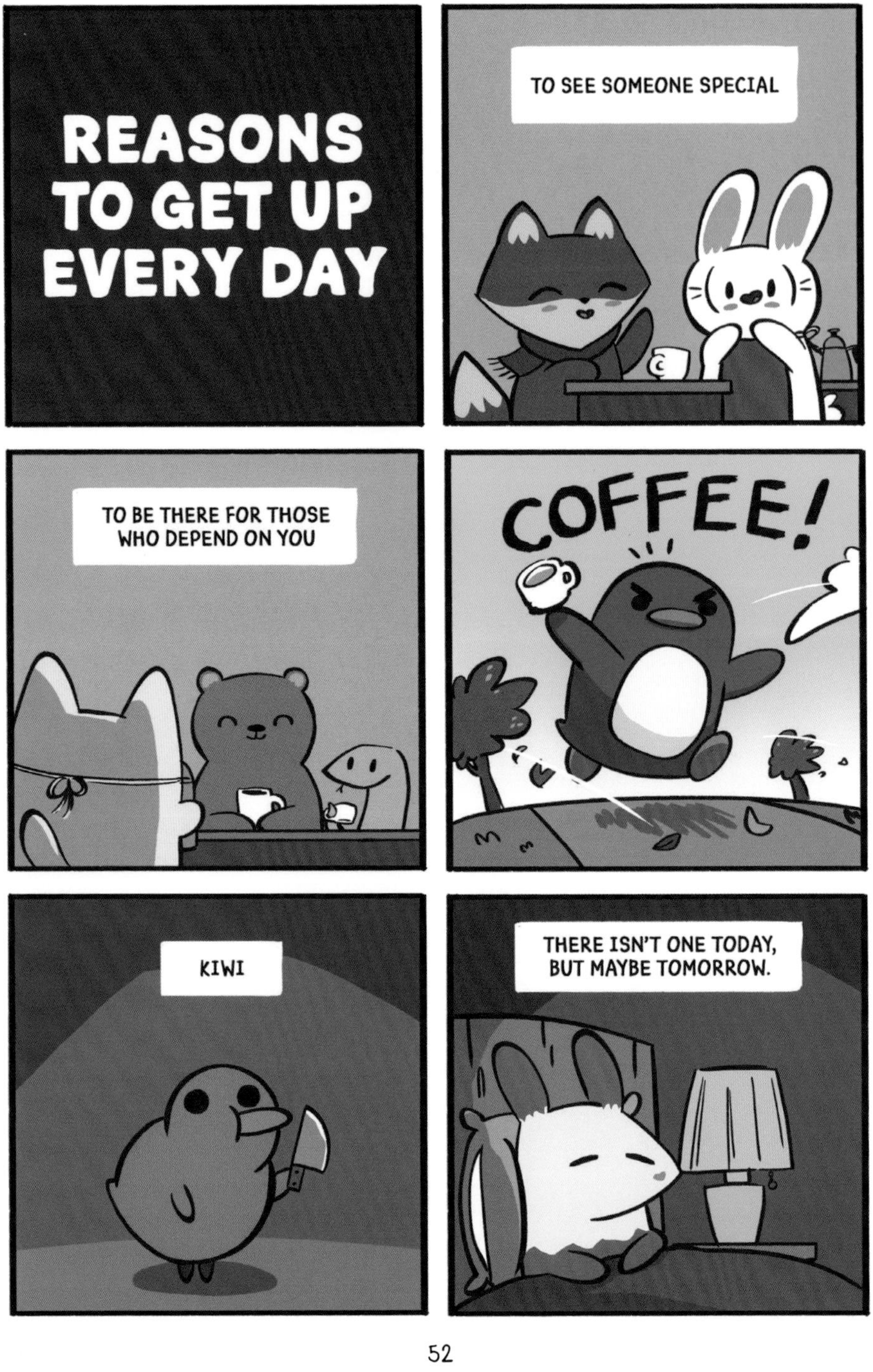
REASONS TO GET UP EVERY DAY
TO SEE SOMEONE SPECIAL
TO BE THERE FOR THOSE WHO DEPEND ON YOU
COFFEE!
KIWI
THERE ISN'T ONE TODAY, BUT MAYBE TOMORROW.

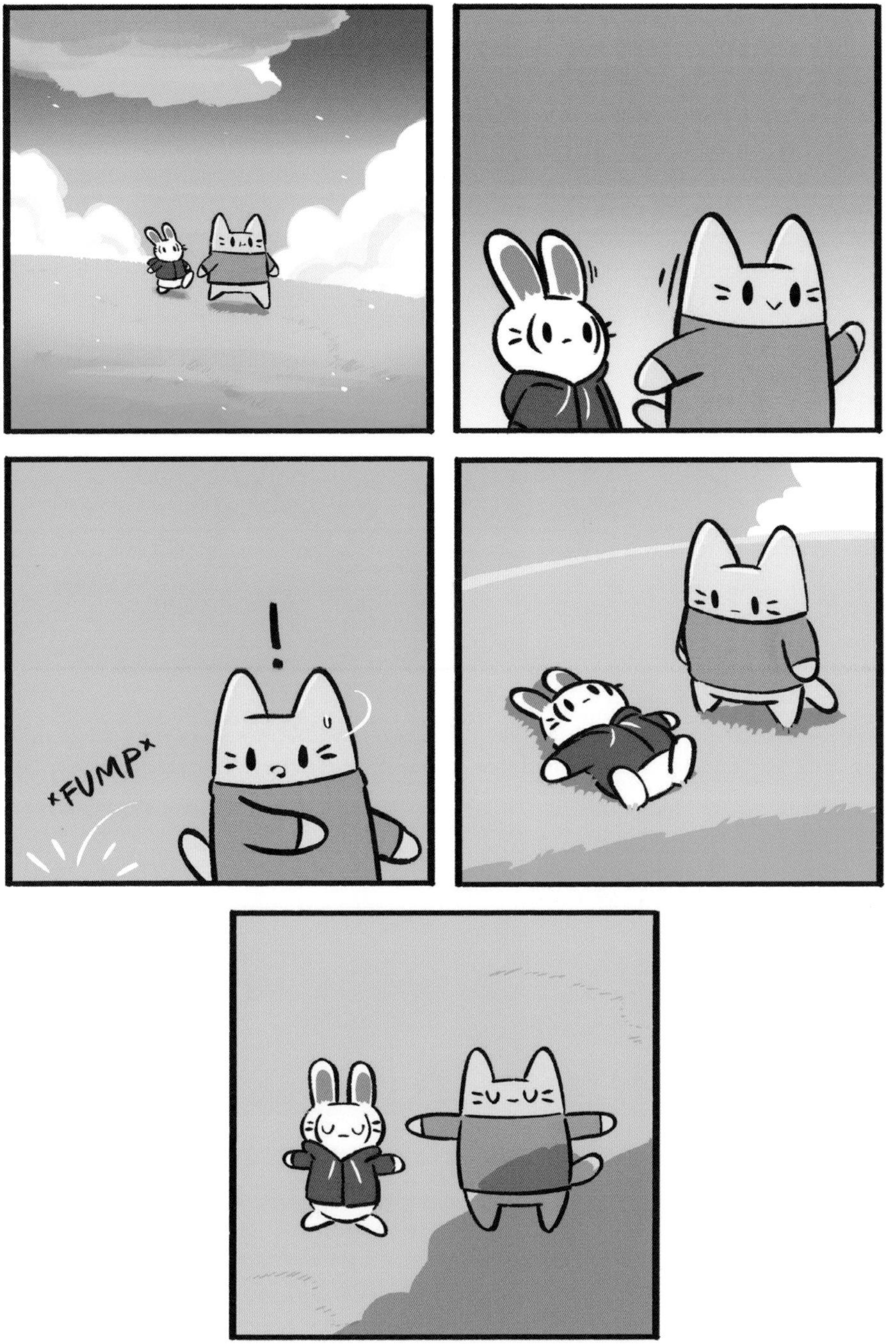
!
FUMP

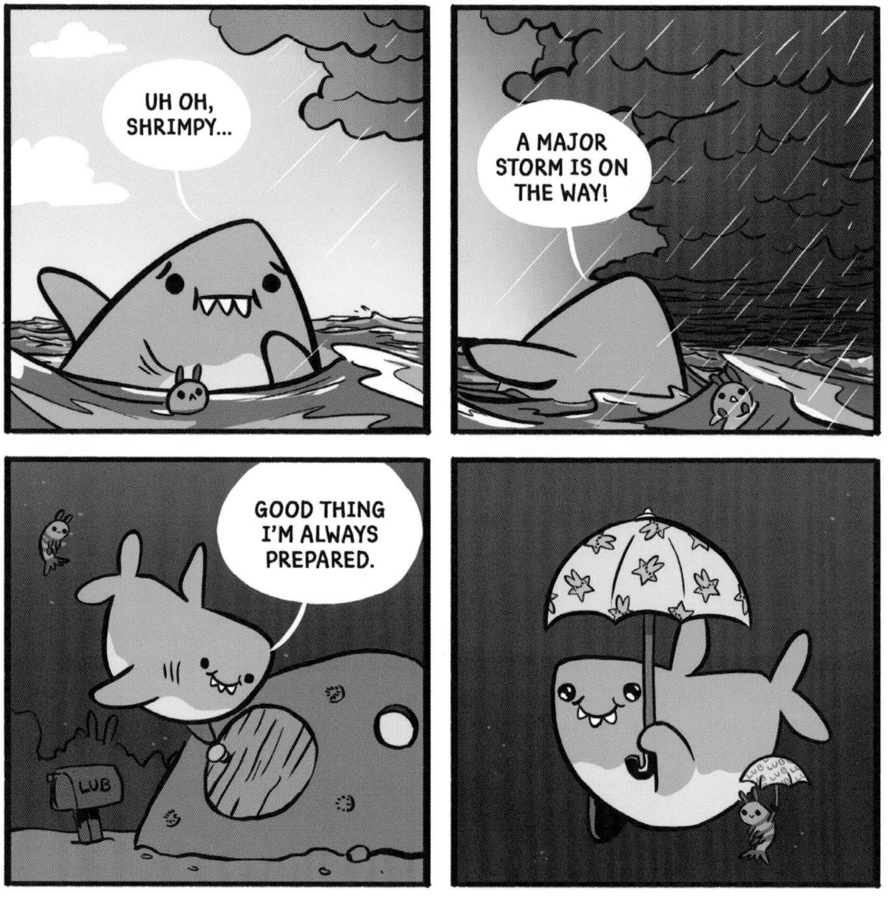
UH OH, SHRIMPY...
A MAJOR STORM IS ON THE WAY!
GOOD THING I'M ALWAYS PREPARED.
LUB

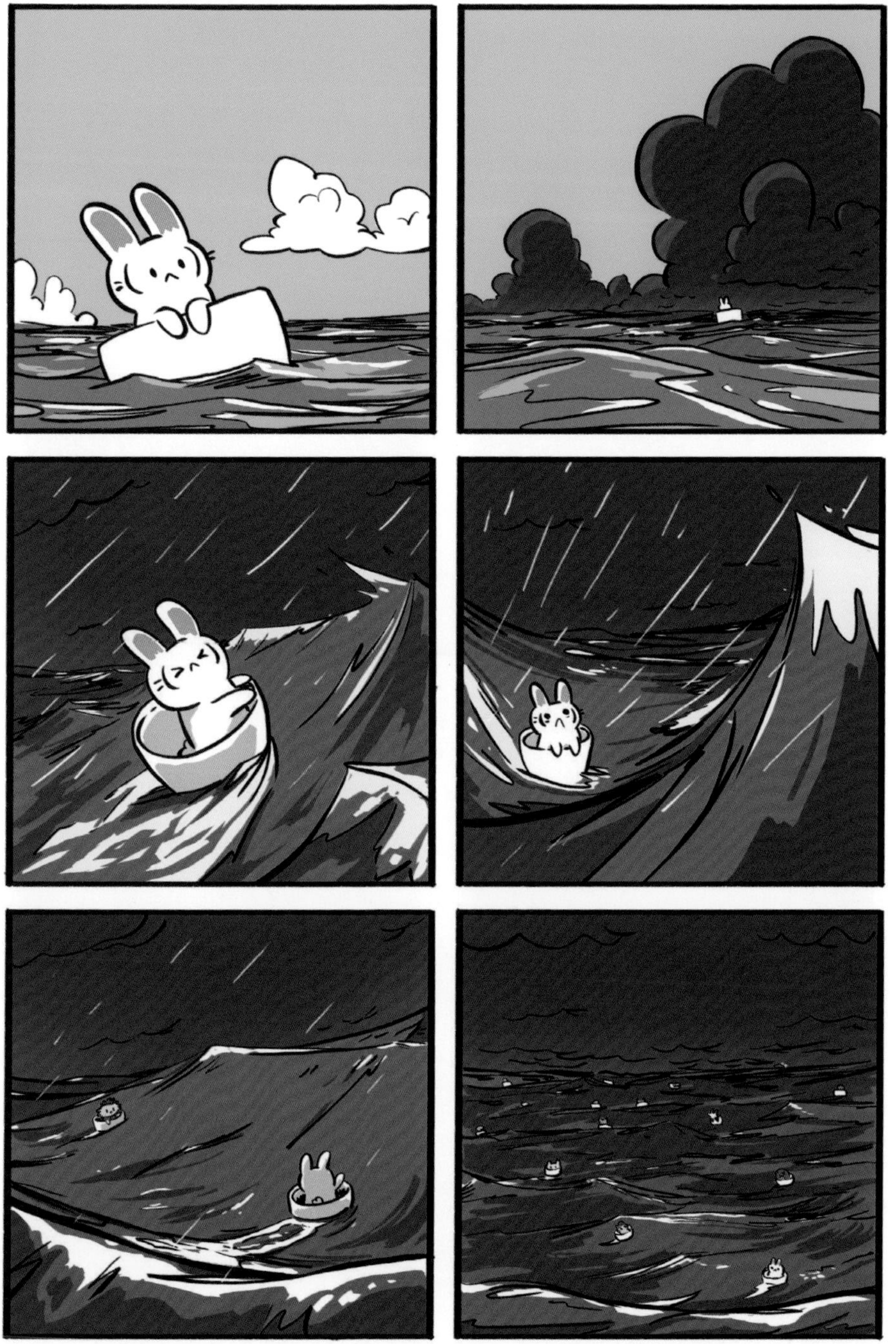

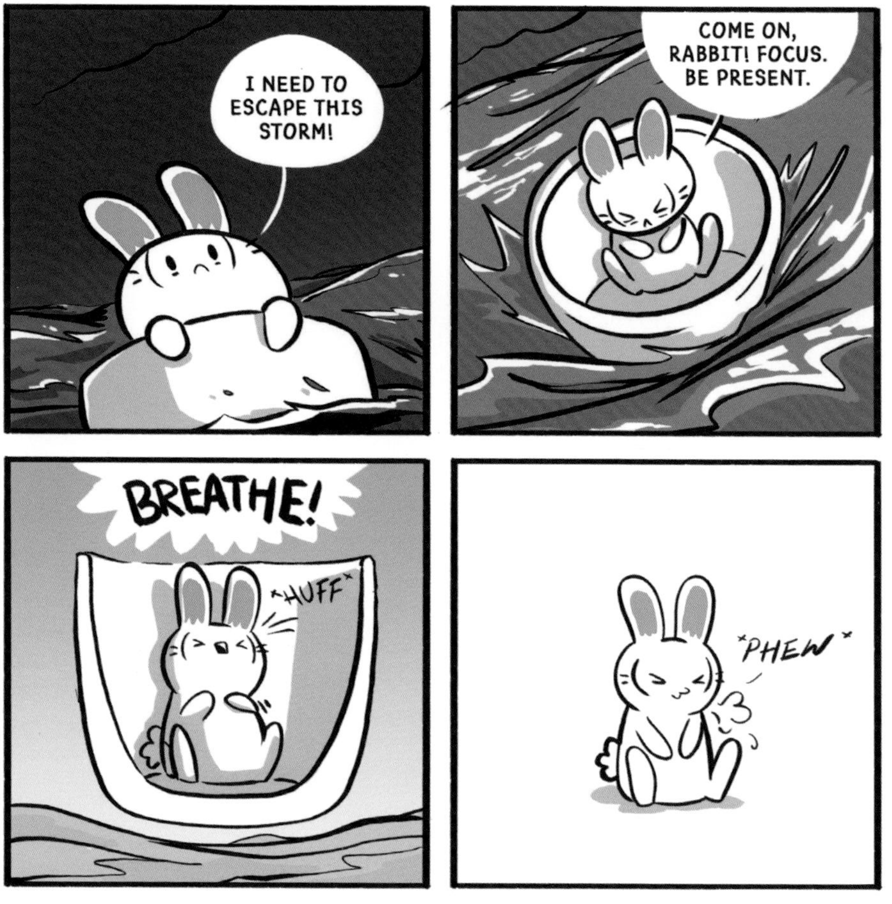
I NEED TO ESCAPE THIS STORM!
COME ON, RABBIT! FOCUS. BE PRESENT.
BREATHE!
HUFF
PHEW

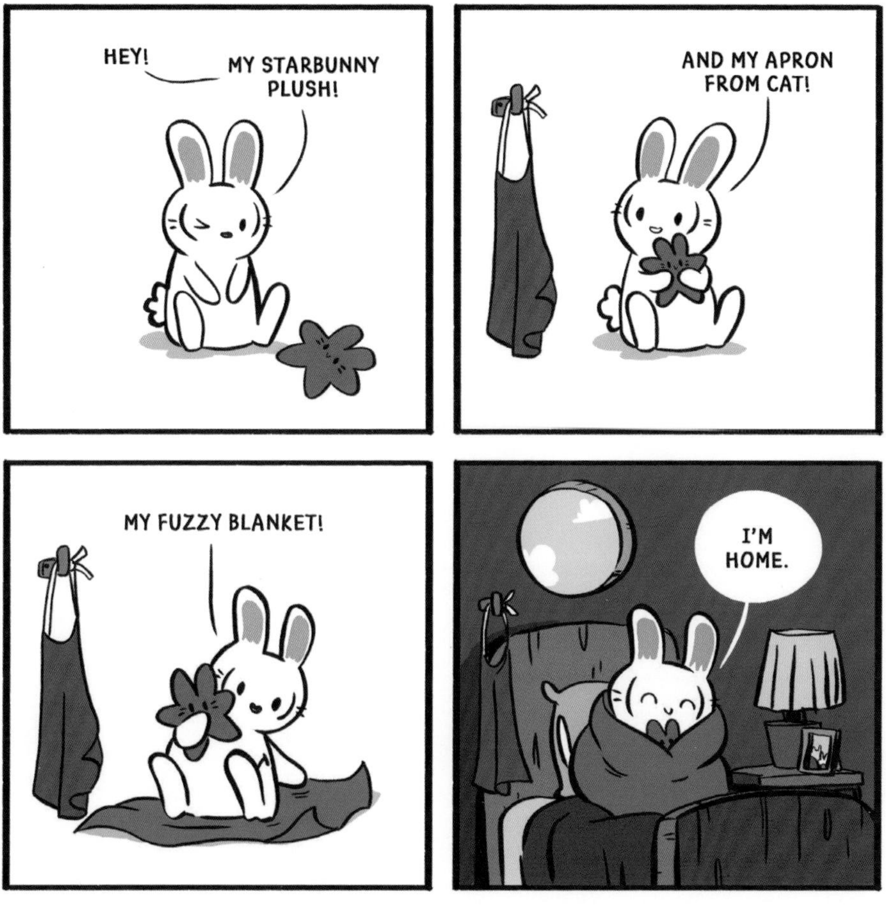
HEY!
MY STARBUNNY PLUSH!
AND MY APRON FROM CAT!
MY FUZZY BLANKET!
I'M HOME.

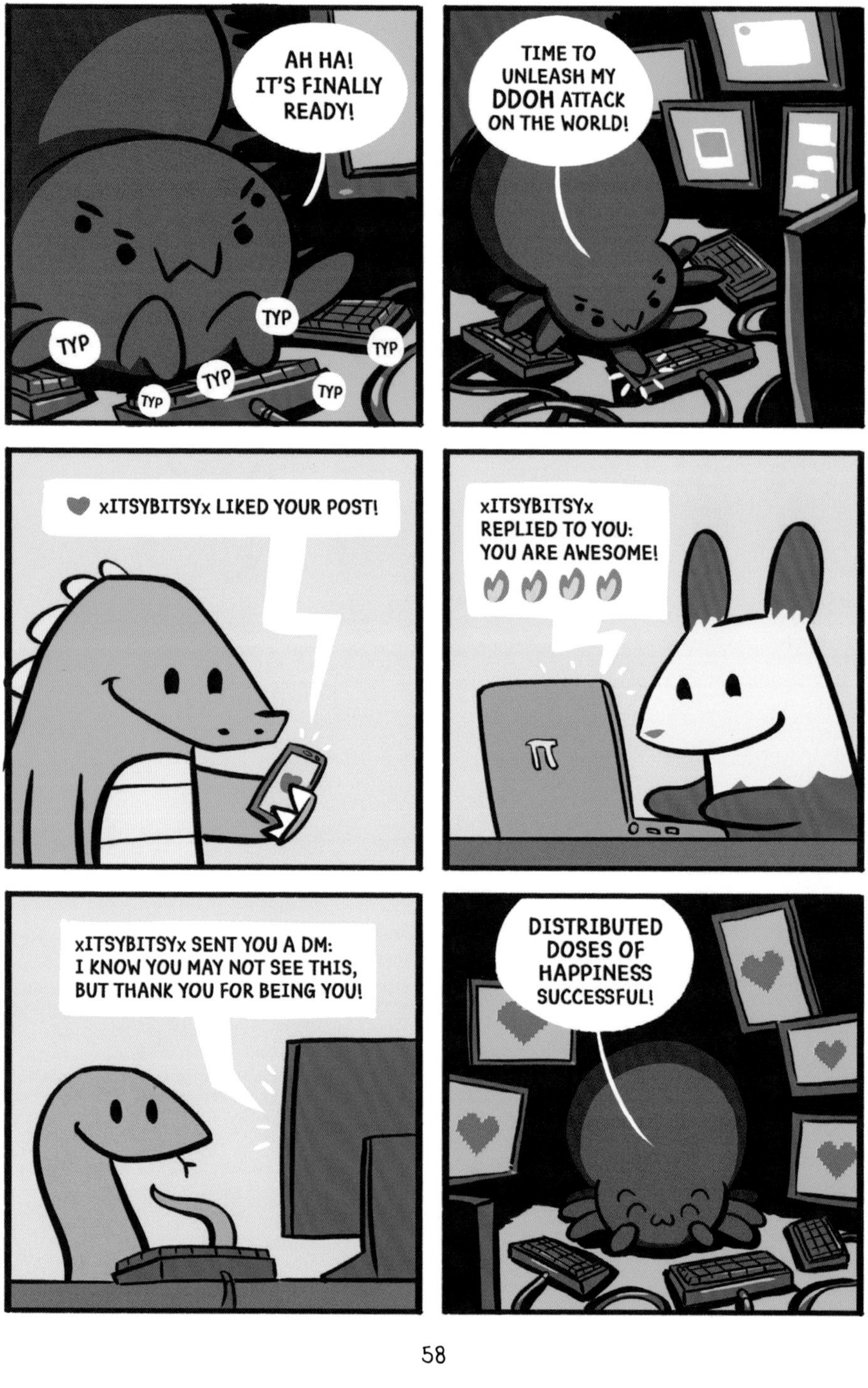
AH HA! IT'S FINALLY READY!
TYP
TYP
TYP
TYP
TYP
TYP
TIME TO UNLEASH MY DDOH ATTACK ON THE WORLD!
xITSYBITSYx LIKED YOUR POST!
xITSYBITSYx REPLIED TO YOU: YOU ARE AWESOME!
xITSYBITSYx SENT YOU A DM: I KNOW YOU MAY NOT SEE THIS, BUT THANK YOU FOR BEING YOU!
DISTRIBUTED DOSES OF HAPPINESS SUCCESSFUL!

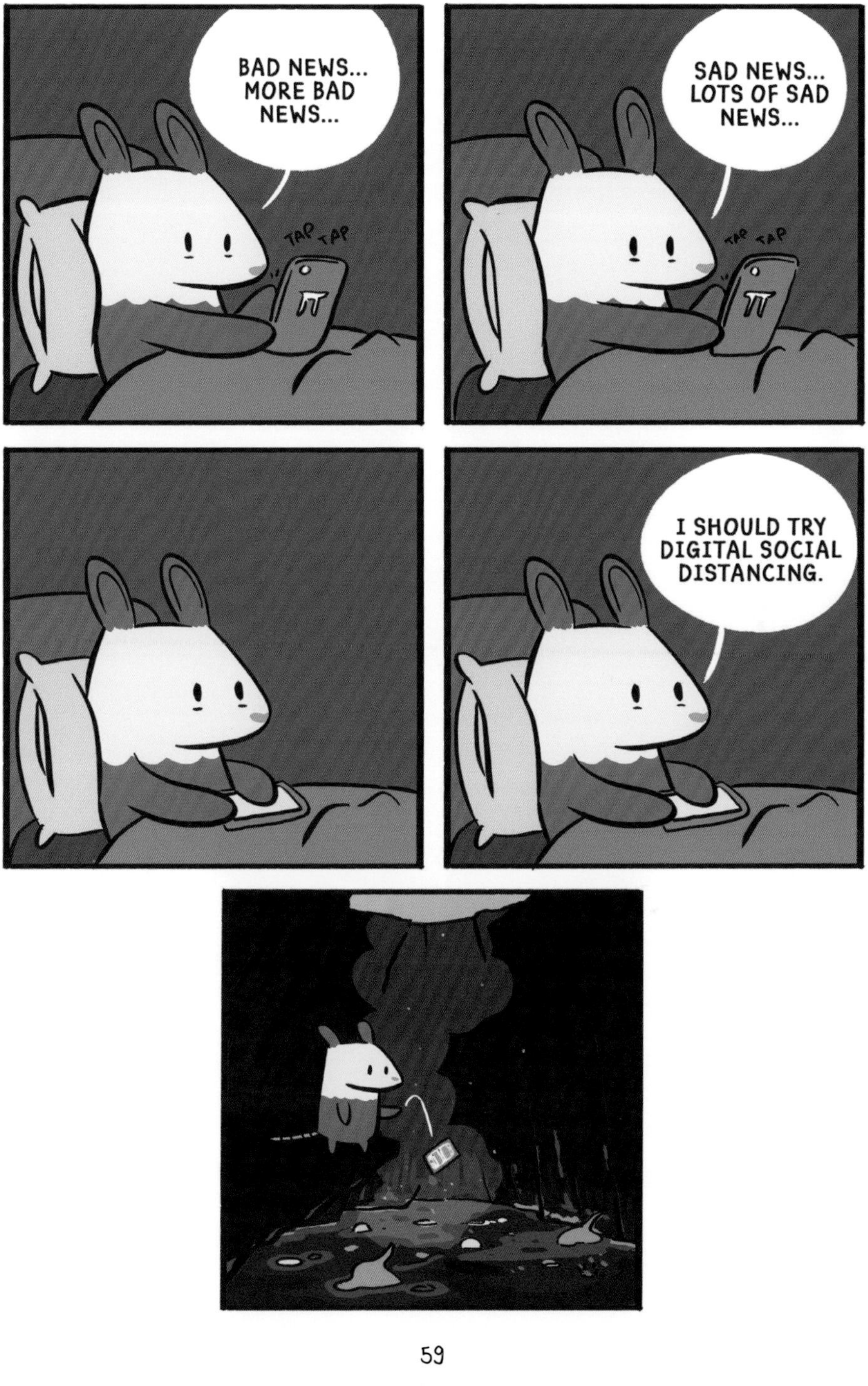
BAD NEWS... MORE BAD NEWS...
TAP TAP
SAD NEWS... LOTS OF SAD NEWS...
TAP TAP
I SHOULD TRY DIGITAL SOCIAL DISTANCING.

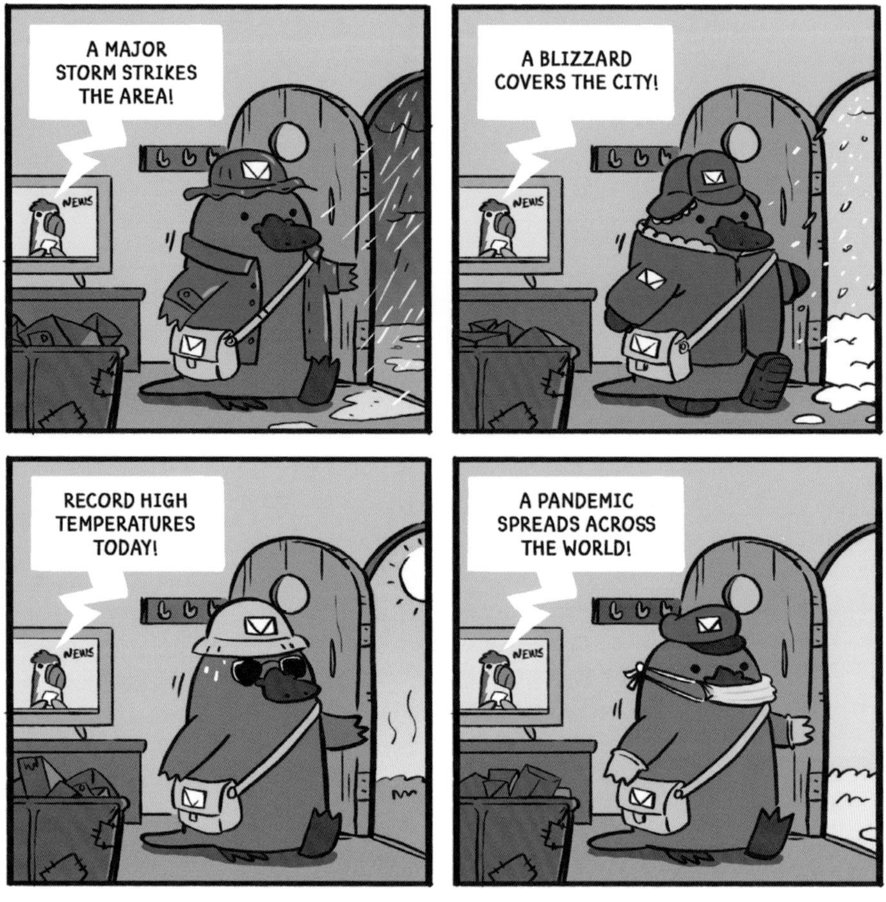
A MAJOR STORM STRIKES THE AREA!
NEWS
A BLIZZARD COVERS THE CITY!
NEWS
RECORD HIGH TEMPERATURES TODAY!
NEWS
A PANDEMIC SPREADS ACROSS THE WORLD!
NEWS

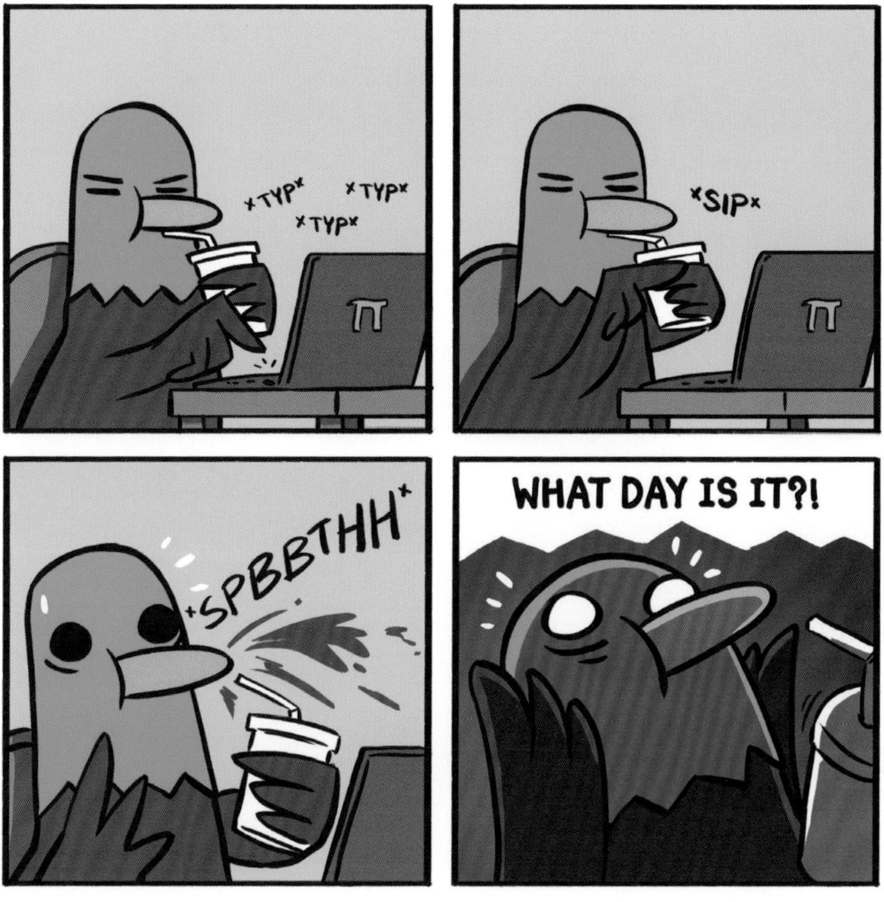
TYP
TYP
TYP
SIP
SPBBTHH
WHAT DAY IS IT?!

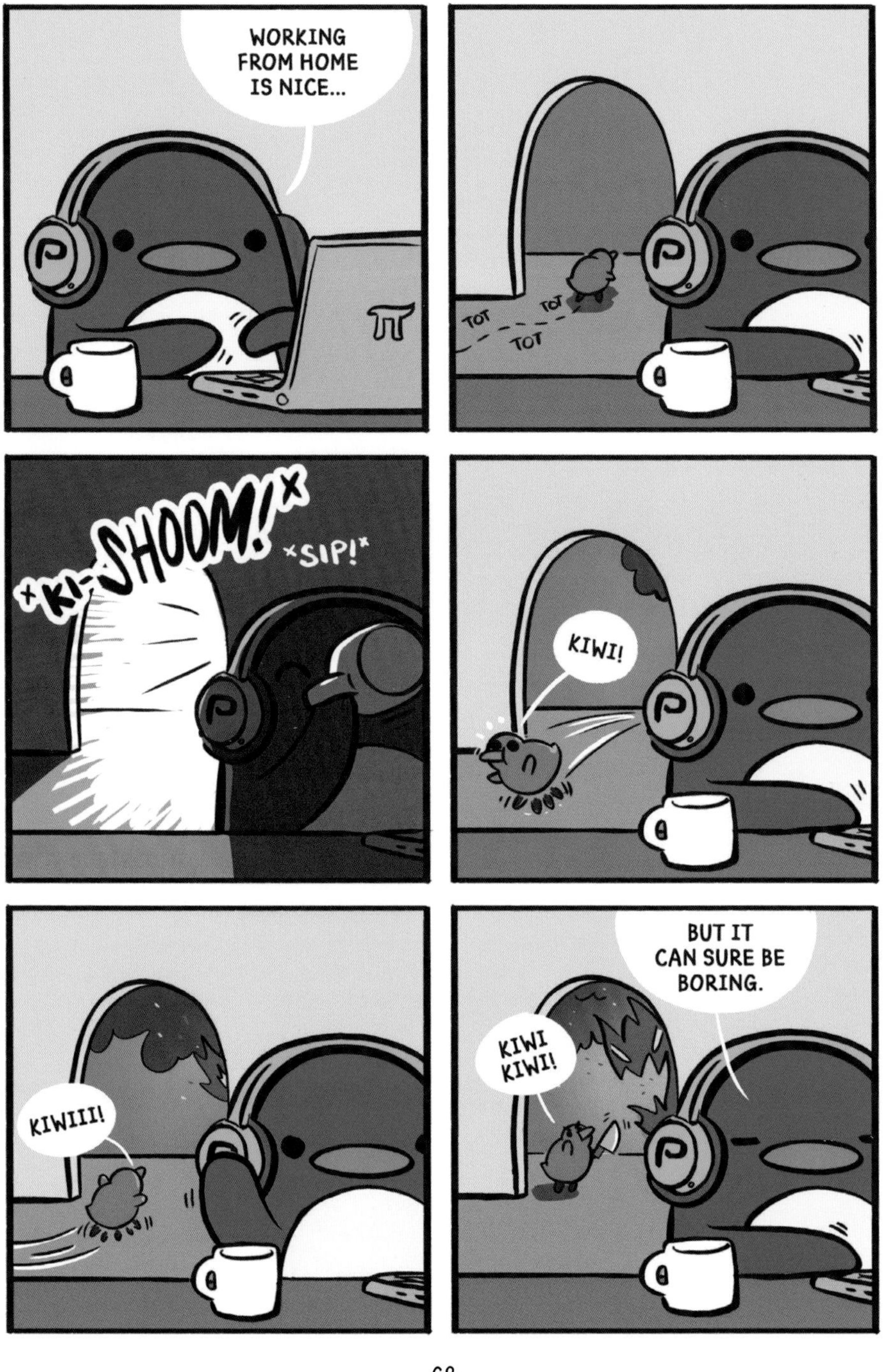
WORKING FROM HOME IS NICE...
TOT
TOT
TOT
KI-SHOOM!
SIP!
KIWI!
KIWIII!
BUT IT CAN SURE BE BORING.
KIWI KIWI!

QUARANTINE HAIRSTYLES

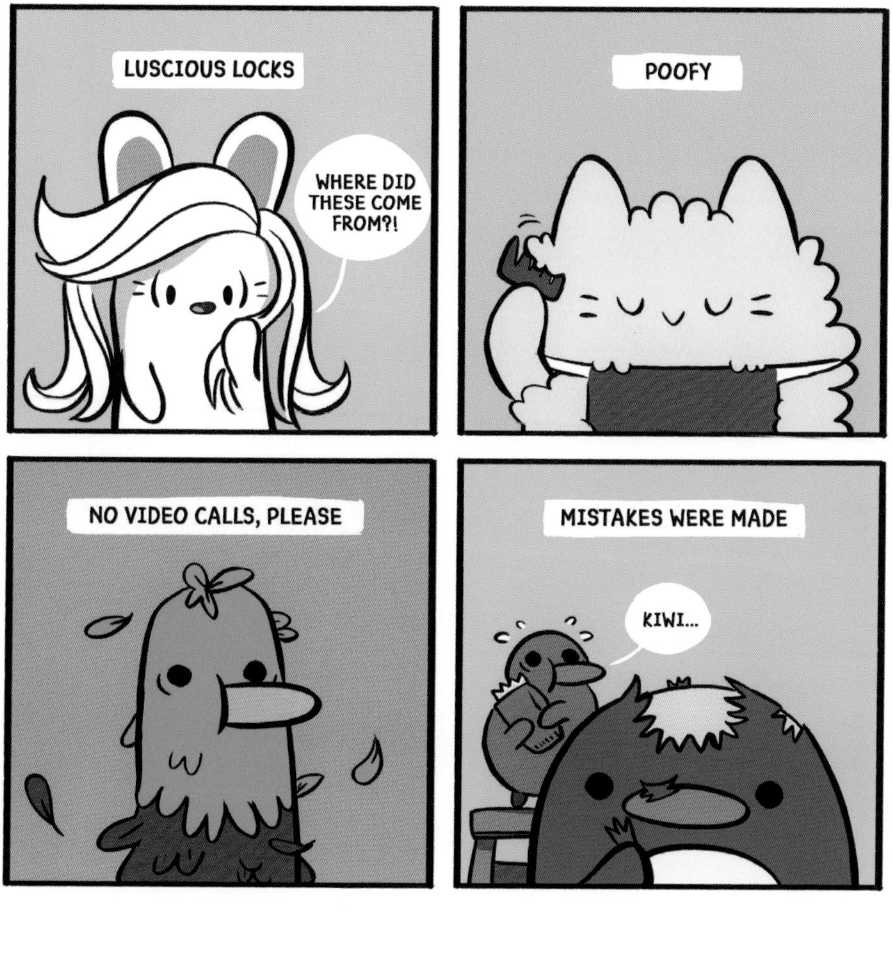
LUSCIOUS LOCKS
WHERE DID THESE COME FROM?!
POOFY
NO VIDEO CALLS, PLEASE
MISTAKES WERE MADE
KIWI...

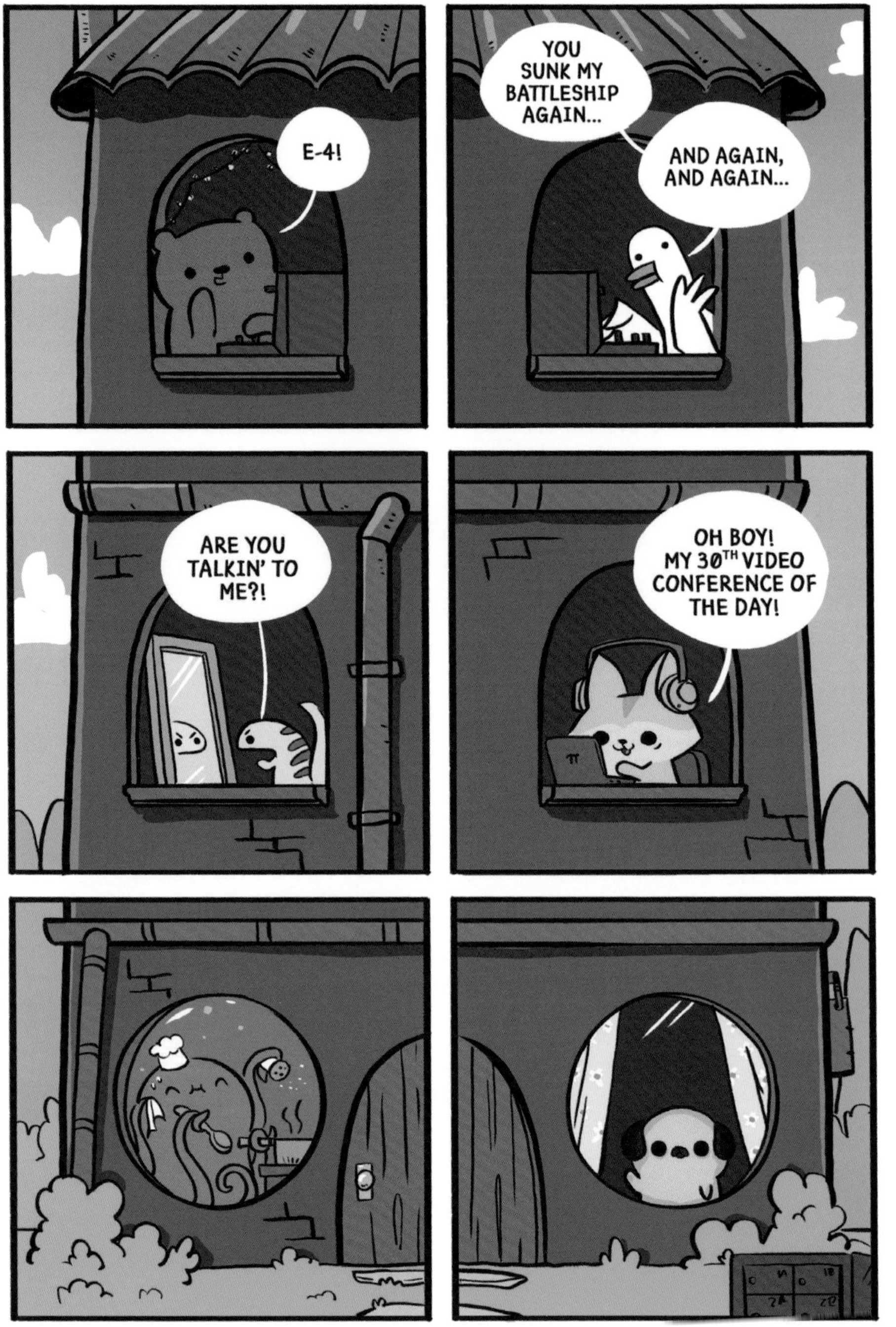
E-4!
YOU SUNK MY BATTLESHIP AGAIN...
AND AGAIN, AND AGAIN...
ARE YOU TALKIN' TO ME?!
OH BOY! MY 30TH VIDEO CONFERENCE OF THE DAY!

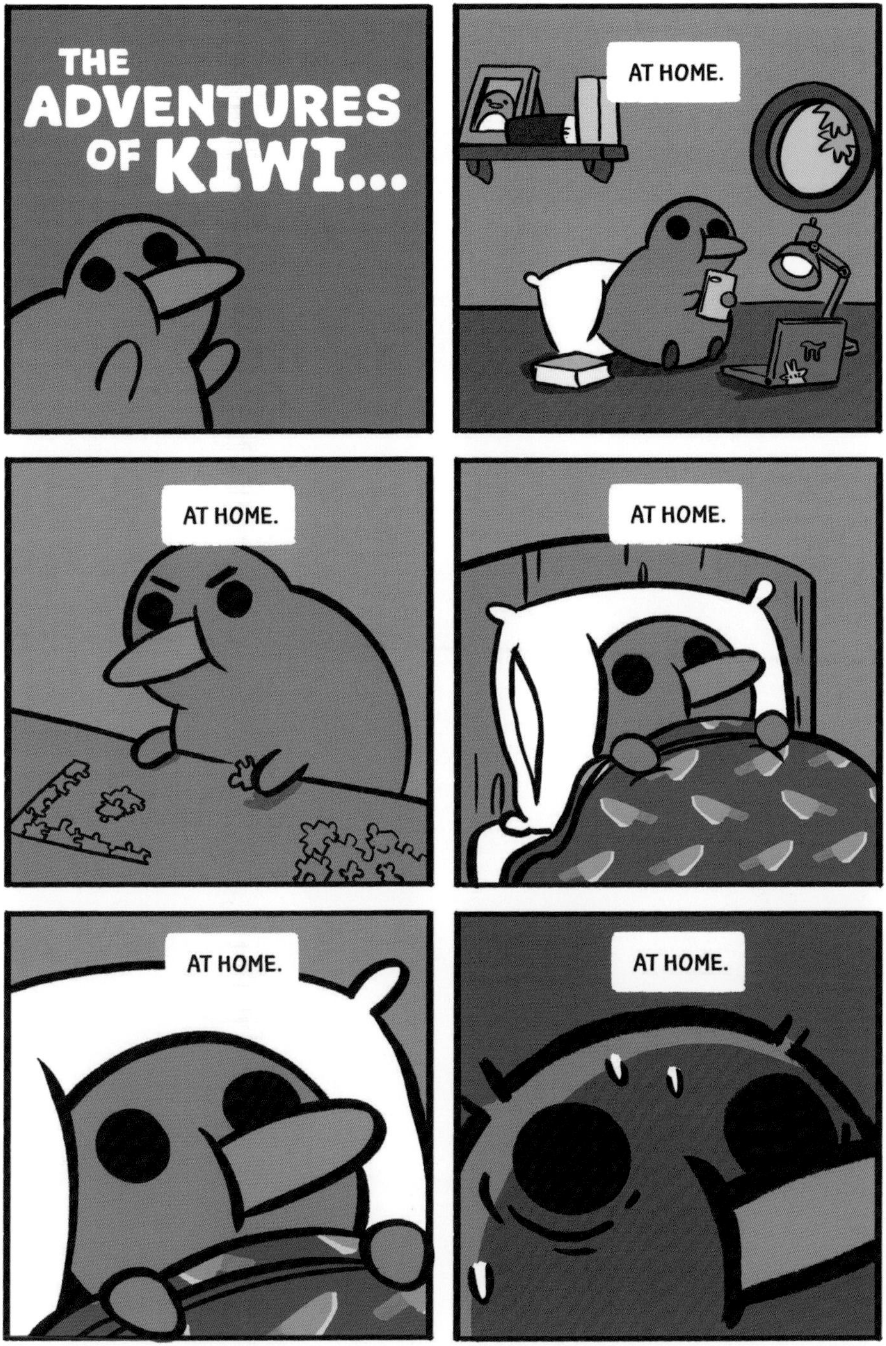
THE ADVENTURES OF KIWI...
AT HOME.
AT HOME.
AT HOME.
AT HOME.
AT HOME.

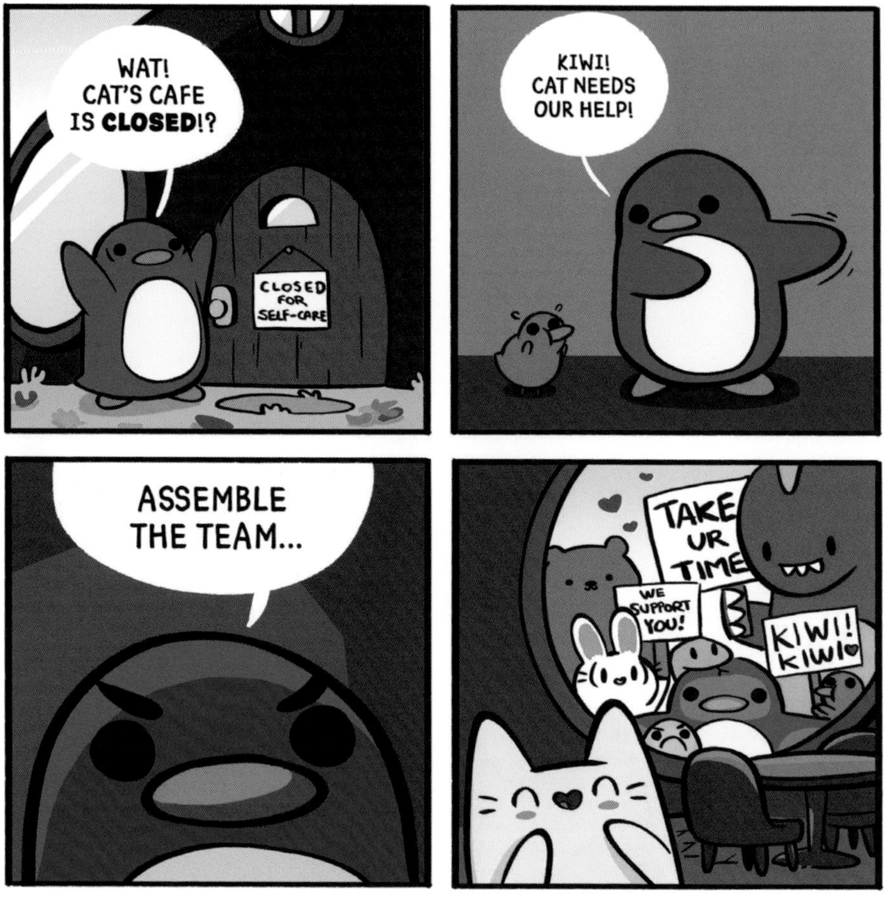
WAT! CAT'S CAFE IS **CLOSED**!?
CLOSED FOR SELF-CARE
KIWI! CAT NEEDS OUR HELP!
ASSEMBLE THE TEAM...
TAKE UR TIME
WE SUPPORT YOU!
KIWI! KIWI

SCIENTISTS HAVE WORKED TIRELESSLY FOR A VACCINE...
DESPERATE FOR HELP...
THEY CALL UPON THEIR LAST RESORT...
KIWI KIWI!

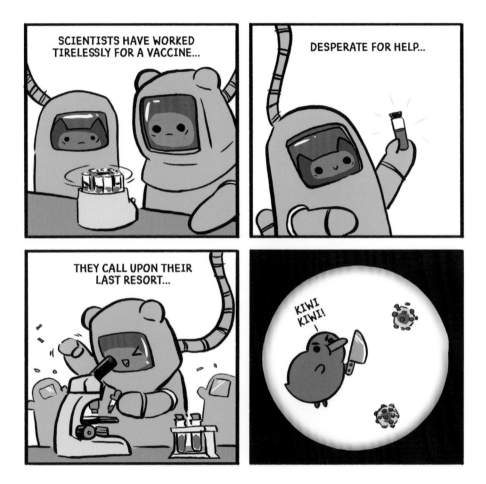

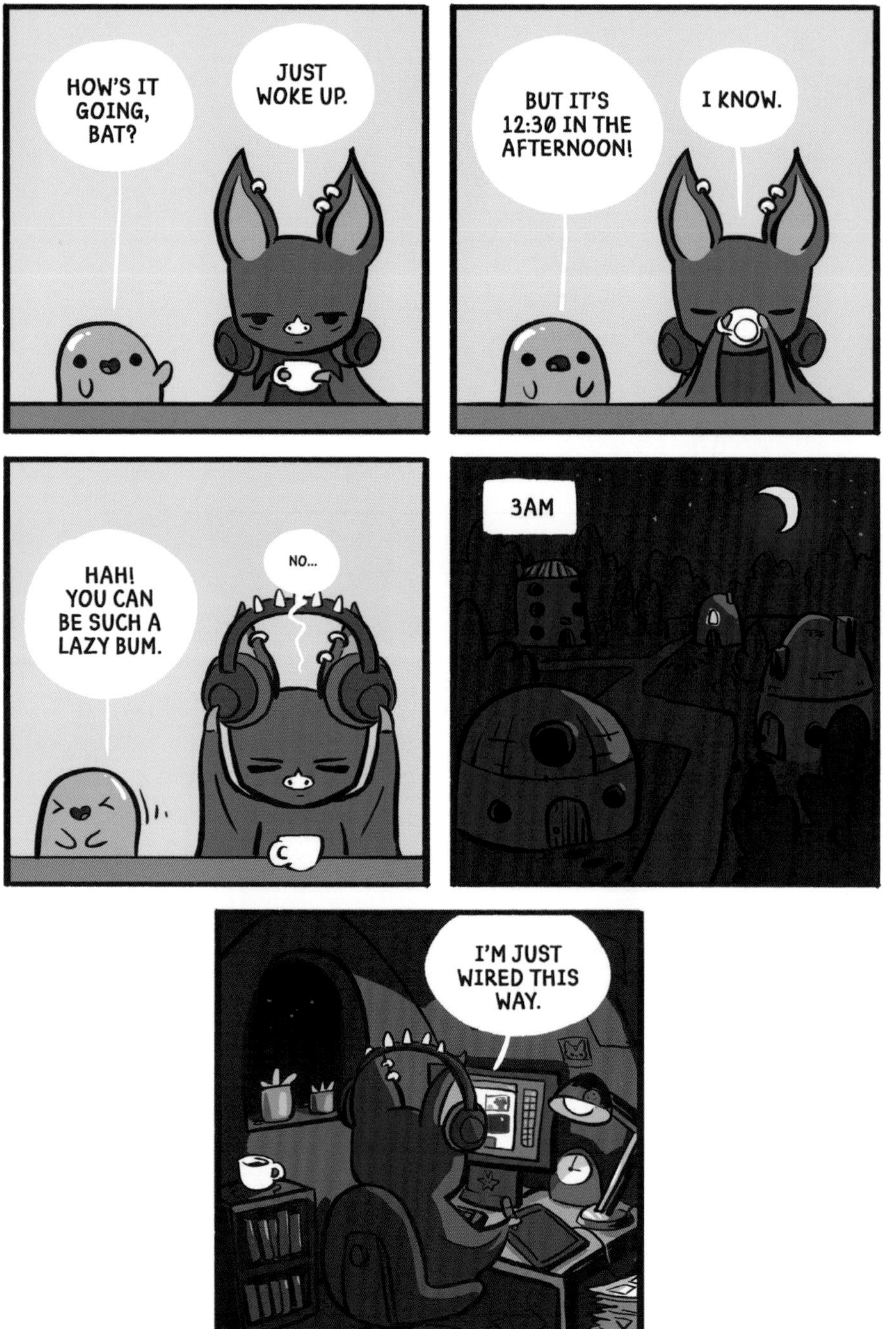
HOW'S IT GOING, BAT?
JUST WOKE UP.
BUT IT'S 12:30 IN THE AFTERNOON!
I KNOW.
HAH! YOU CAN BE SUCH A LAZY BUM.
NO...
3AM
I'M JUST WIRED THIS WAY.

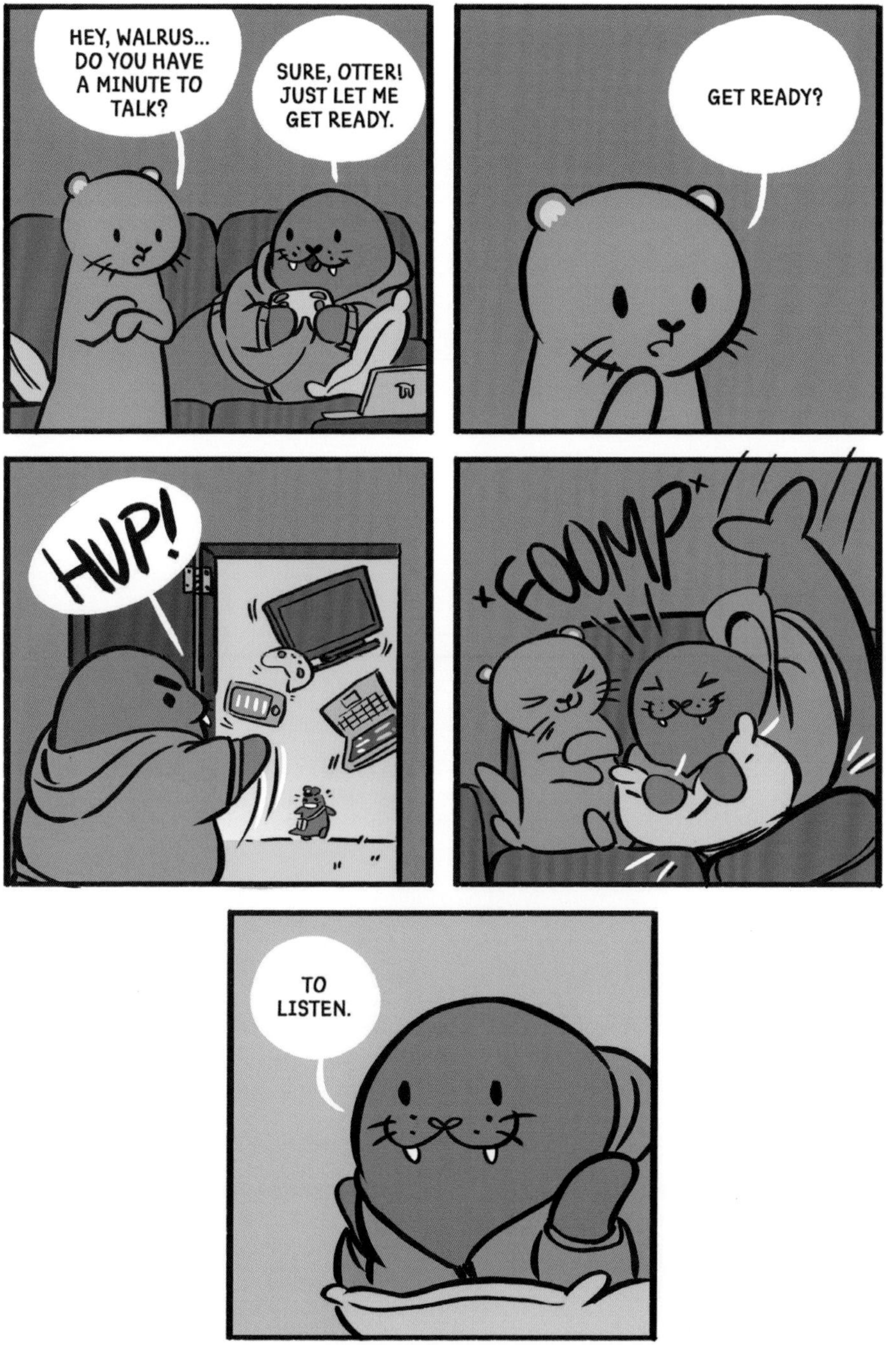
HEY, WALRUS... DO YOU HAVE A MINUTE TO TALK?
SURE, OTTER! JUST LET ME GET READY.
GET READY?
HUP!
FOOMP
TO LISTEN.

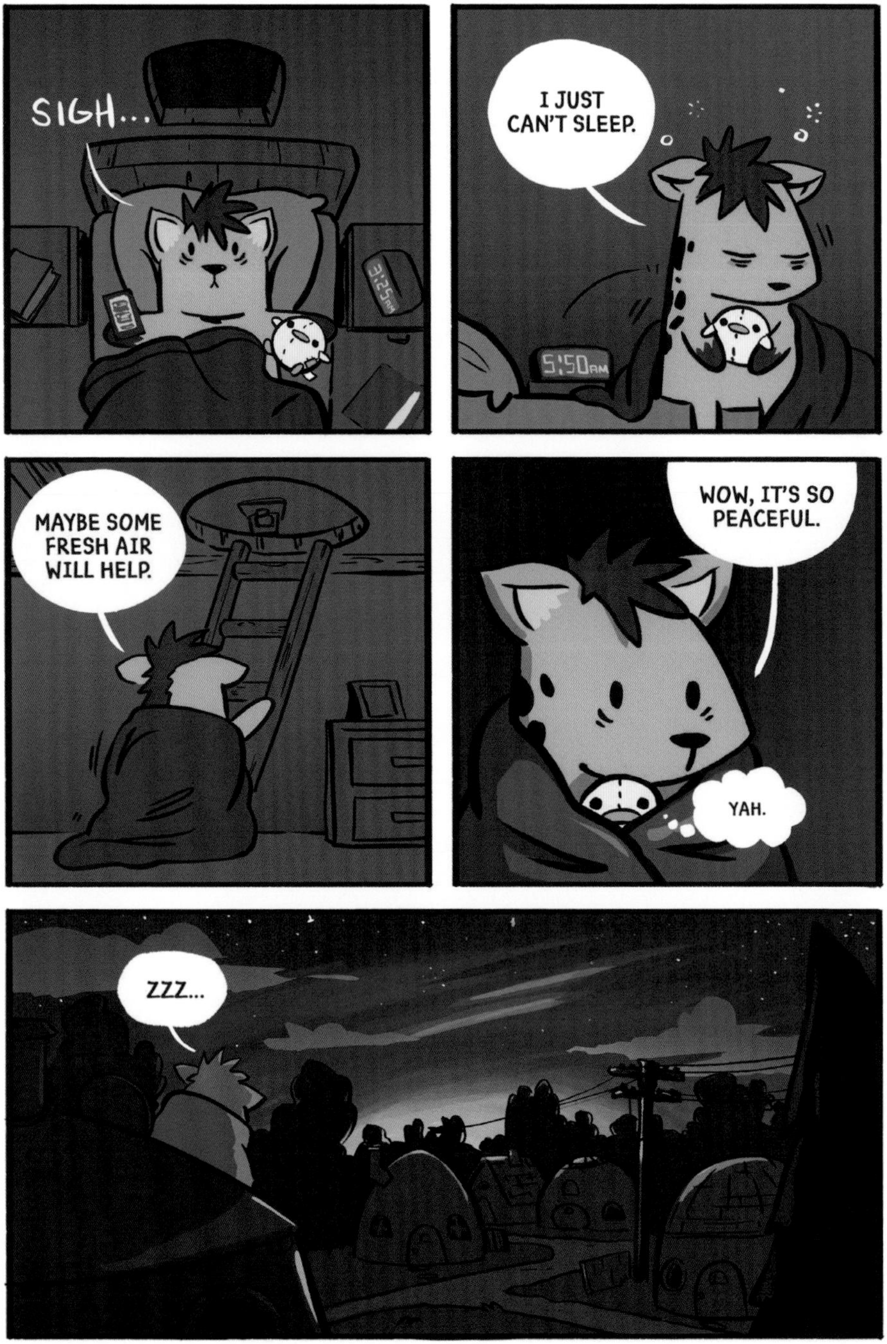
SIGH...
I JUST CAN'T SLEEP.
MAYBE SOME FRESH AIR WILL HELP.
WOW, IT'S SO PEACEFUL.
YAH.
ZZZ...

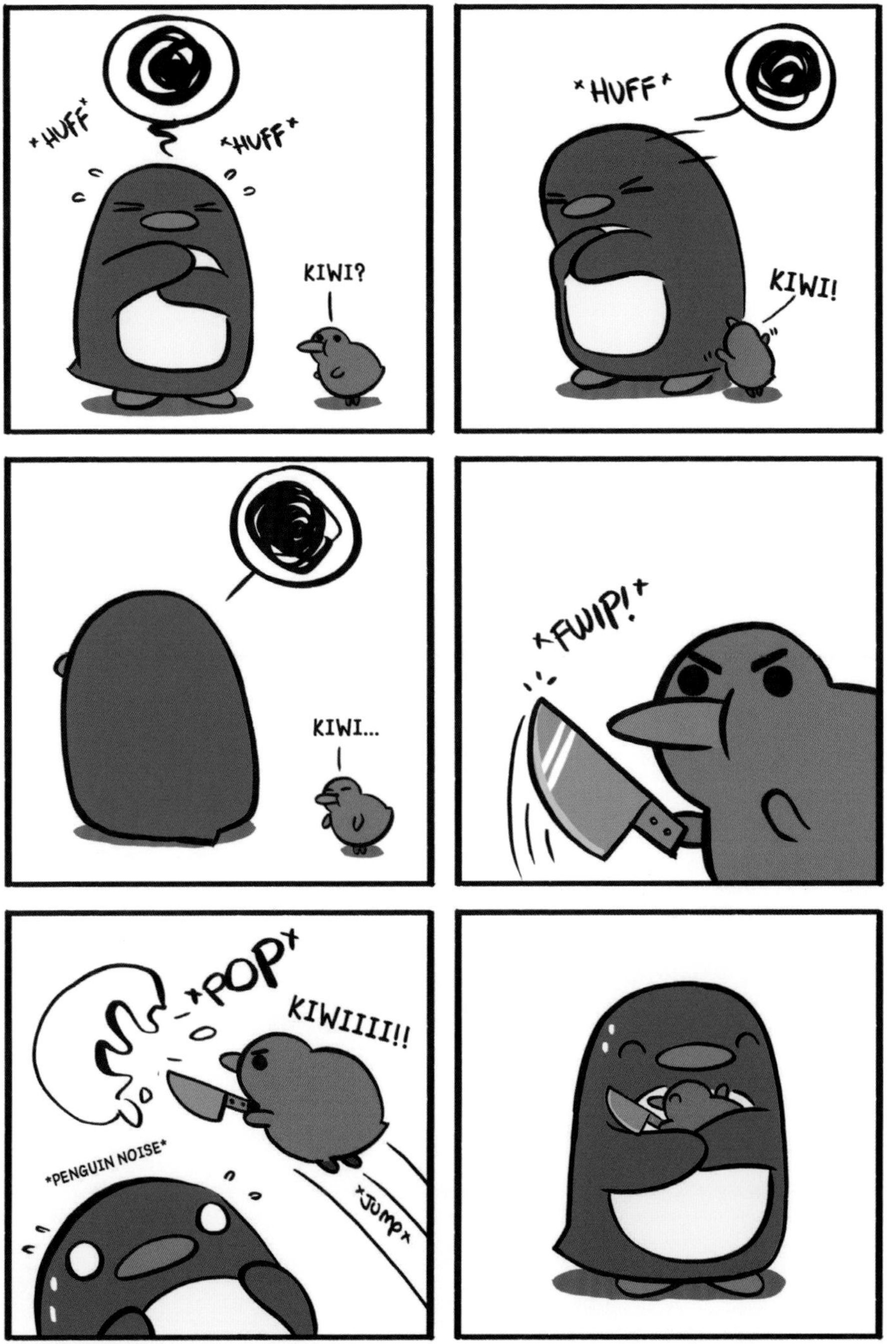
HUFF
HUFF
KIWI?
HUFF
KIWI!
KIWI...
FWIP!
POP
KIWIIII!!
PENGUIN NOISE
JUMP

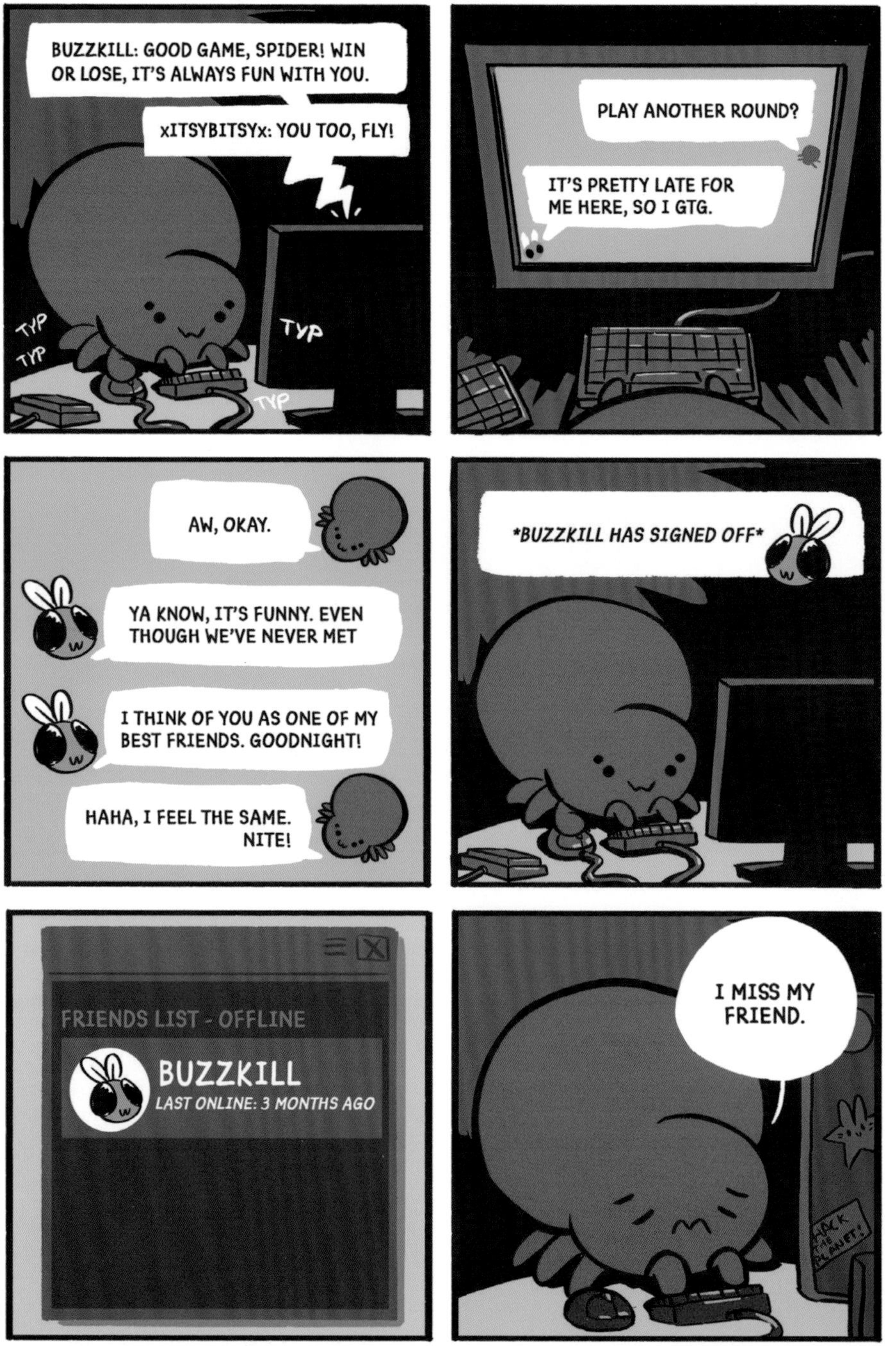
BUZZKILL: GOOD GAME, SPIDER! WIN OR LOSE, IT'S ALWAYS FUN WITH YOU.
xITSYBITSYx: YOU TOO, FLY!
TYP
TYP
TYP
TYP
PLAY ANOTHER ROUND?
IT'S PRETTY LATE FOR ME HERE, SO I GTG.
AW, OKAY.
YA KNOW, IT'S FUNNY. EVEN THOUGH WE'VE NEVER MET
I THINK OF YOU AS ONE OF MY BEST FRIENDS. GOODNIGHT!
HAHA, I FEEL THE SAME. NITE!
BUZZKILL HAS SIGNED OFF
FRIENDS LIST - OFFLINE
BUZZKILL
LAST ONLINE: 3 MONTHS AGO
I MISS MY FRIEND.

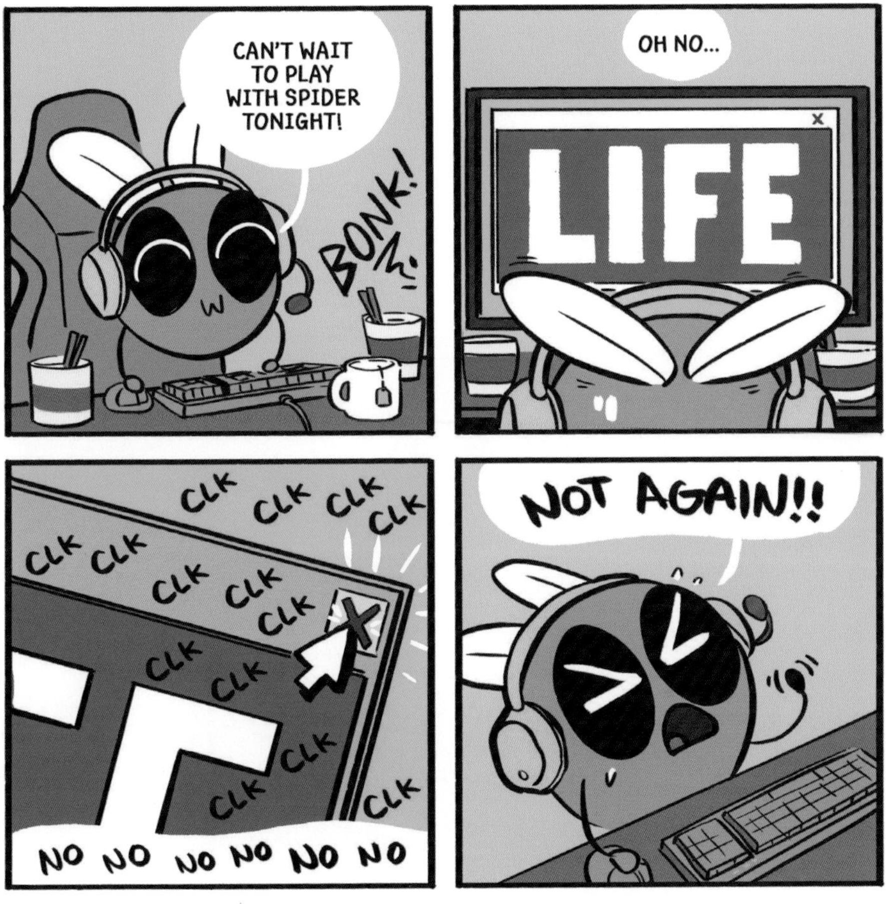
CAN'T WAIT TO PLAY WITH SPIDER TONIGHT!
BONK!
OH NO...
LIFE
CLK CLK CLK CLK CLK CLK CLK CLK CLK CLK CLK CLK CLK CLK CLK
NO NO NO NO NO NO
NOT AGAIN!!

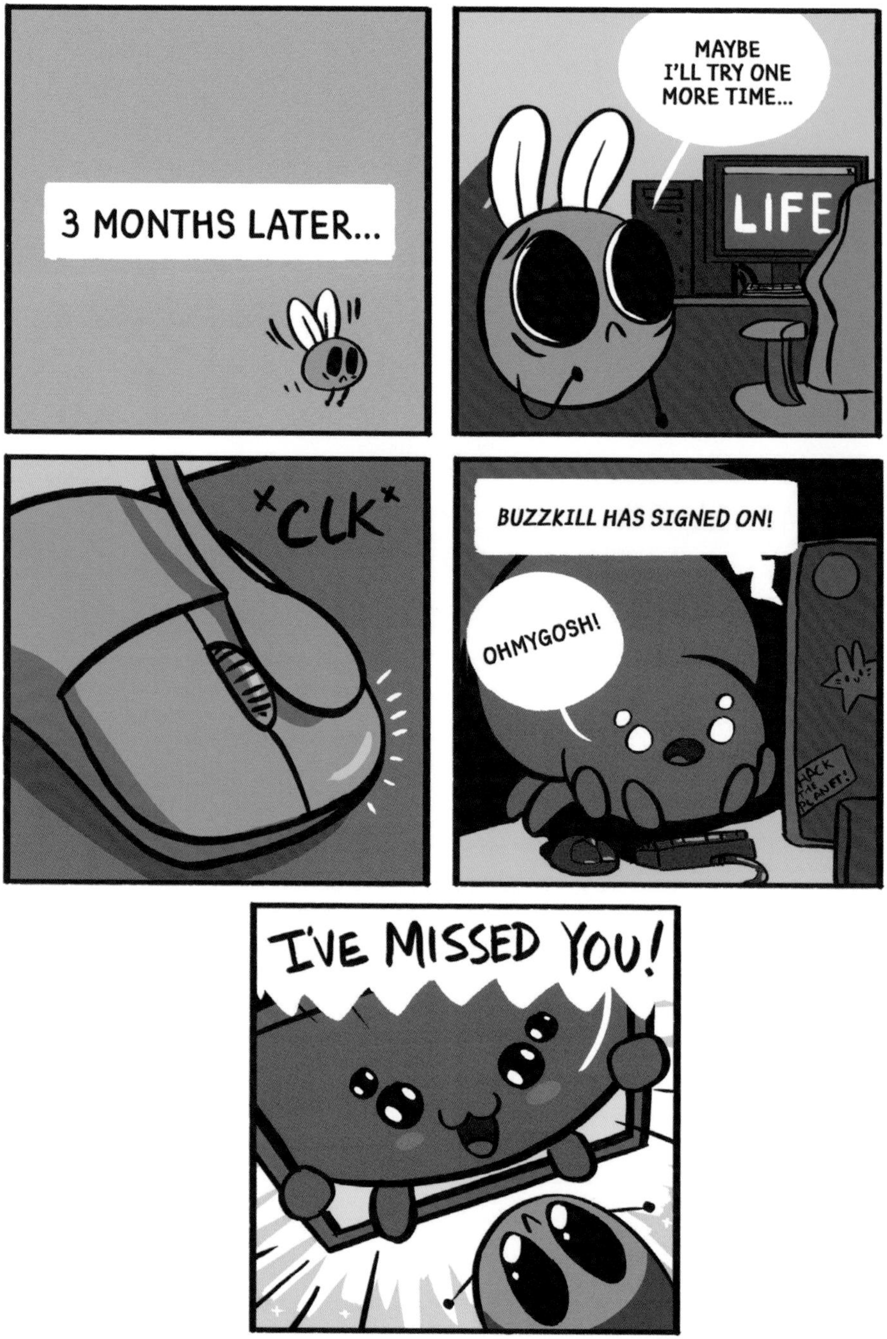
3 MONTHS LATER...
MAYBE I'LL TRY ONE MORE TIME...
LIFE
CLK
BUZZKILL HAS SIGNED ON!
OHMYGOSH!
HACK THE PLANET!
I'VE MISSED YOU!

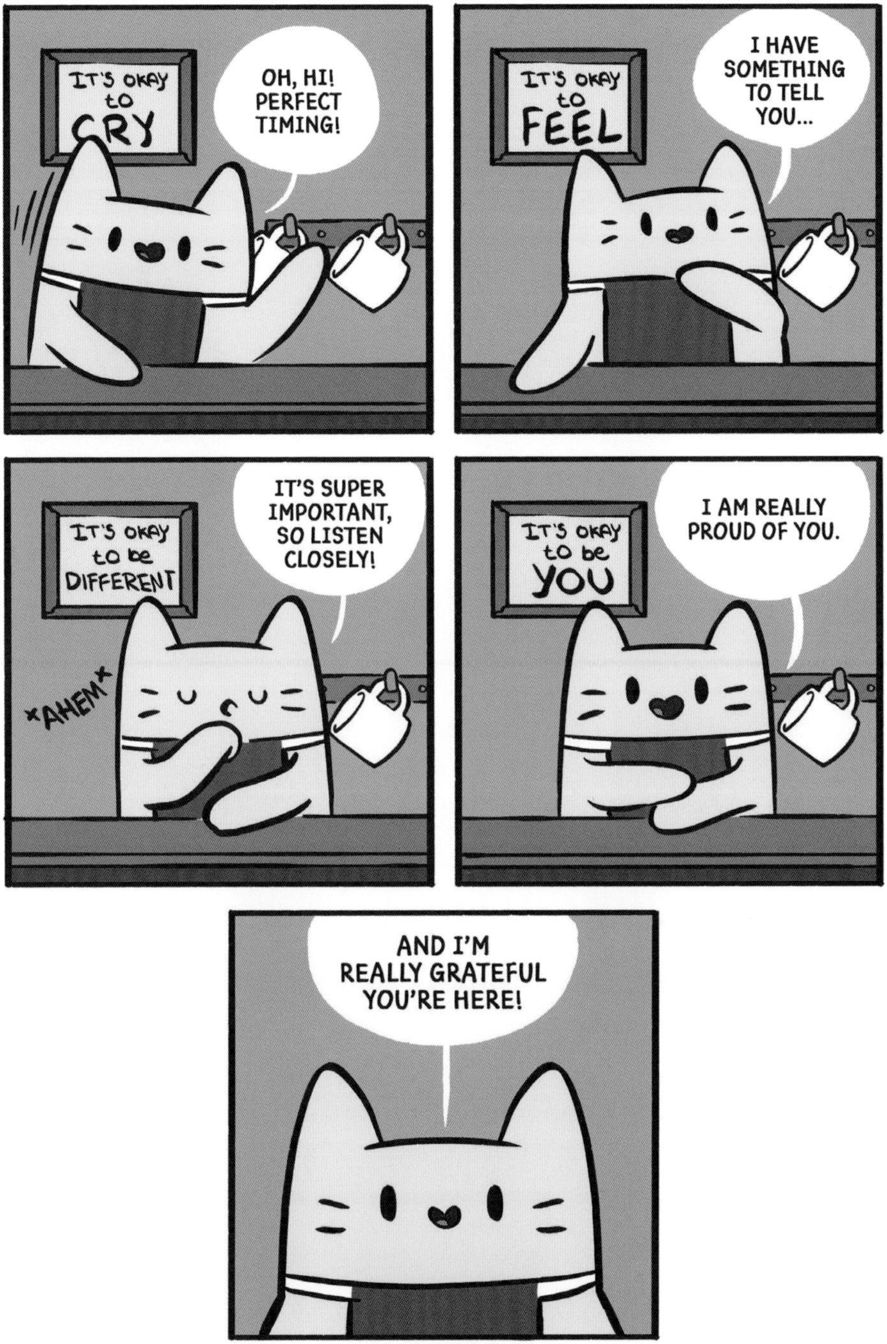
IT'S OKAY to CRY
OH, HI! PERFECT TIMING!
IT'S OKAY to FEEL
I HAVE SOMETHING TO TELL YOU...
IT'S OKAY to be DIFFERENT
IT'S SUPER IMPORTANT, SO LISTEN CLOSELY!
AHEM
IT'S OKAY to be YOU
I AM REALLY PROUD OF YOU.
AND I'M REALLY GRATEFUL YOU'RE HERE!

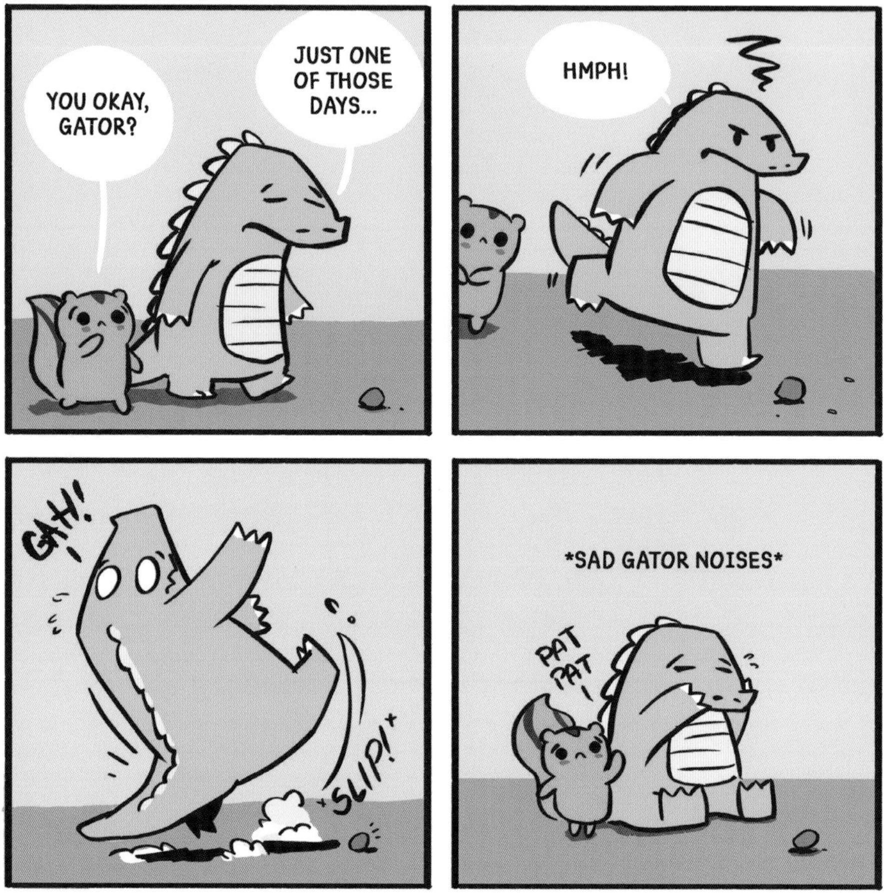
YOU OKAY, GATOR?
JUST ONE OF THOSE DAYS...
HMPH!
GAH!
SLIP!
SAD GATOR NOISES
PAT PAT

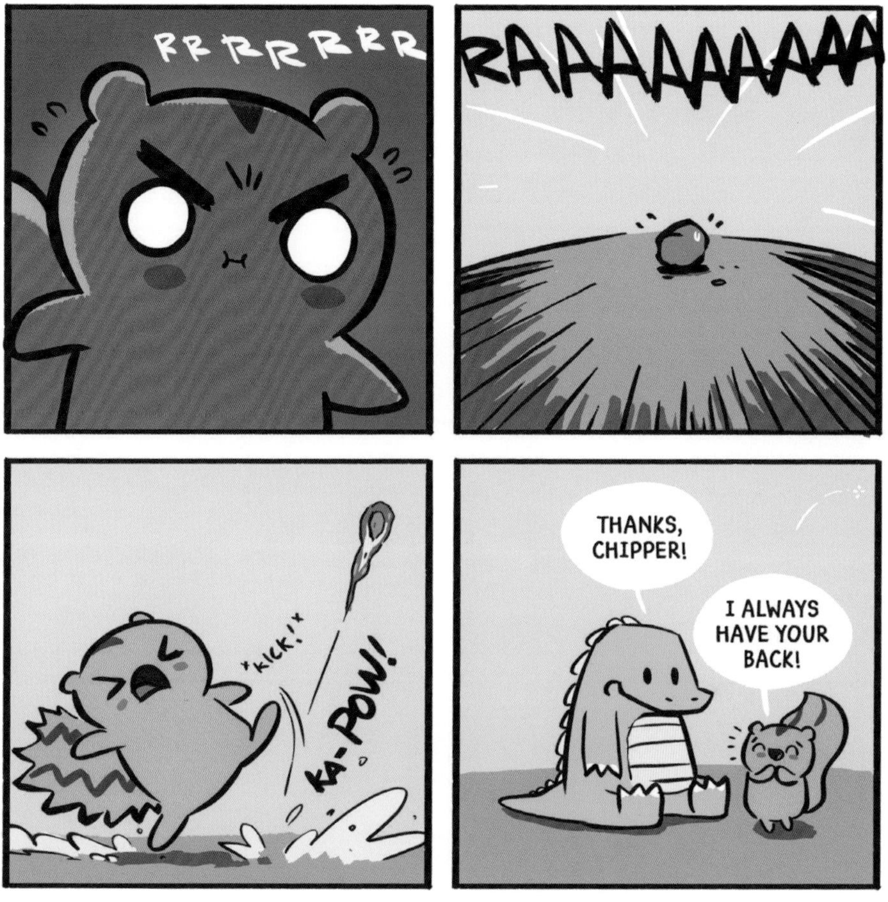
RRRRRRRR
RAAAAAAAAA
KICK!
KA-POW!
THANKS, CHIPPER!
I ALWAYS HAVE YOUR BACK!

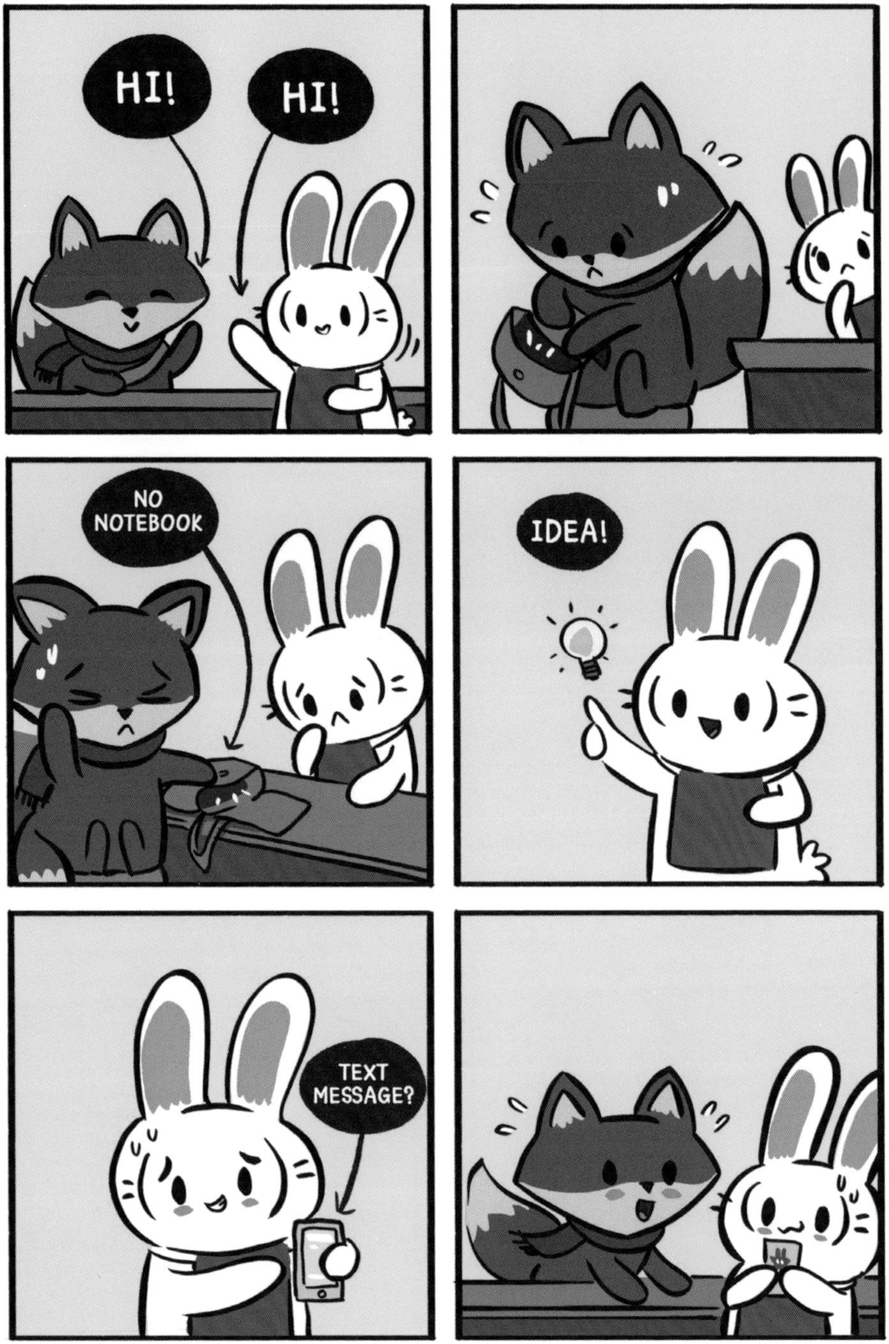
HI!
HI!
NO NOTEBOOK
IDEA!
TEXT MESSAGE?

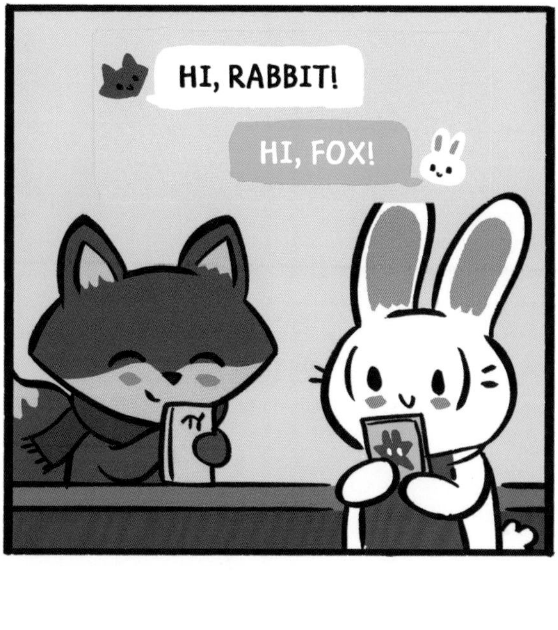
HI, RABBIT!
HI, FOX!

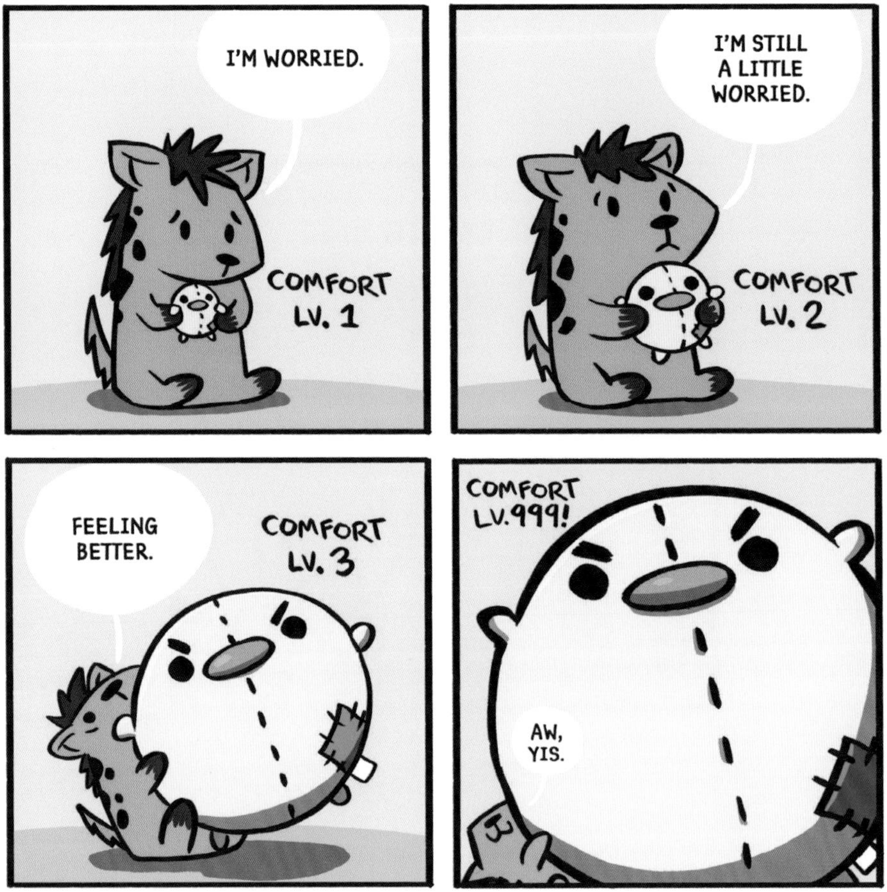
I'M WORRIED.
COMFORT LV. 1
I'M STILL A LITTLE WORRIED.
COMFORT LV. 2
FEELING BETTER.
COMFORT LV. 3
COMFORT LV.999!
AW, YIS.

A DAY IN THE LIFE OF RABBIT

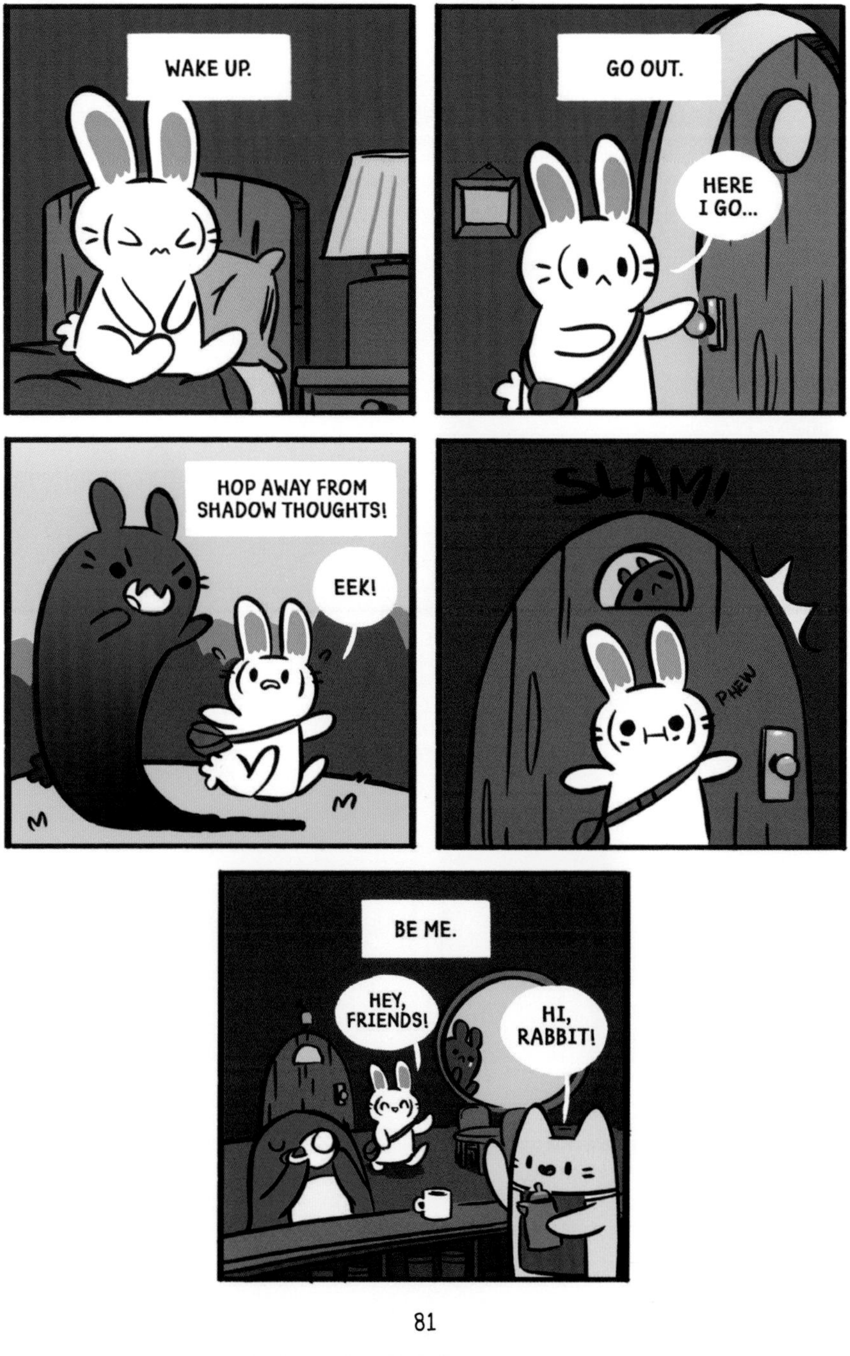
WAKE UP.
GO OUT.
HERE I GO...
HOP AWAY FROM SHADOW THOUGHTS!
EEK!
SLAM!
PHEW
BE ME.
HEY, FRIENDS!
HI, RABBIT!

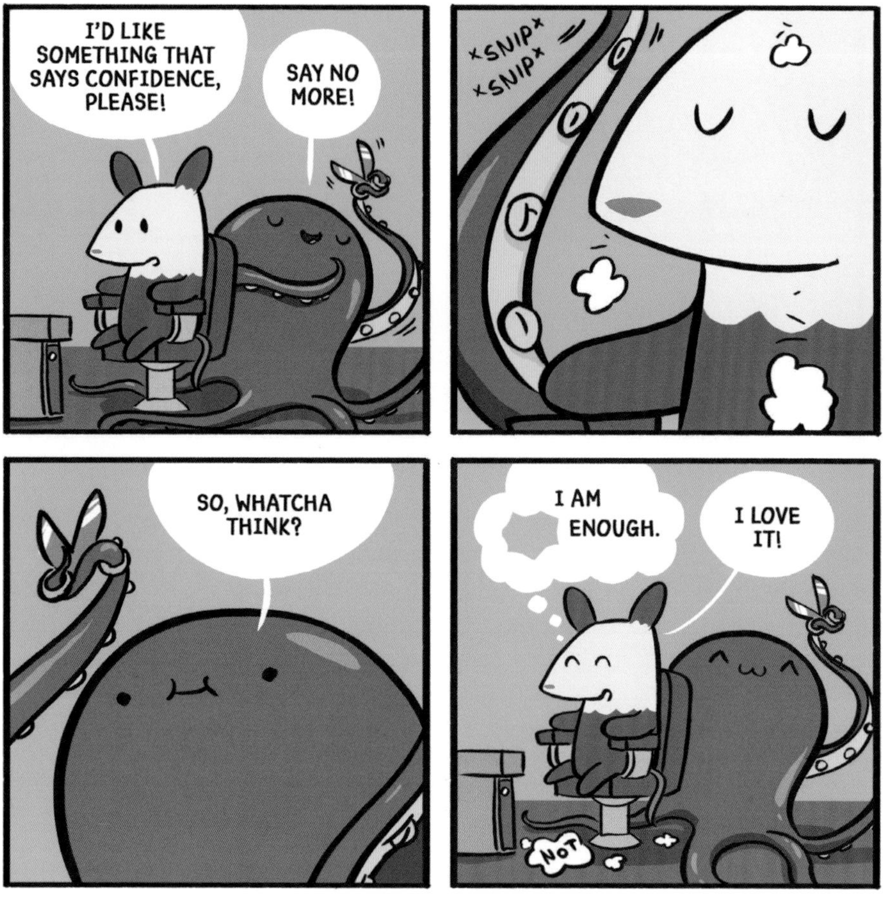
I'D LIKE SOMETHING THAT SAYS CONFIDENCE, PLEASE!
SAY NO MORE!
SNIP *SNIP*
SO, WHATCHA THINK?
I AM ENOUGH.
I LOVE IT!
NOT

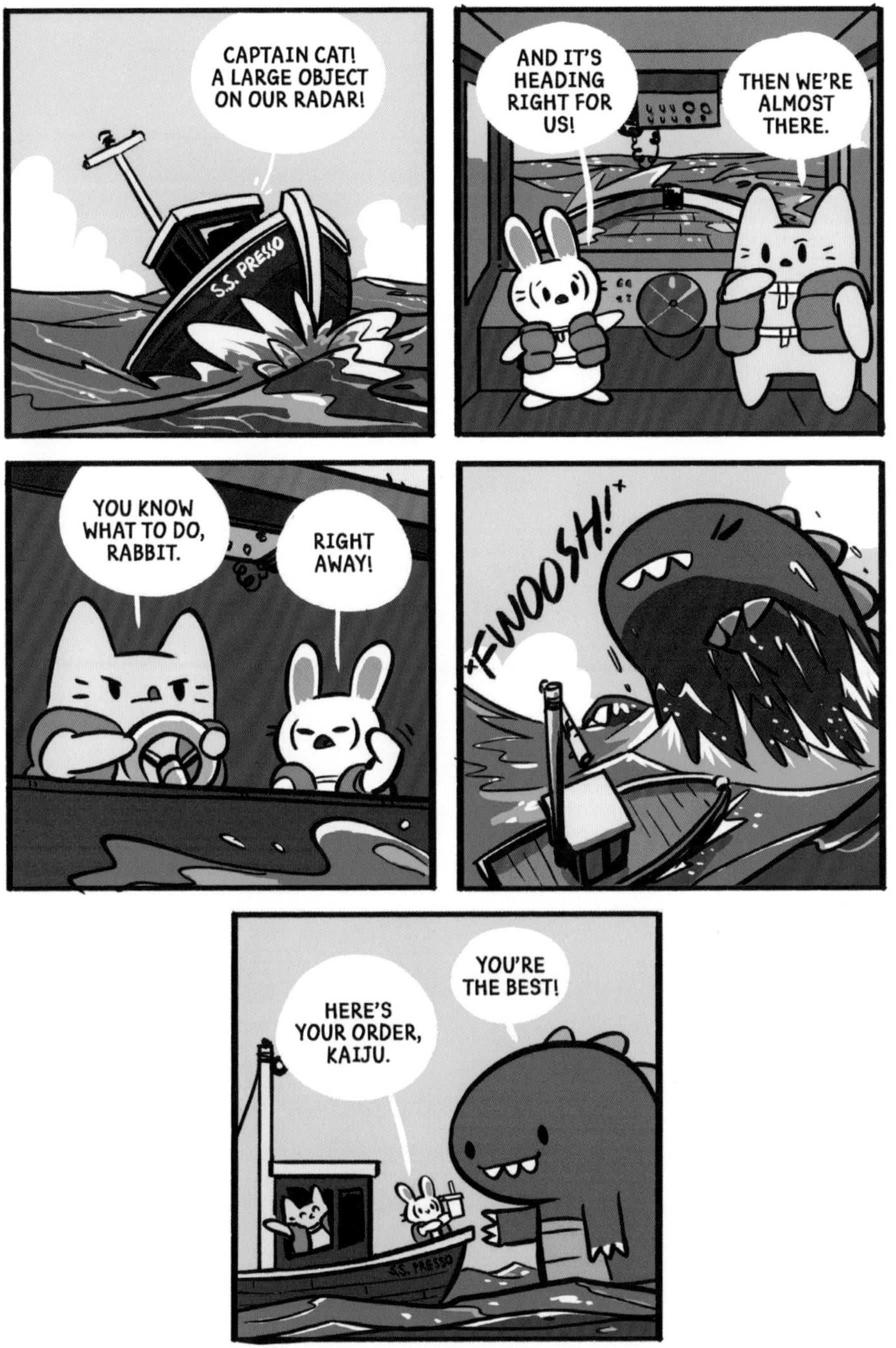
CAPTAIN CAT! A LARGE OBJECT ON OUR RADAR!
S.S. PRESSO
AND IT'S HEADING RIGHT FOR US!
THEN WE'RE ALMOST THERE.
YOU KNOW WHAT TO DO, RABBIT.
RIGHT AWAY!
FWOOSH!
HERE'S YOUR ORDER, KAIJU.
YOU'RE THE BEST!
S.S. PRESSO

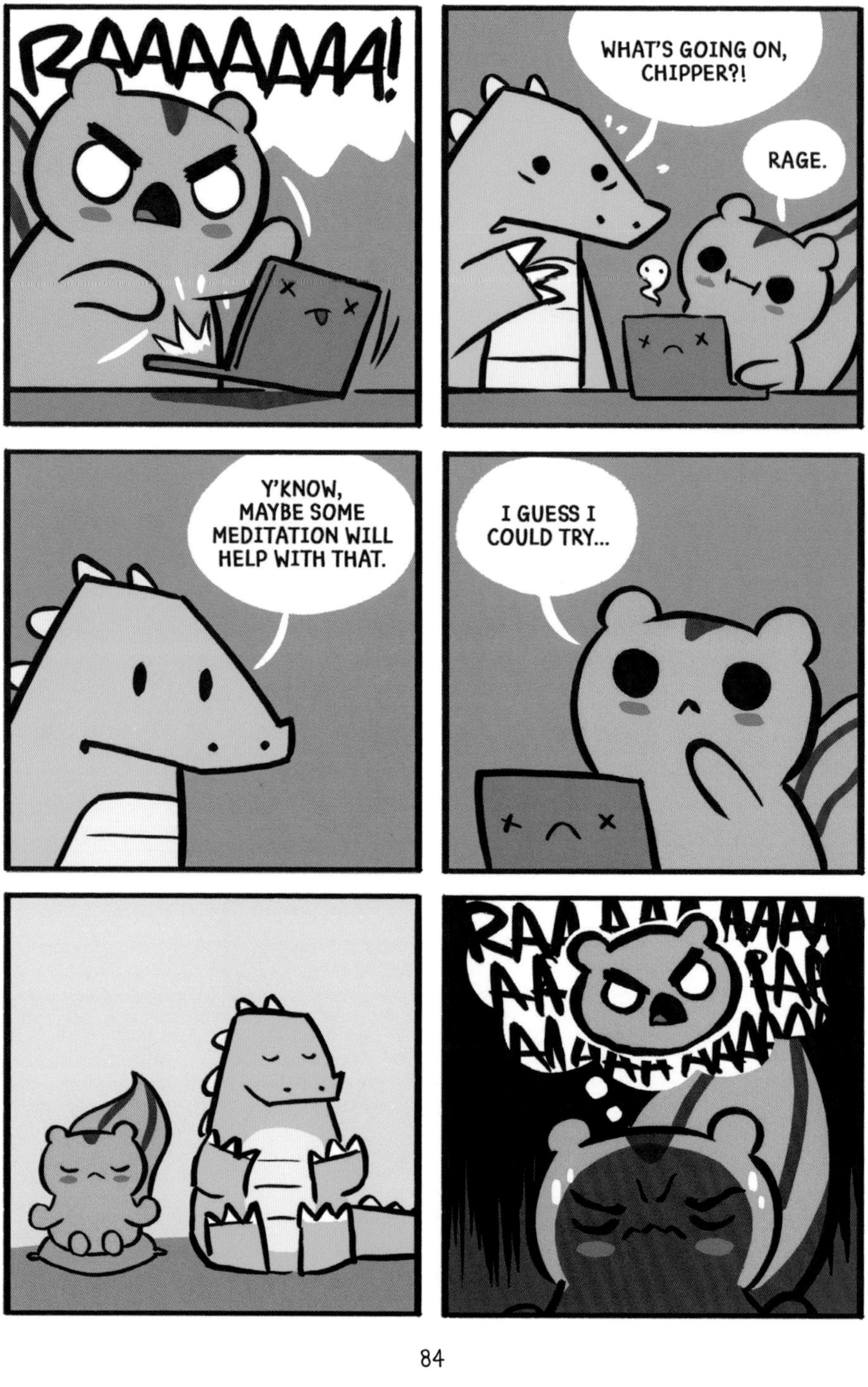
RAAAAAAA!
WHAT'S GOING ON, CHIPPER?!
RAGE.
Y'KNOW, MAYBE SOME MEDITATION WILL HELP WITH THAT.
I GUESS I COULD TRY...

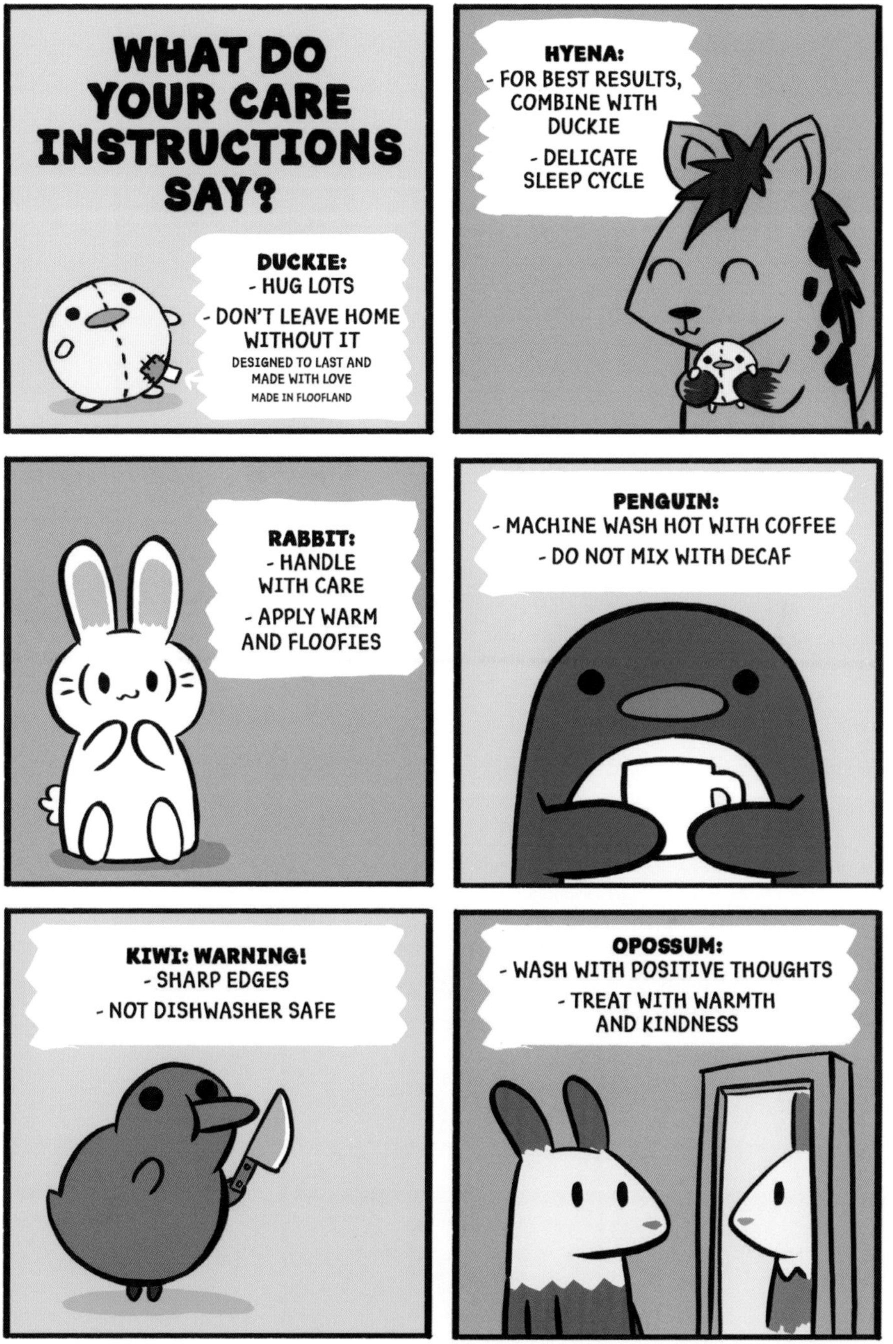
WHAT DO YOUR CARE INSTRUCTIONS SAY?
DUCKIE:
- HUG LOTS
- DON'T LEAVE HOME WITHOUT IT
DESIGNED TO LAST AND MADE WITH LOVE
MADE IN FLOOFLAND
HYENA:
- FOR BEST RESULTS, COMBINE WITH DUCKIE
- DELICATE SLEEP CYCLE
RABBIT:
- HANDLE WITH CARE
- APPLY WARM AND FLOOFIES
PENGUIN:
- MACHINE WASH HOT WITH COFFEE
- DO NOT MIX WITH DECAF
KIWI: WARNING!
- SHARP EDGES
- NOT DISHWASHER SAFE
OPOSSUM:
- WASH WITH POSITIVE THOUGHTS
- TREAT WITH WARMTH AND KINDNESS

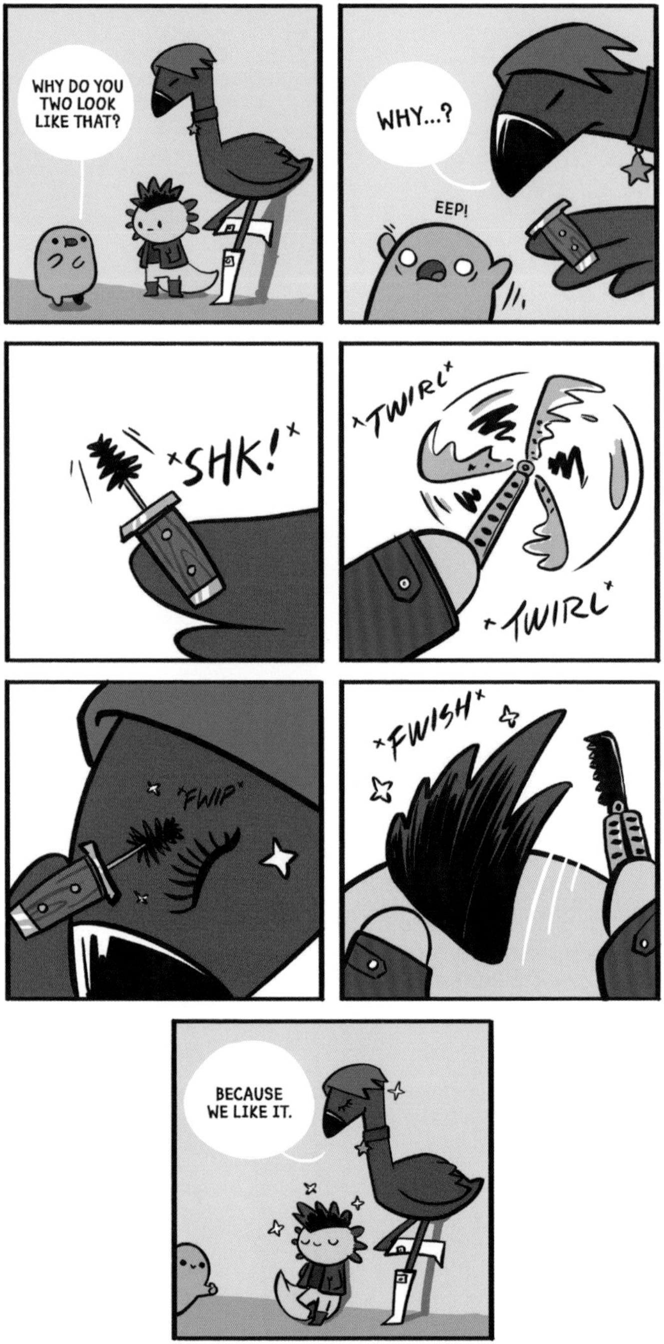
WHY DO YOU TWO LOOK LIKE THAT?
WHY...?
EEP!
SHK!
TWIRL
TWIRL
FWIP
FWISH
BECAUSE WE LIKE IT.

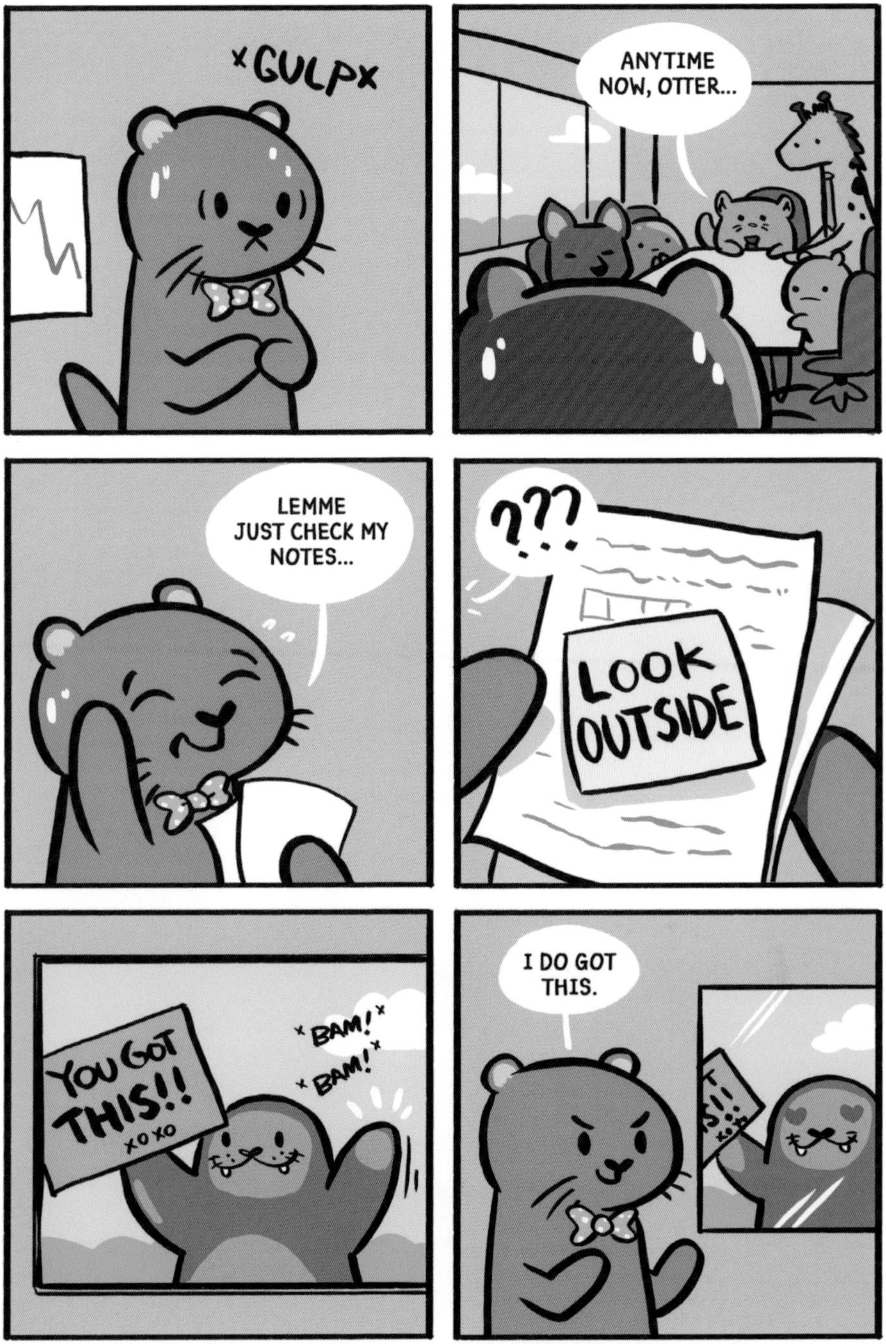
×GULP×
ANYTIME NOW, OTTER...
LEMME JUST CHECK MY NOTES...
???
LOOK OUTSIDE
YOU GOT THIS!! XOXO
×BAM!×
×BAM!×
I DO GOT THIS.

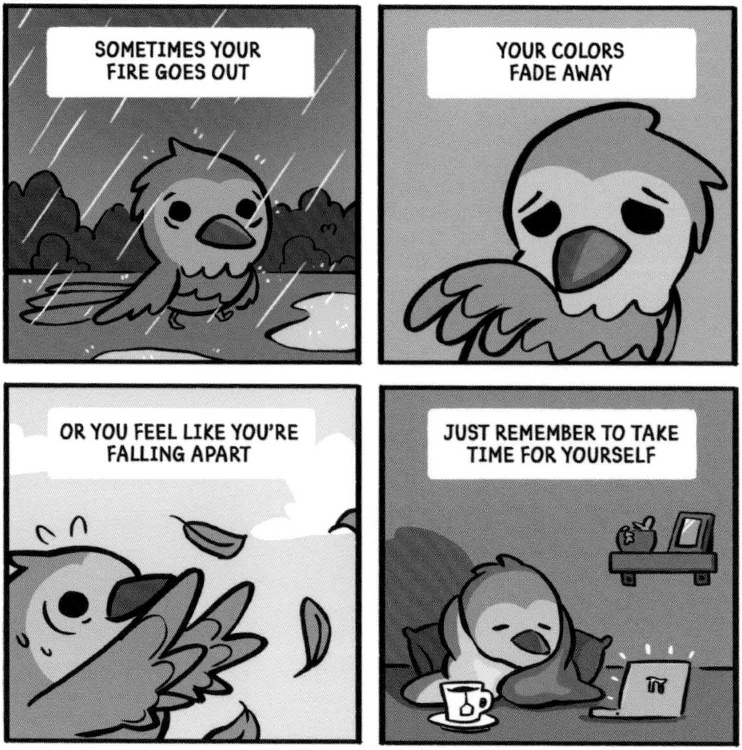
SOMETIMES YOUR FIRE GOES OUT
YOUR COLORS FADE AWAY
OR YOU FEEL LIKE YOU'RE FALLING APART
JUST REMEMBER TO TAKE TIME FOR YOURSELF

AND YOU CAN BE REIGNITED LIKE NEVER BEFORE!

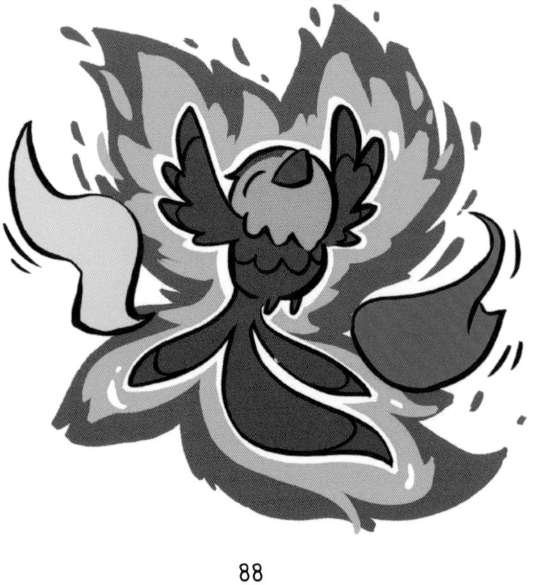

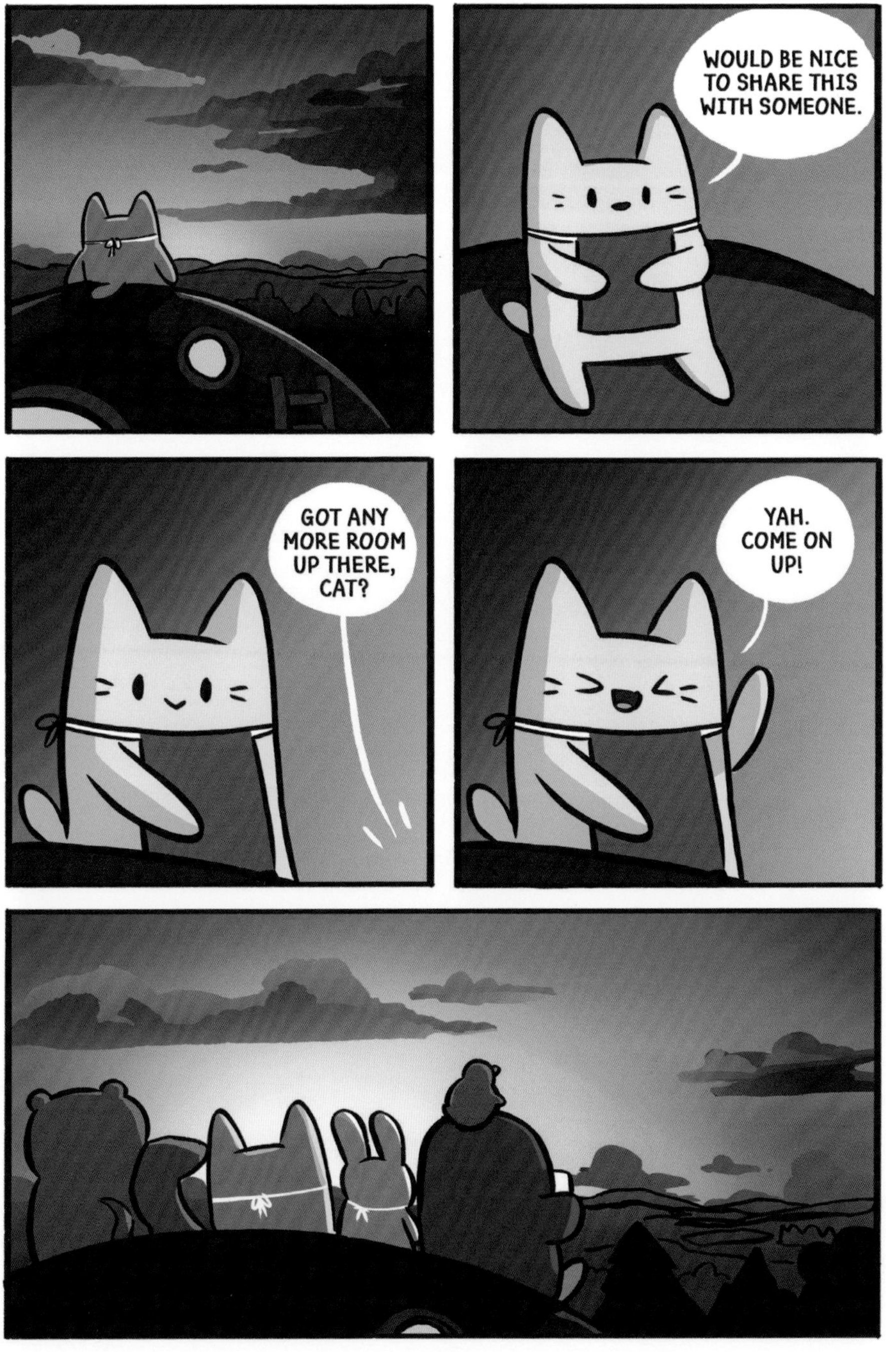
WOULD BE NICE TO SHARE THIS WITH SOMEONE.
GOT ANY MORE ROOM UP THERE, CAT?
YAH. COME ON UP!

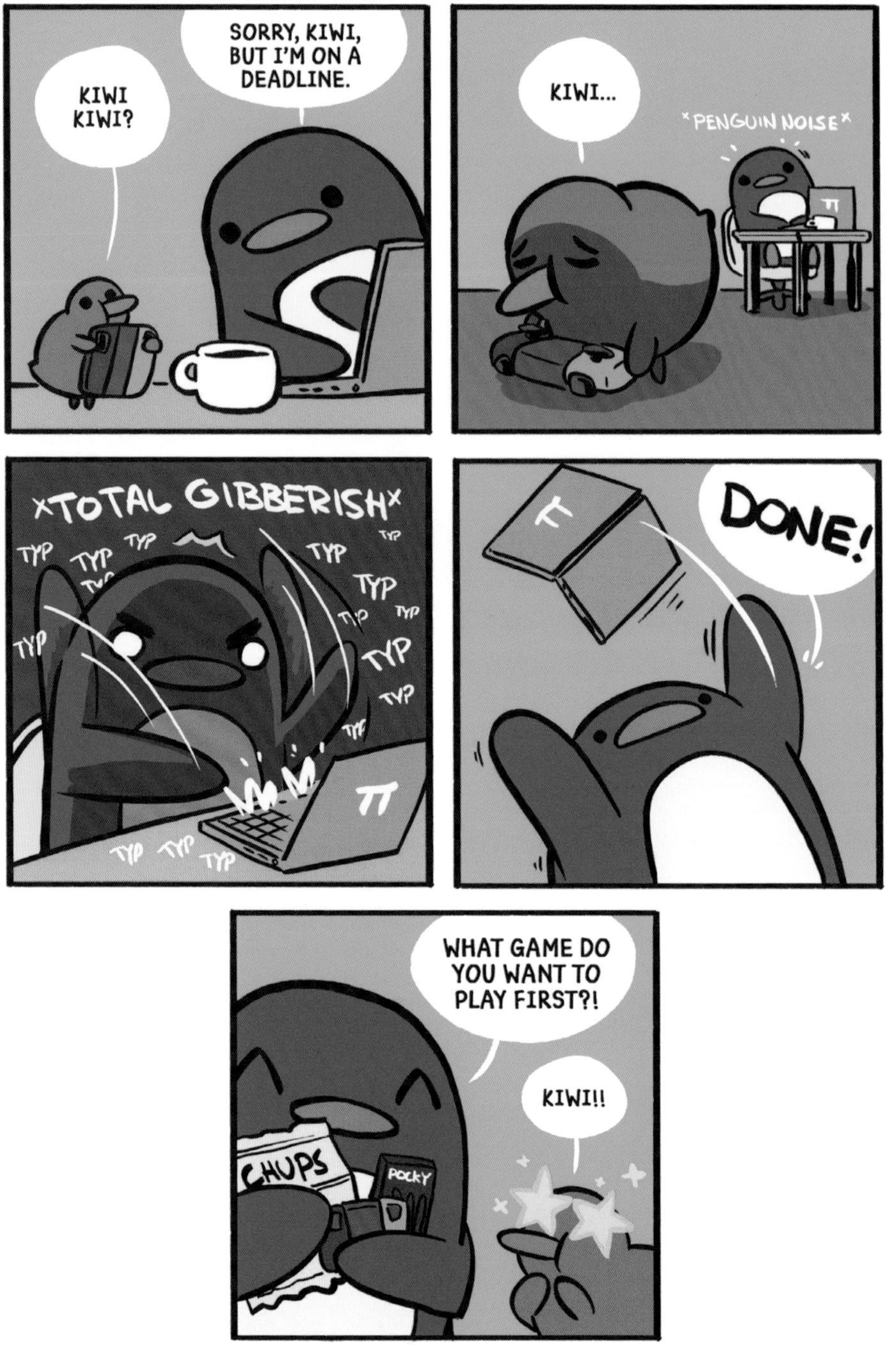
KIWI
KIWI?
SORRY, KIWI, BUT I'M ON A DEADLINE.
KIWI...
PENGUIN NOISE
TOTAL GIBBERISH
TYP TYP TYP TYP TYP TYP TYP TYP TYP TYP TYP TYP TYP TYP TYP
DONE!
WHAT GAME DO YOU WANT TO PLAY FIRST?!
KIWI!!
CHUPS
POCKY

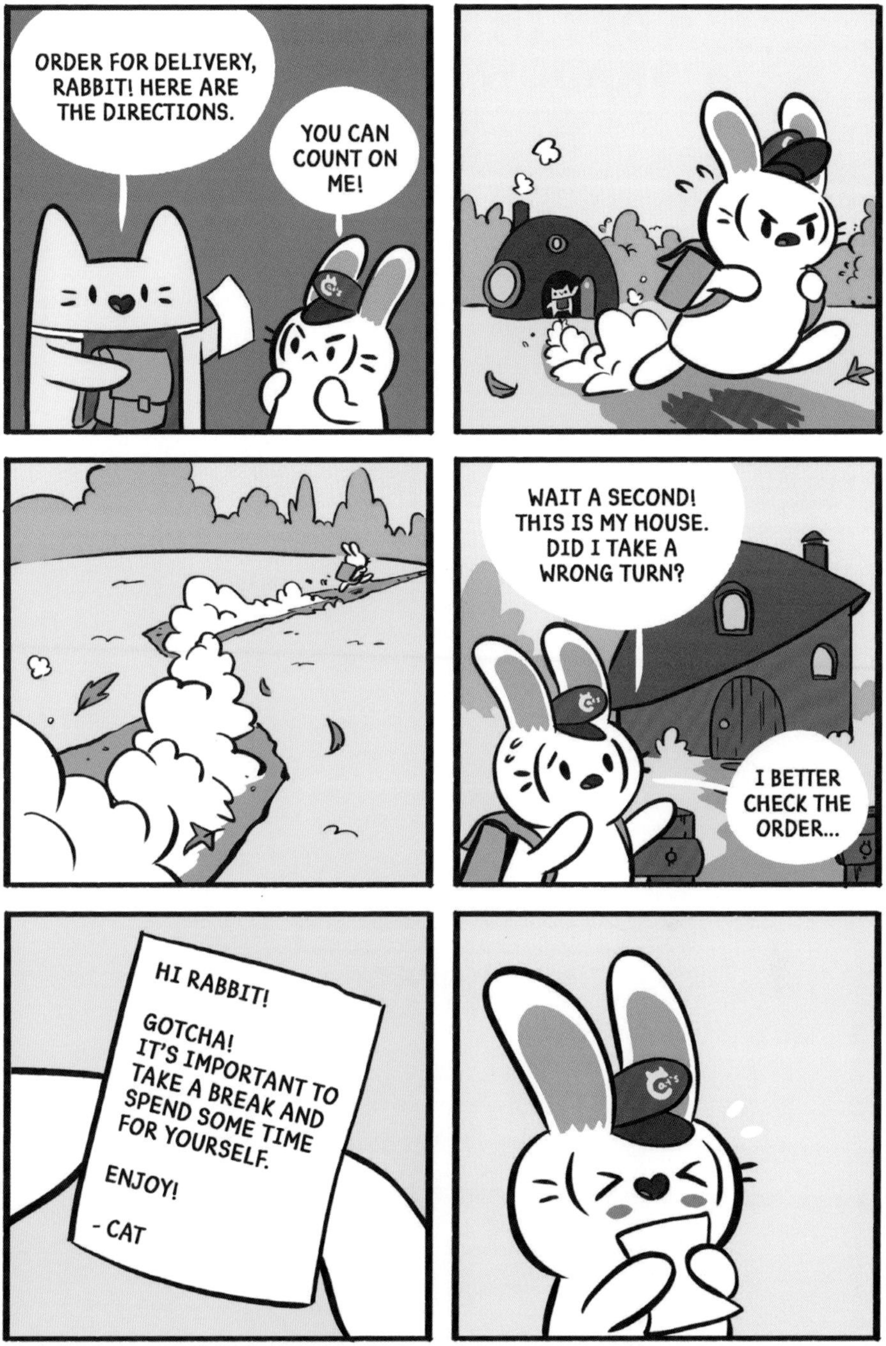

ORDER FOR DELIVERY, RABBIT! HERE ARE THE DIRECTIONS.
YOU CAN COUNT ON ME!
WAIT A SECOND! THIS IS MY HOUSE. DID I TAKE A WRONG TURN?
I BETTER CHECK THE ORDER...
HI RABBIT!
GOTCHA! IT'S IMPORTANT TO TAKE A BREAK AND SPEND SOME TIME FOR YOURSELF.
ENJOY!
- CAT

A DAY IN THE LIFE OF SHADOW THOUGHTS

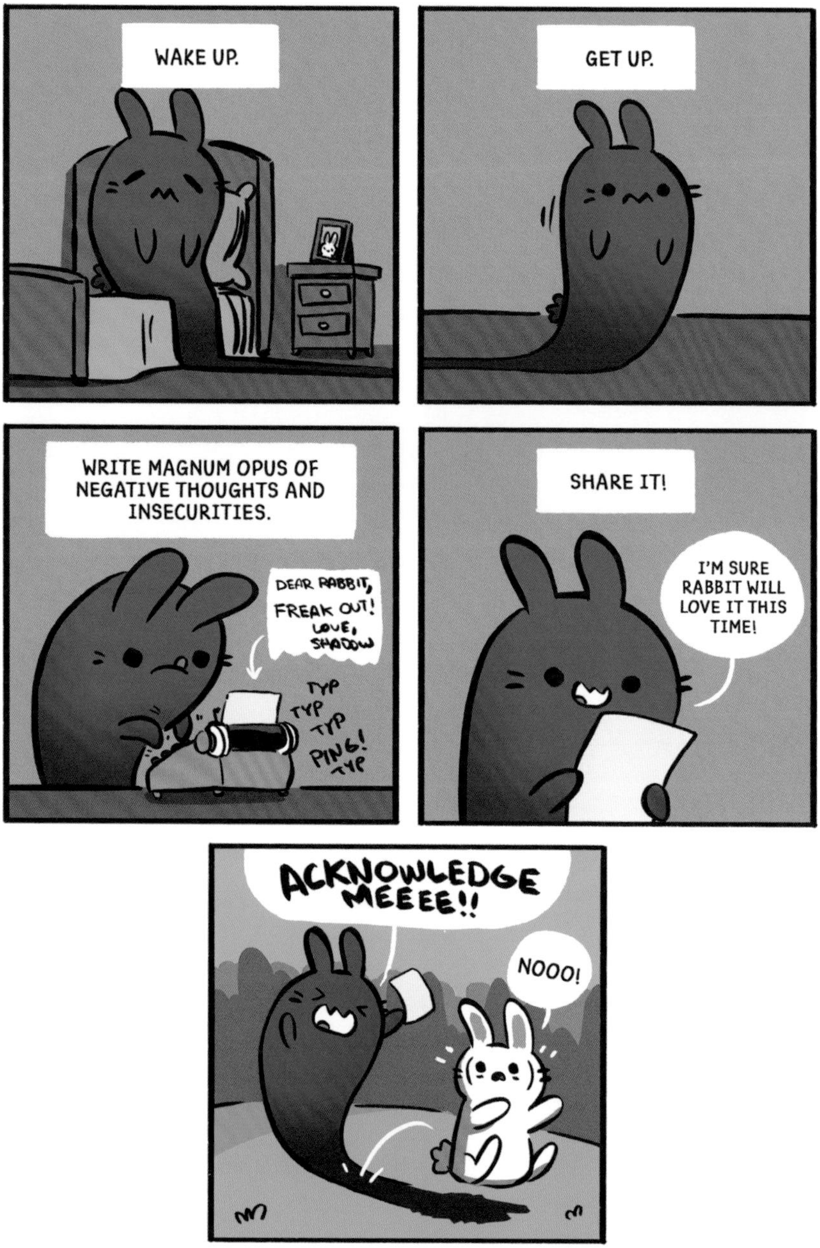

WAKE UP.
GET UP.
WRITE MAGNUM OPUS OF NEGATIVE THOUGHTS AND INSECURITIES.
DEAR RABBIT, FREAK OUT! LOVE, SHADOW
TYP TYP TYP PING! TYP
SHARE IT!
I'M SURE RABBIT WILL LOVE IT THIS TIME!
ACKNOWLEDGE MEEEE!!
NOOO!

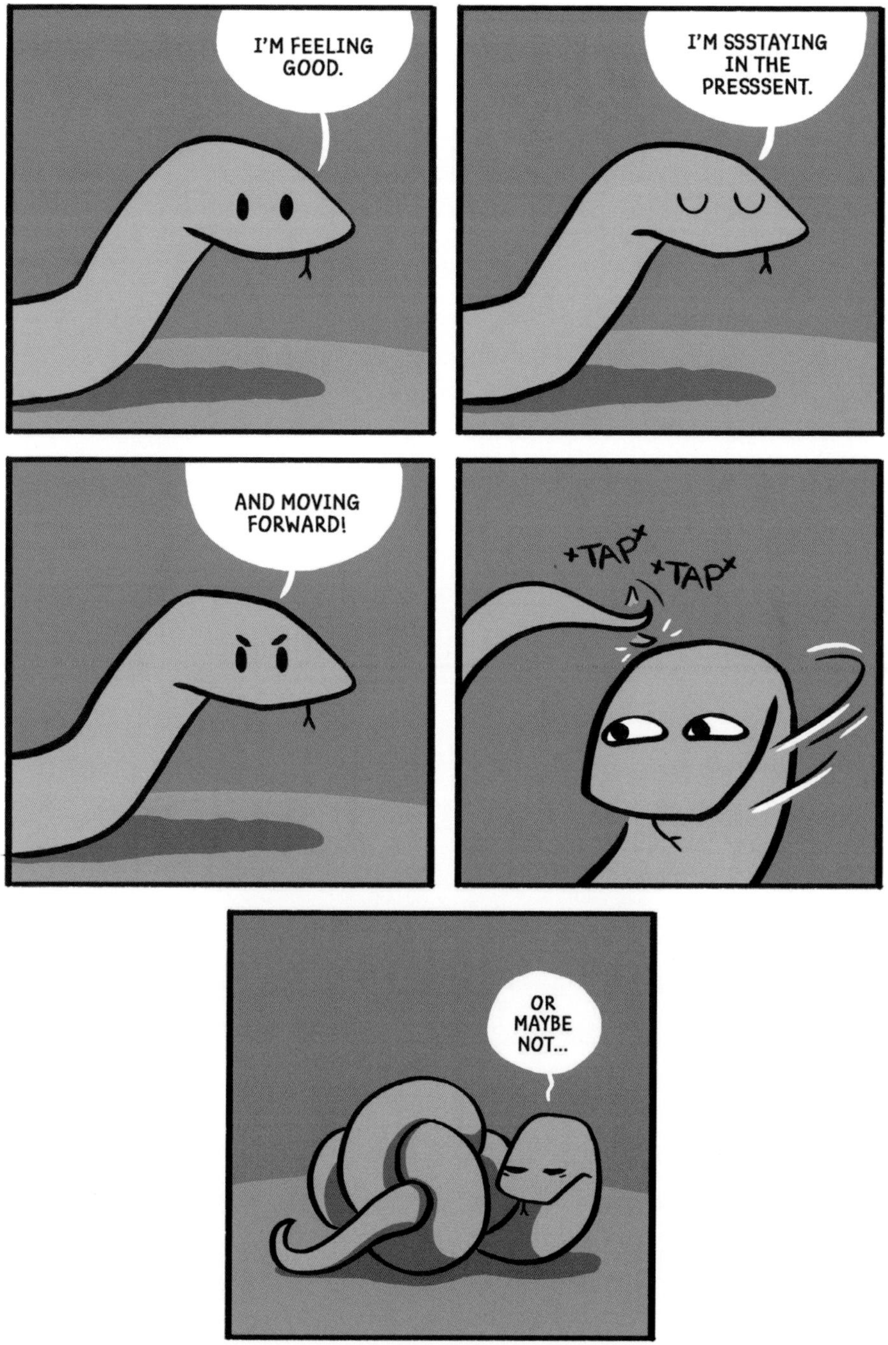
I'M FEELING GOOD.
I'M SSSTAYING IN THE PRESSSENT.
AND MOVING FORWARD!
TAP *TAP*
OR MAYBE NOT...

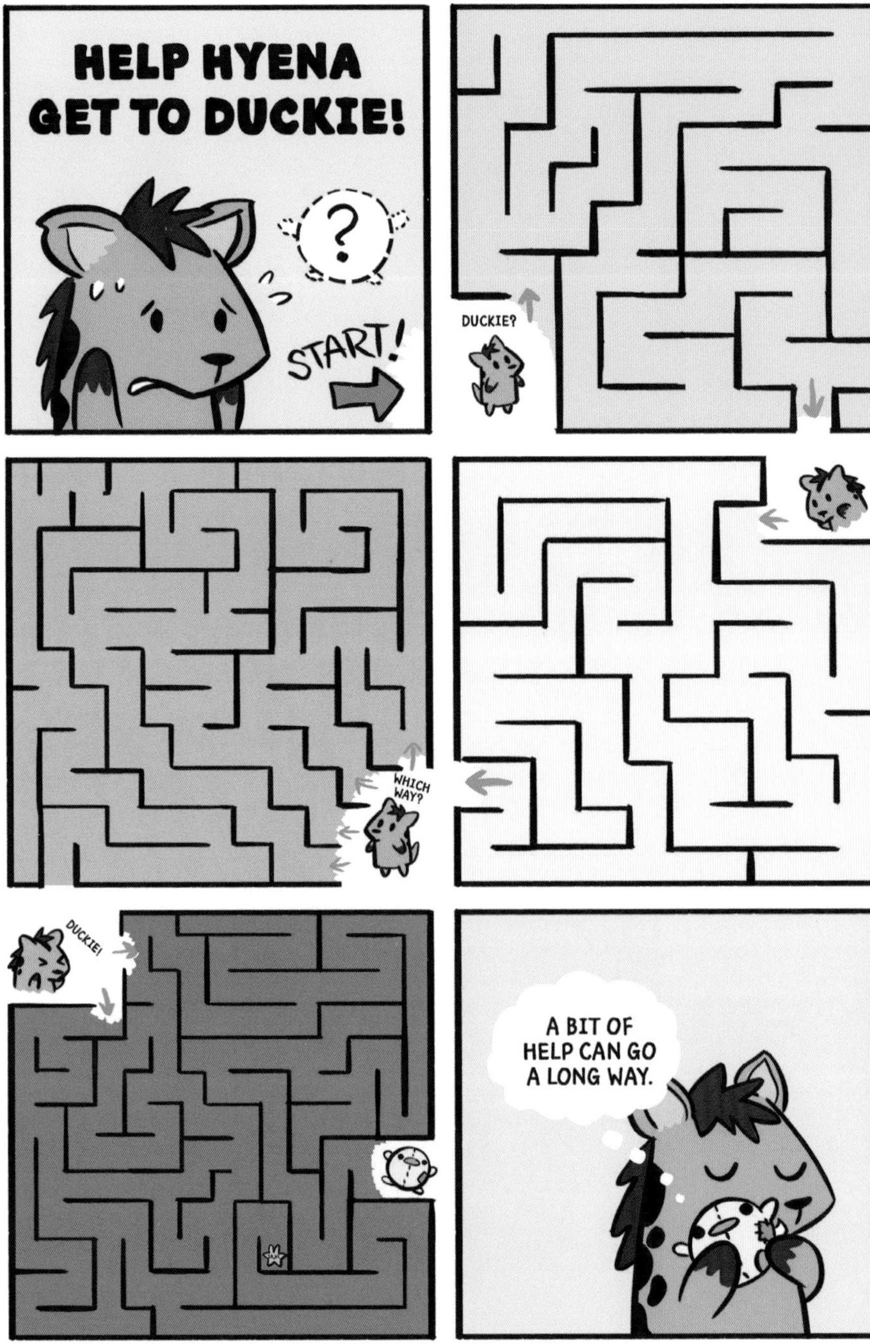
HELP HYENA GET TO DUCKIE!
START!
DUCKIE?
WHICH WAY?
DUCKIE!
A BIT OF HELP CAN GO A LONG WAY.

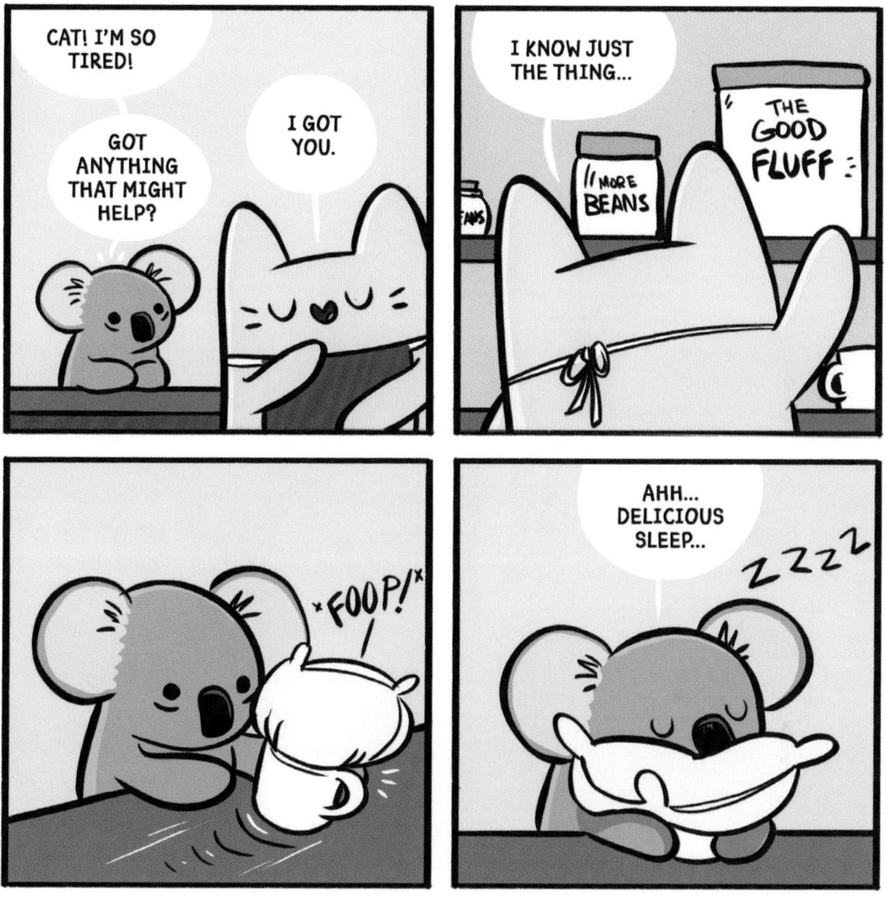
CAT! I'M SO TIRED!
GOT ANYTHING THAT MIGHT HELP?
I GOT YOU.
I KNOW JUST THE THING...
MORE BEANS
THE GOOD FLUFF
FOOP!
AHH... DELICIOUS SLEEP...
ZZZZ

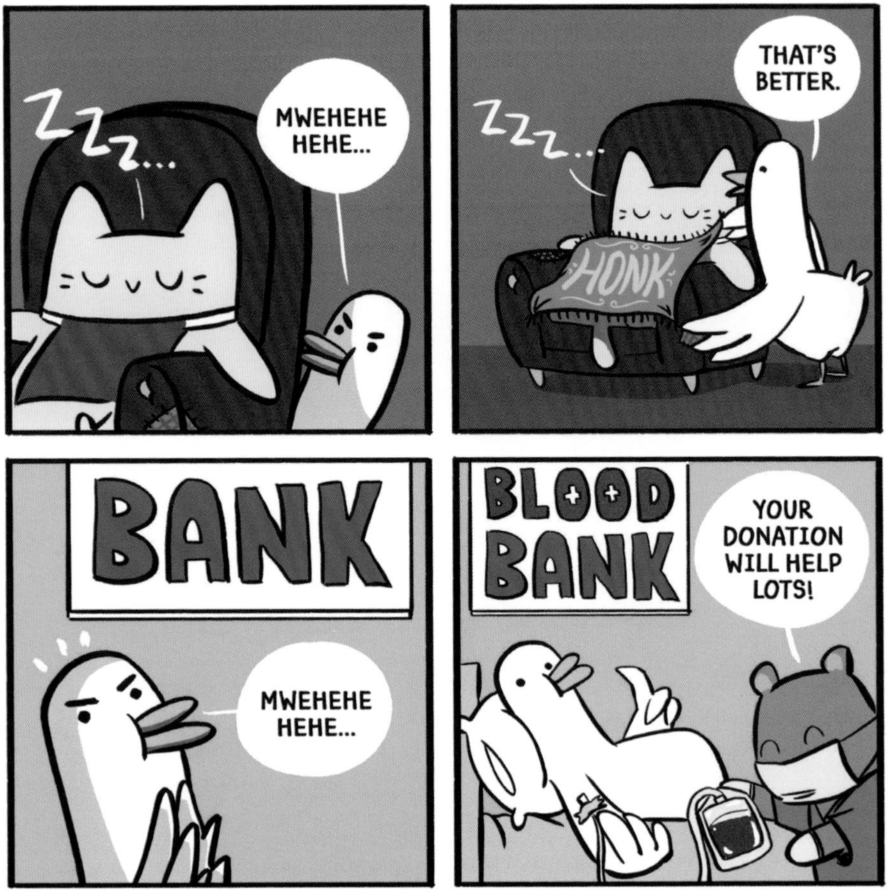
ZZZ...
MWEHEHE HEHE...
ZZZ...
THAT'S BETTER.
HONK
BANK
MWEHEHE HEHE...
BLOOD BANK
YOUR DONATION WILL HELP LOTS!

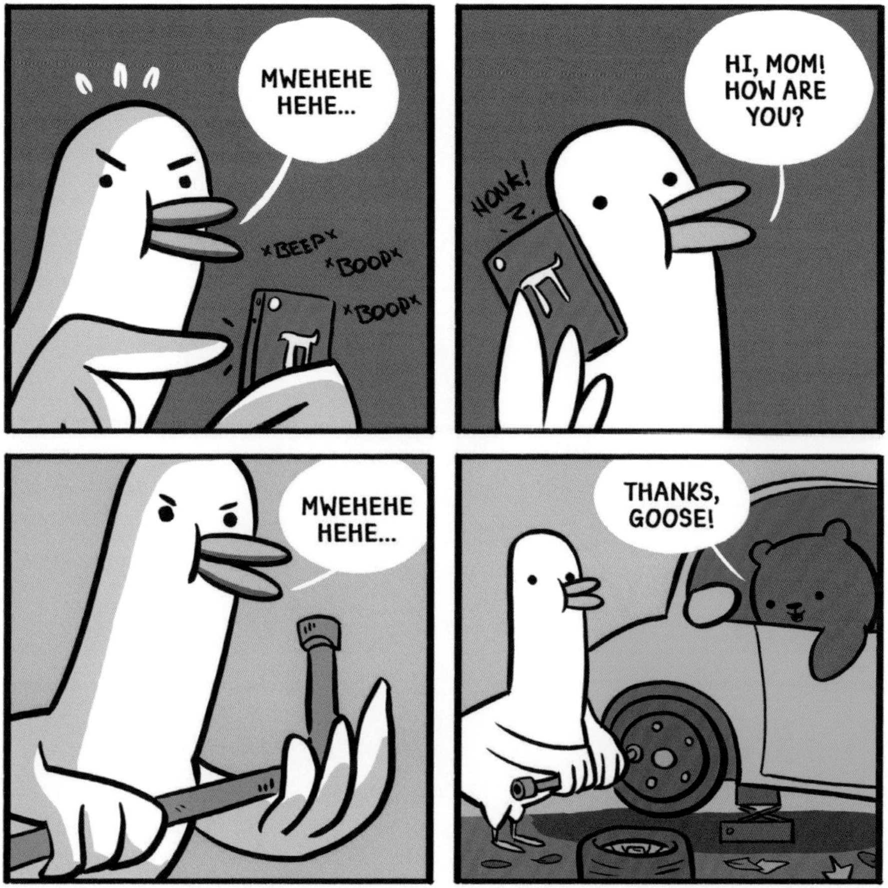
MWEHEHE HEHE...
BEEP
BOOP
BOOP
HONK!
HI, MOM! HOW ARE YOU?
MWEHEHE HEHE...
THANKS, GOOSE!

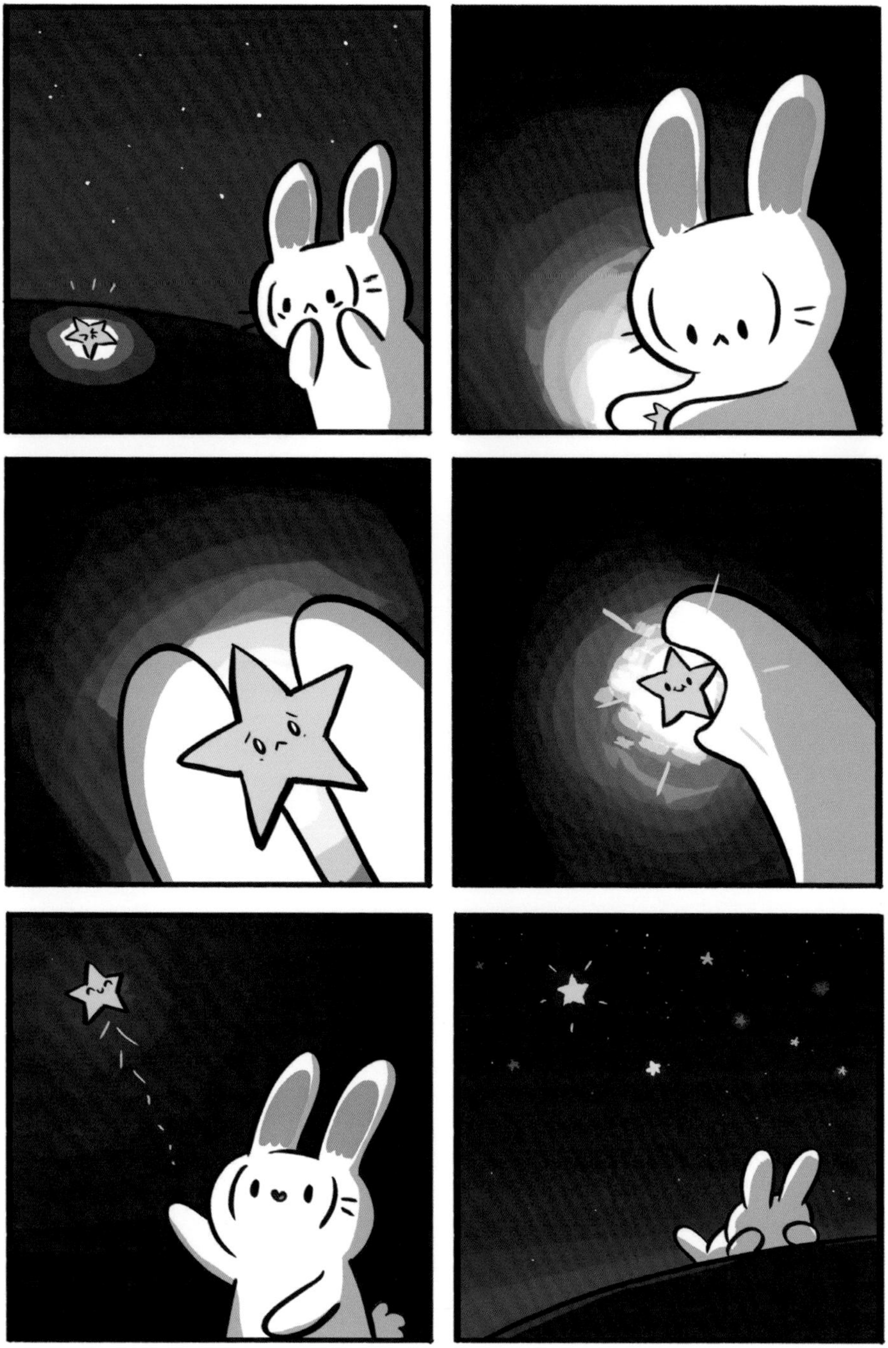

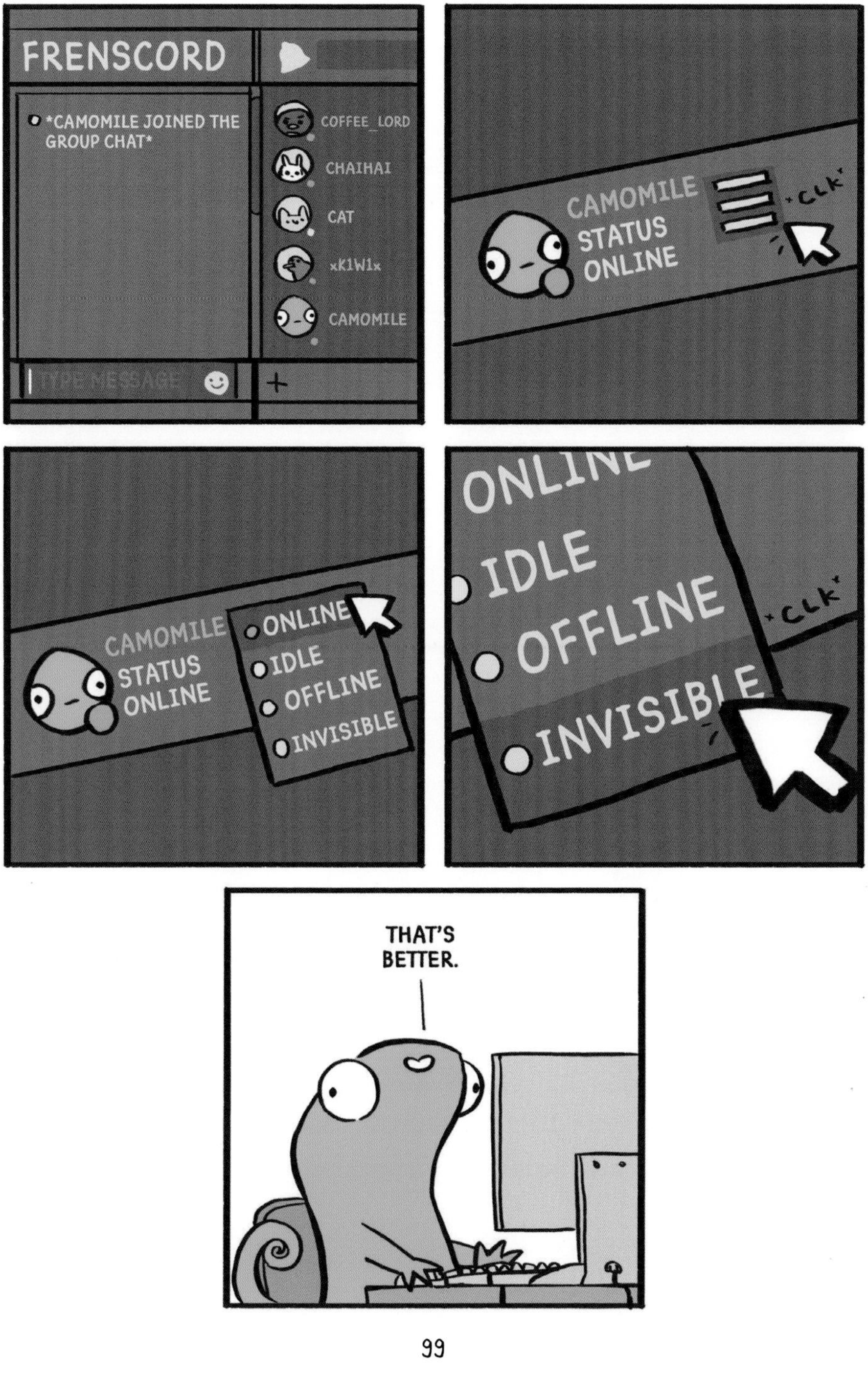
FRENSCORD
CAMOMILE JOINED THE GROUP CHAT
COFFEE_LORD
CHAIHAI
CAT
xKIWIx
CAMOMILE
TYPE MESSAGE
CAMOMILE
STATUS
ONLINE
CLK
CAMOMILE
STATUS
ONLINE
ONLINE
IDLE
OFFLINE
INVISIBLE
ONLINE
IDLE
OFFLINE
INVISIBLE
CLK
THAT'S BETTER.

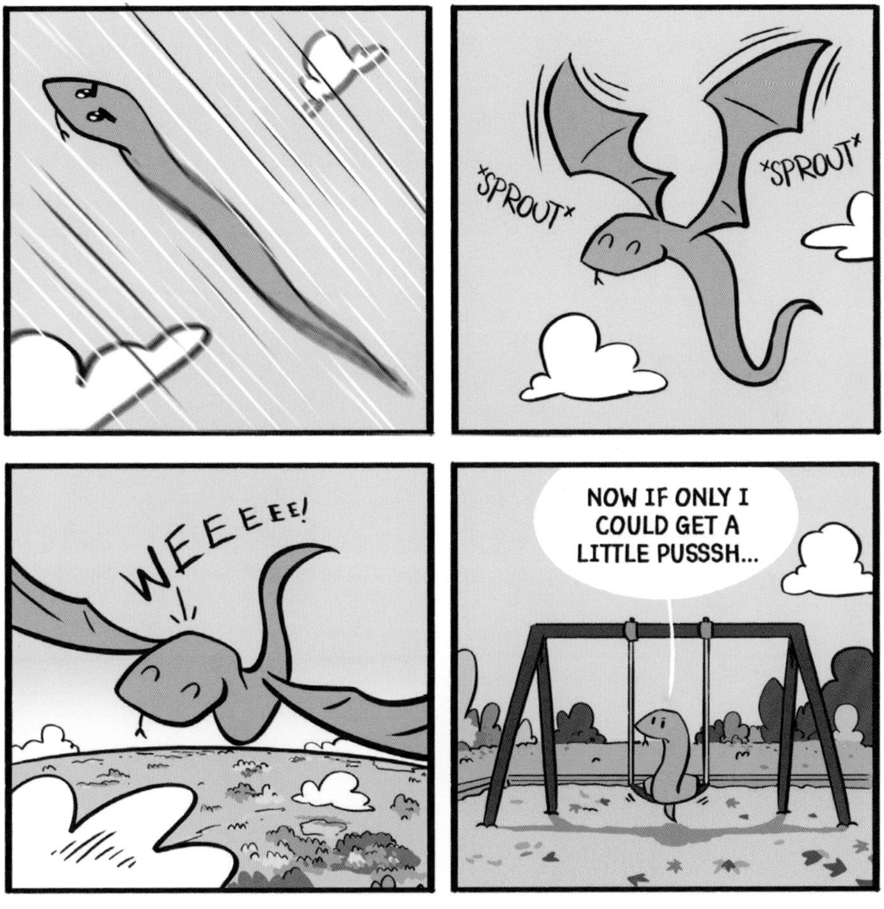
SPROUT
SPROUT
WEEEEEE!
NOW IF ONLY I COULD GET A LITTLE PUSSSH...

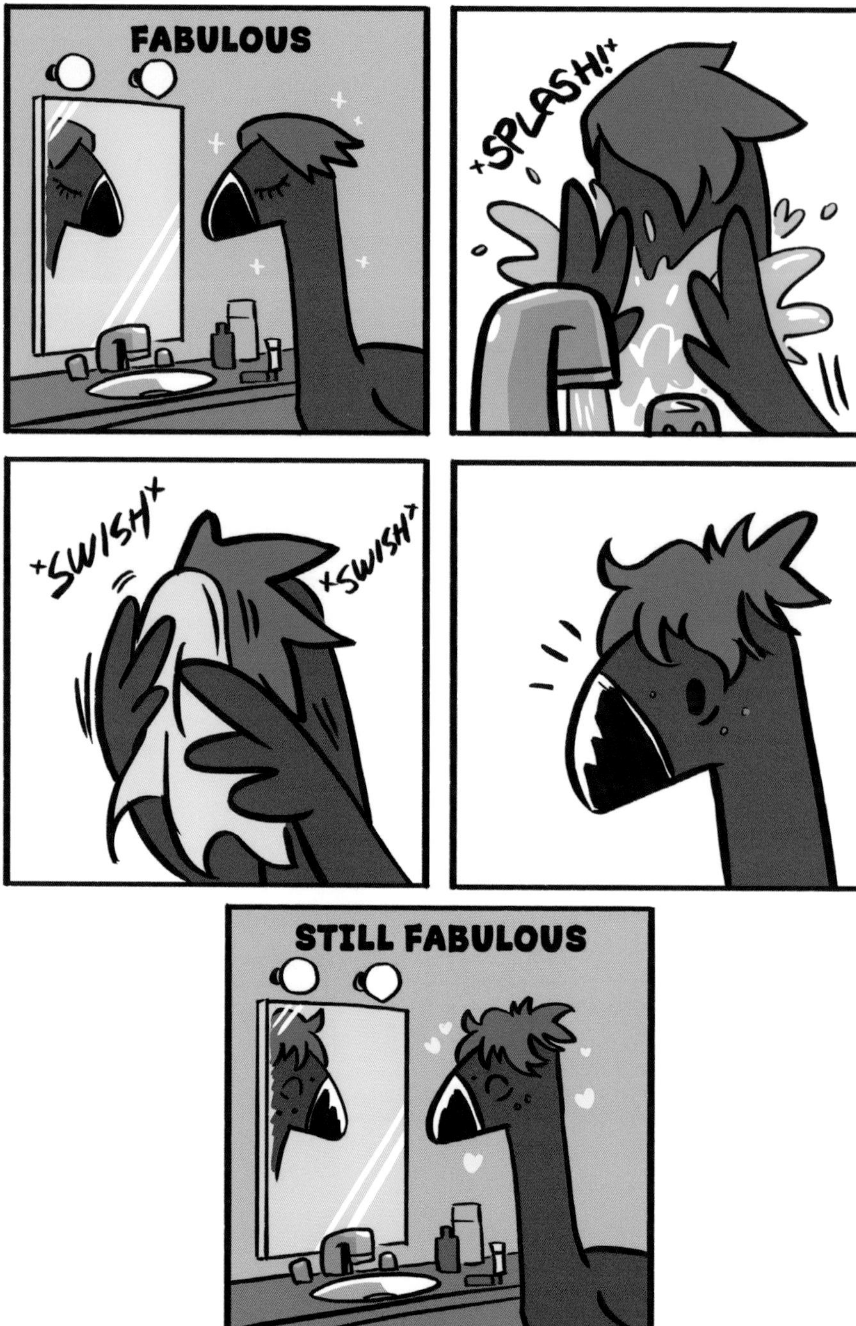
FABULOUS
SPLASH!
SWISH
SWISH
STILL FABULOUS

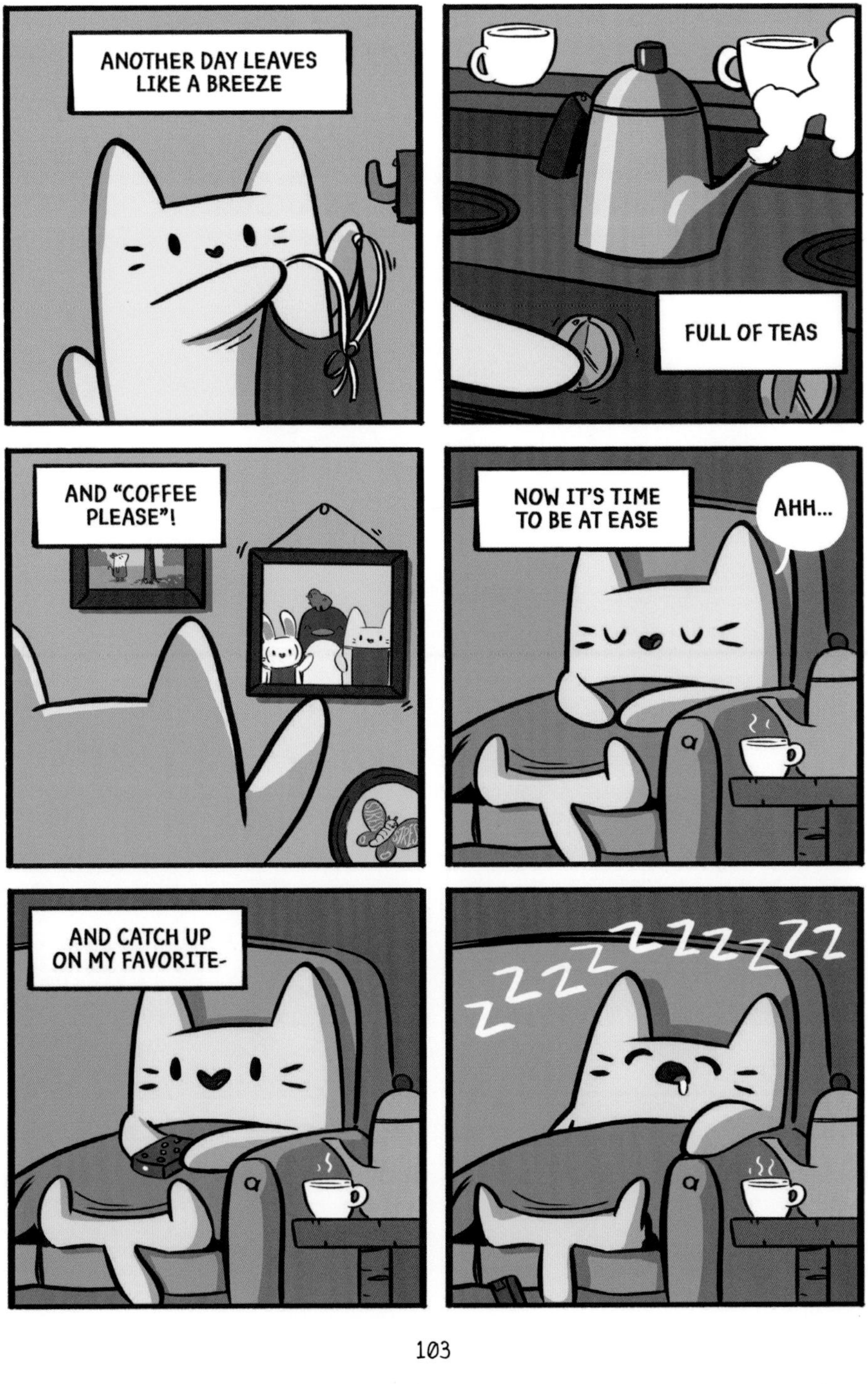
ANOTHER DAY LEAVES LIKE A BREEZE
FULL OF TEAS
AND "COFFEE PLEASE"!
NOW IT'S TIME TO BE AT EASE
AHH...
AND CATCH UP ON MY FAVORITE-
ZZZZZZZZZZZ

FAR FROM HOME

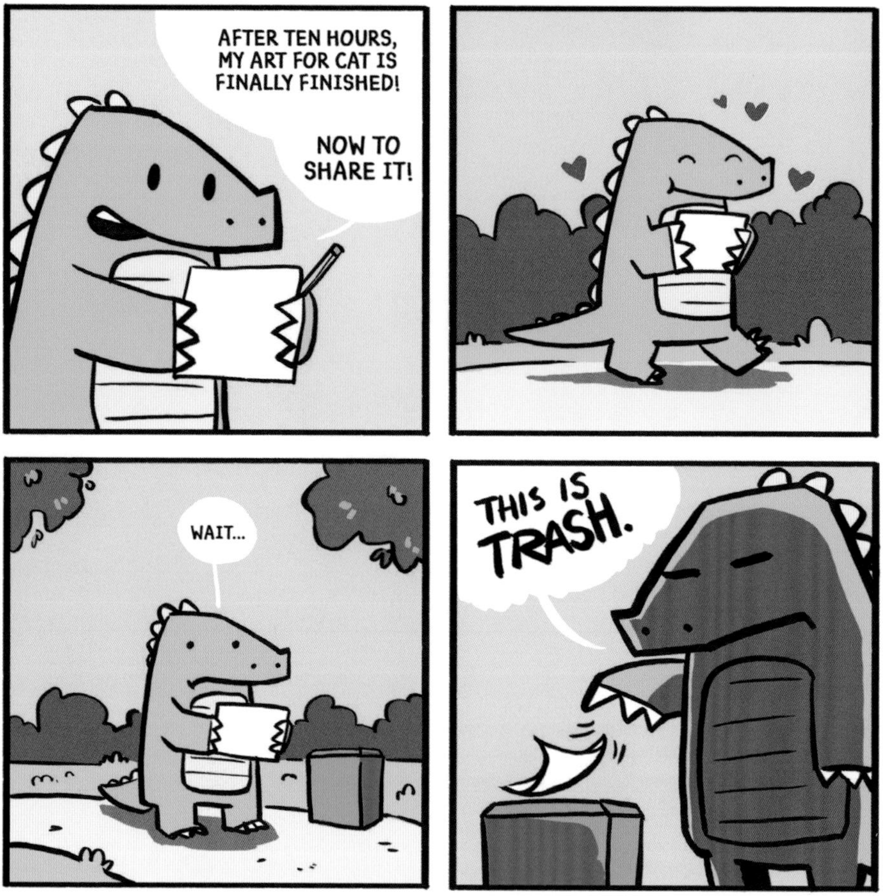
AFTER TEN HOURS, MY ART FOR CAT IS FINALLY FINISHED!
NOW TO SHARE IT!
WAIT...
THIS IS TRASH.

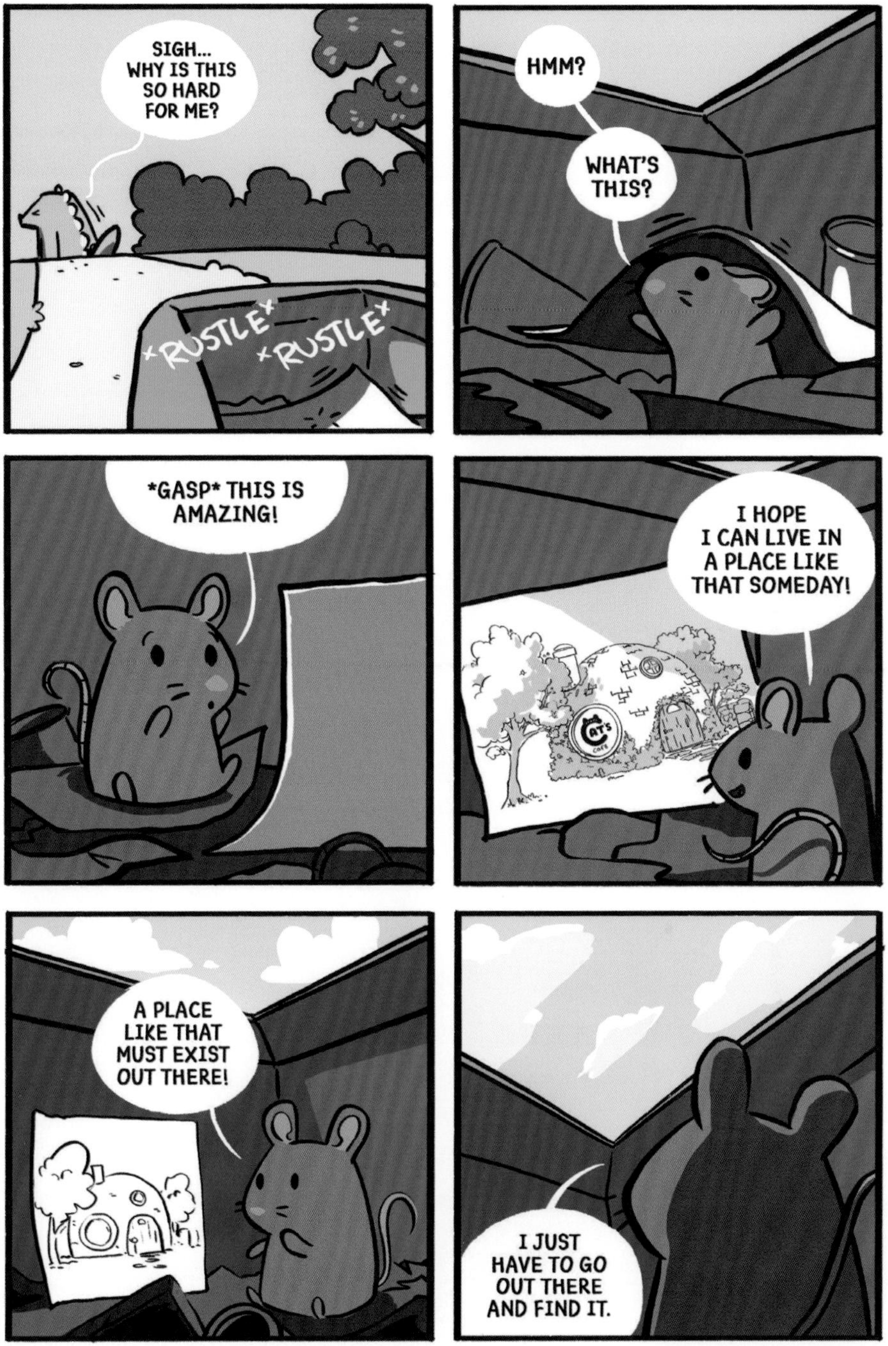
SIGH... WHY IS THIS SO HARD FOR ME?
RUSTLE RUSTLE
HMM?
WHAT'S THIS?
GASP THIS IS AMAZING!
I HOPE I CAN LIVE IN A PLACE LIKE THAT SOMEDAY!
A PLACE LIKE THAT MUST EXIST OUT THERE!
I JUST HAVE TO GO OUT THERE AND FIND IT.

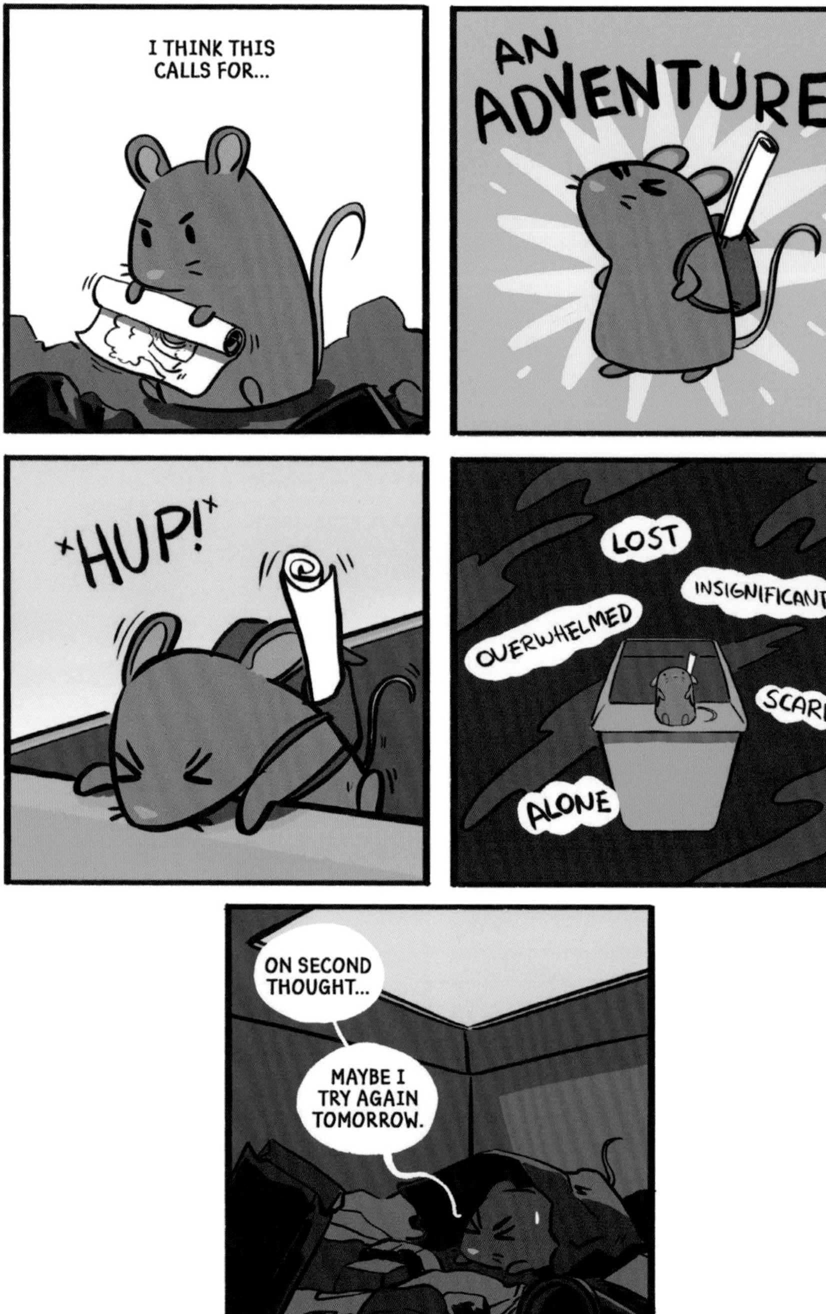
I THINK THIS CALLS FOR...
AN ADVENTURE!
HUP!
LOST
INSIGNIFICANT
OVERWHELMED
SCARED
ALONE
ON SECOND THOUGHT...
MAYBE I TRY AGAIN TOMORROW.

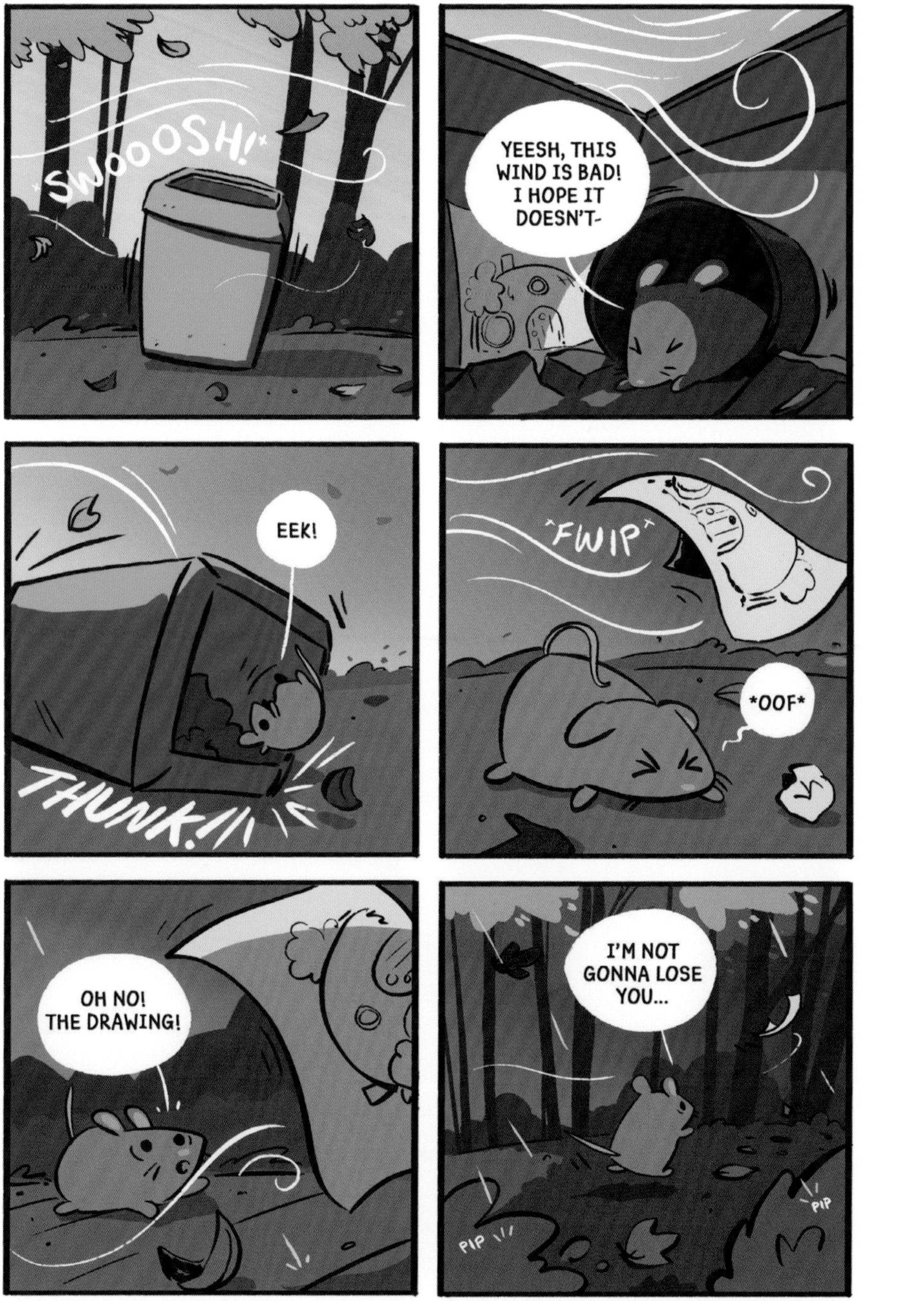
SWOOOSH!
YEESH, THIS WIND IS BAD! I HOPE IT DOESN'T-
EEK!
THUNK!
FWIP
OOF
OH NO! THE DRAWING!
I'M NOT GONNA LOSE YOU...
PIP
PIP

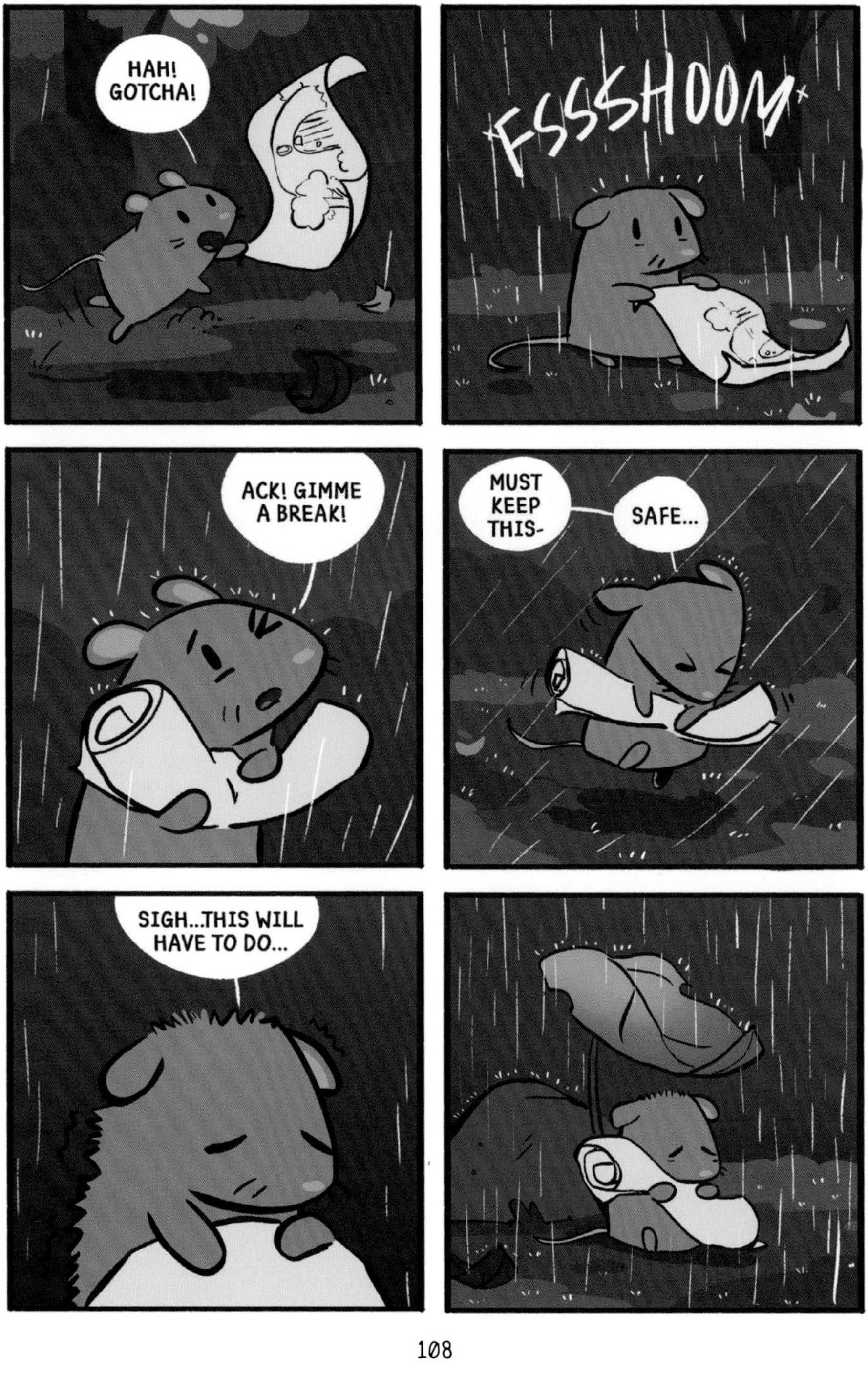
HAH! GOTCHA!
FSSSHOOM
ACK! GIMME A BREAK!
MUST KEEP THIS-
SAFE...
SIGH...THIS WILL HAVE TO DO...

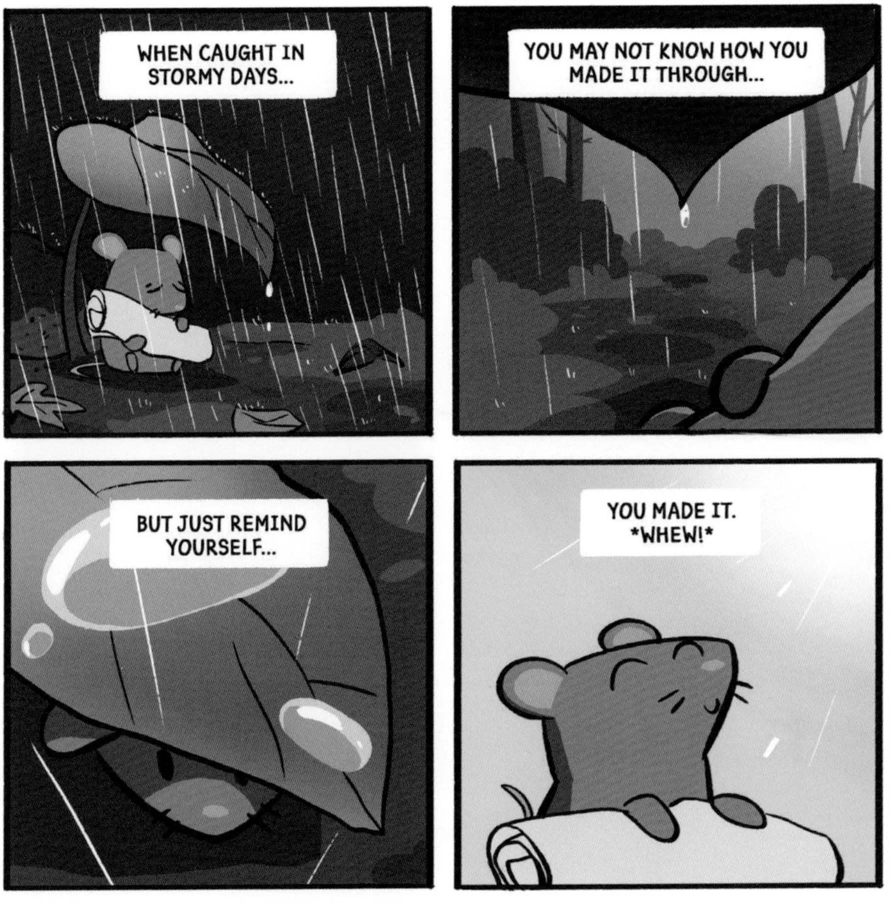
WHEN CAUGHT IN STORMY DAYS...
YOU MAY NOT KNOW HOW YOU MADE IT THROUGH...
BUT JUST REMIND YOURSELF...
YOU MADE IT. *WHEW!*

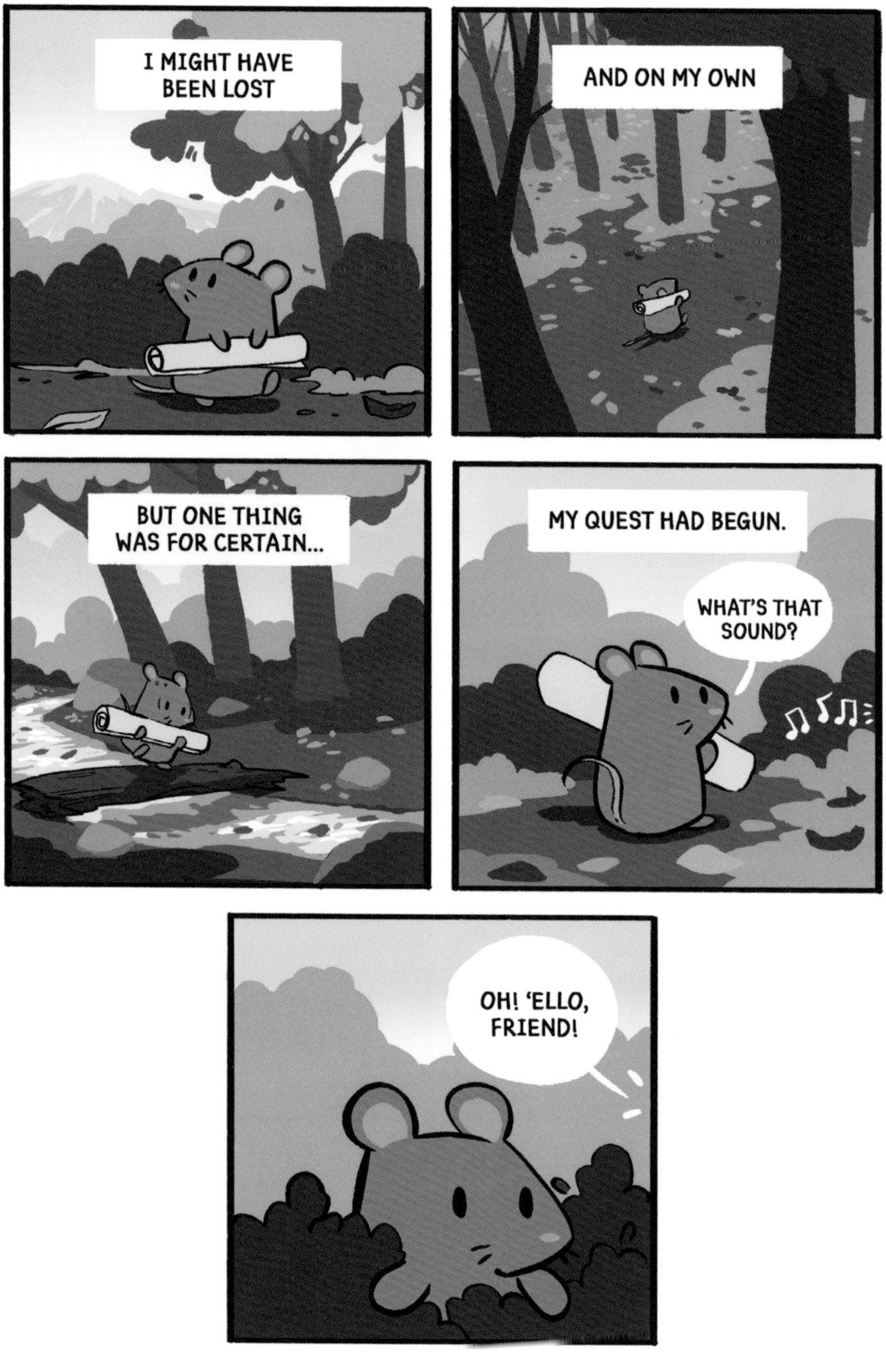
I MIGHT HAVE BEEN LOST
AND ON MY OWN
BUT ONE THING WAS FOR CERTAIN...
MY QUEST HAD BEGUN.
WHAT'S THAT SOUND?
OH! 'ELLO, FRIEND!

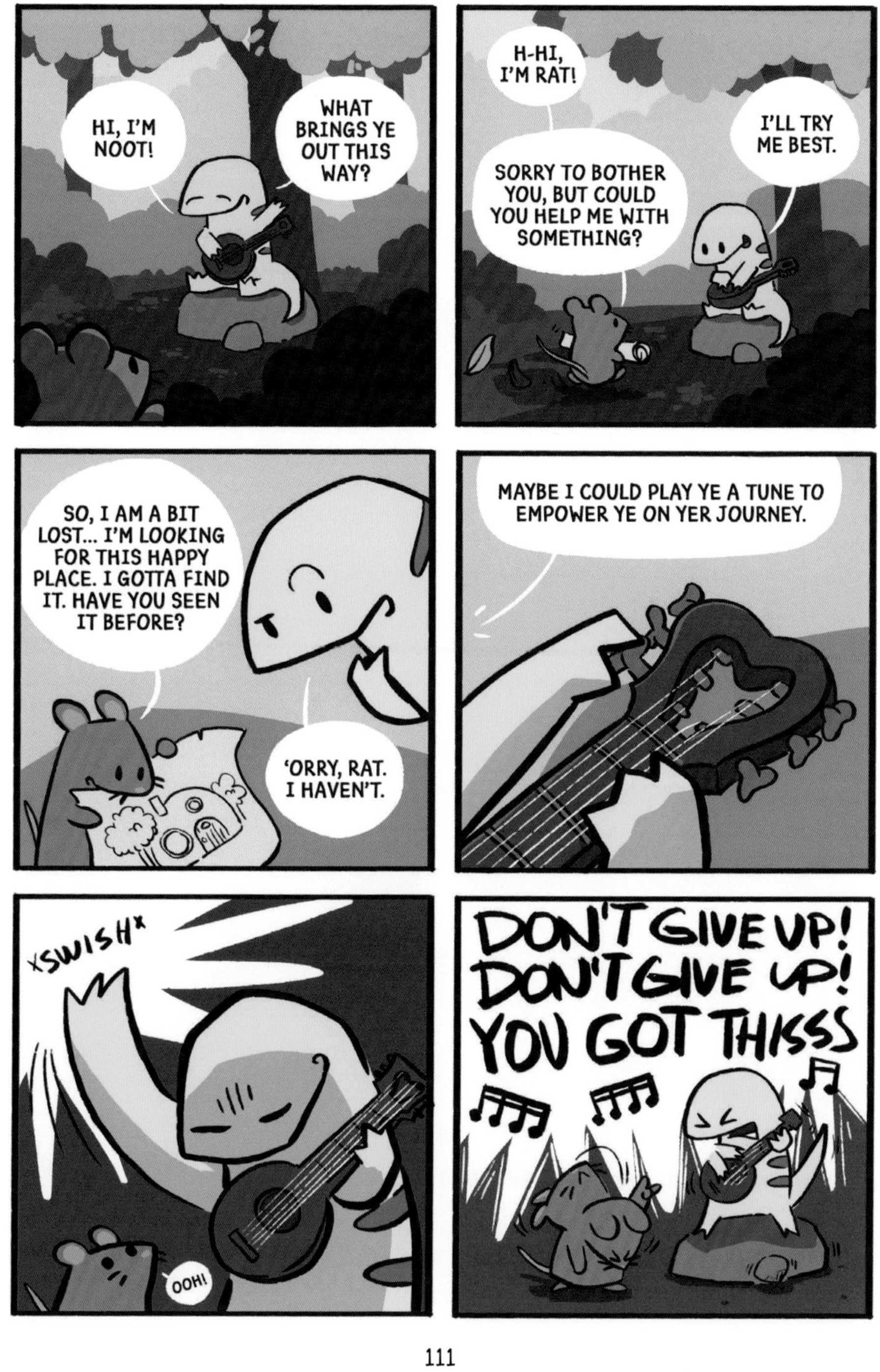
HI, I'M NOOT!
WHAT BRINGS YE OUT THIS WAY?
H-HI, I'M RAT!
SORRY TO BOTHER YOU, BUT COULD YOU HELP ME WITH SOMETHING?
I'LL TRY ME BEST.
SO, I AM A BIT LOST... I'M LOOKING FOR THIS HAPPY PLACE. I GOTTA FIND IT. HAVE YOU SEEN IT BEFORE?
'ORRY, RAT. I HAVEN'T.
MAYBE I COULD PLAY YE A TUNE TO EMPOWER YE ON YER JOURNEY.
xSWISHx
OOH!
DON'T GIVE UP! DON'T GIVE UP! YOU GOT THISSS

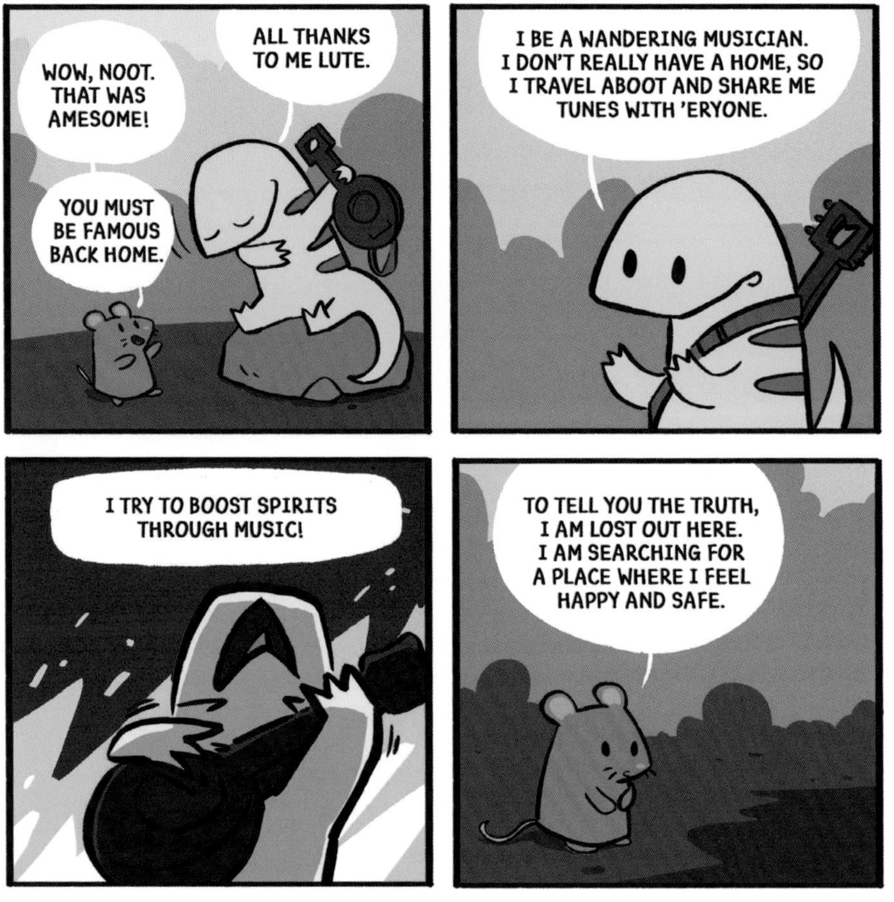
WOW, NOOT. THAT WAS AMESOME!
ALL THANKS TO ME LUTE.
YOU MUST BE FAMOUS BACK HOME.
I BE A WANDERING MUSICIAN. I DON'T REALLY HAVE A HOME, SO I TRAVEL ABOOT AND SHARE ME TUNES WITH 'ERYONE.
I TRY TO BOOST SPIRITS THROUGH MUSIC!
TO TELL YOU THE TRUTH, I AM LOST OUT HERE. I AM SEARCHING FOR A PLACE WHERE I FEEL HAPPY AND SAFE.

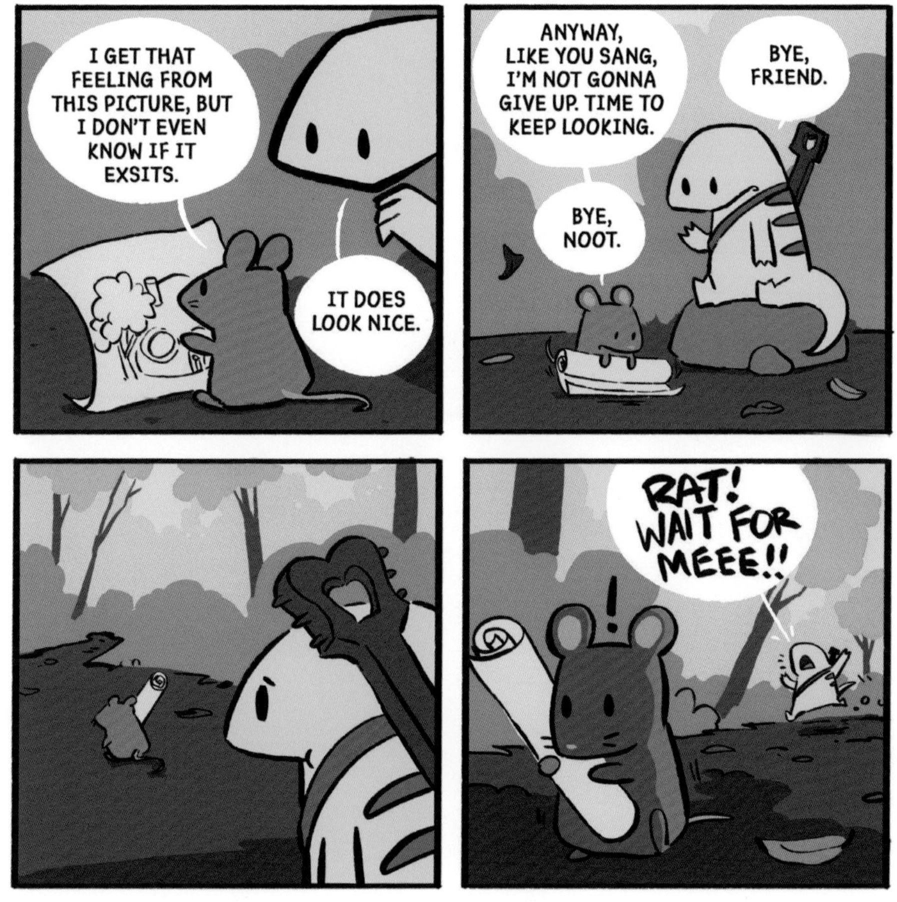
I GET THAT FEELING FROM THIS PICTURE, BUT I DON'T EVEN KNOW IF IT EXSITS.
IT DOES LOOK NICE.
ANYWAY, LIKE YOU SANG, I'M NOT GONNA GIVE UP. TIME TO KEEP LOOKING.
BYE, FRIEND.
BYE, NOOT.
RAT! WAIT FOR MEEE!!
!

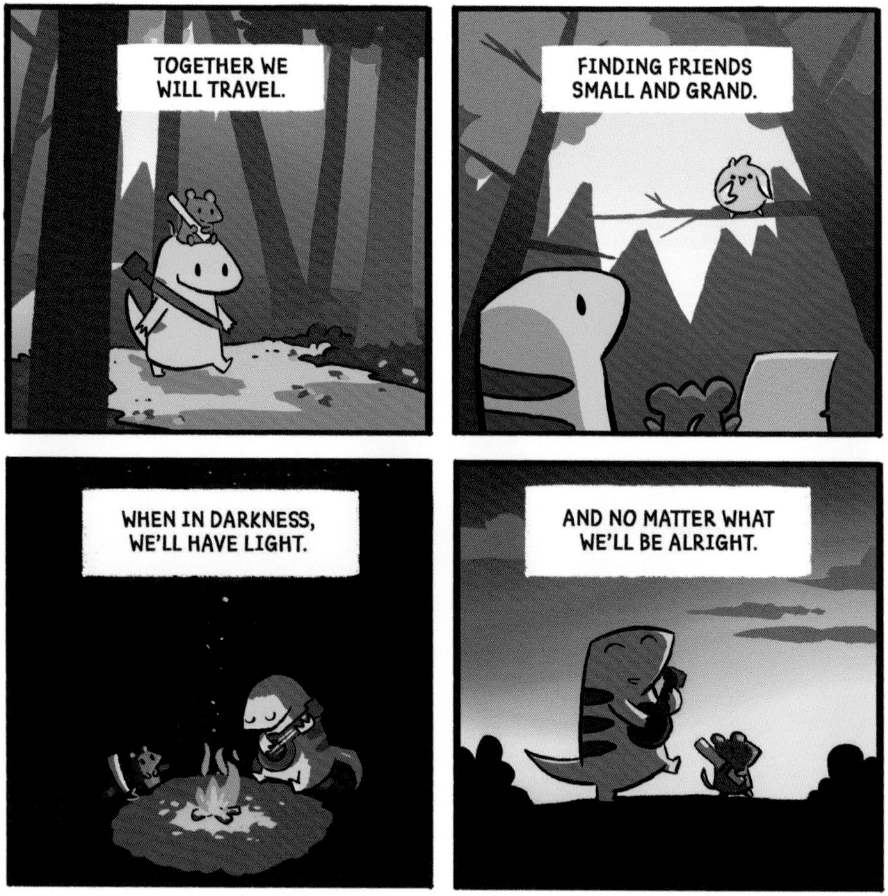
TOGETHER WE
WILL TRAVEL.
FINDING FRIENDS
SMALL AND GRAND.
WHEN IN DARKNESS,
WE'LL HAVE LIGHT.
AND NO MATTER WHAT
WE'LL BE ALRIGHT.

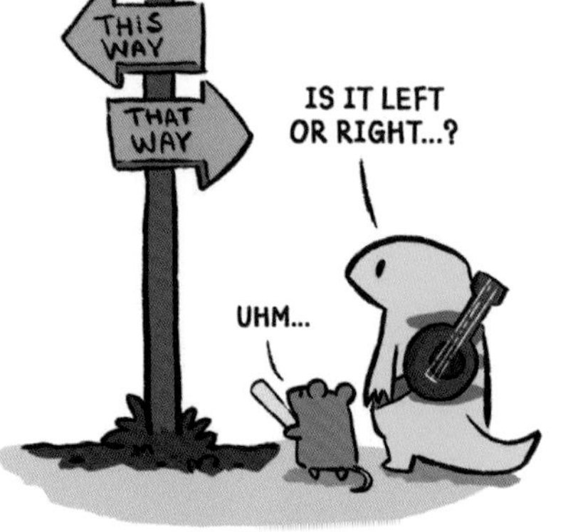
THIS
WAY
THAT
WAY
IS IT LEFT
OR RIGHT...?
UHM...

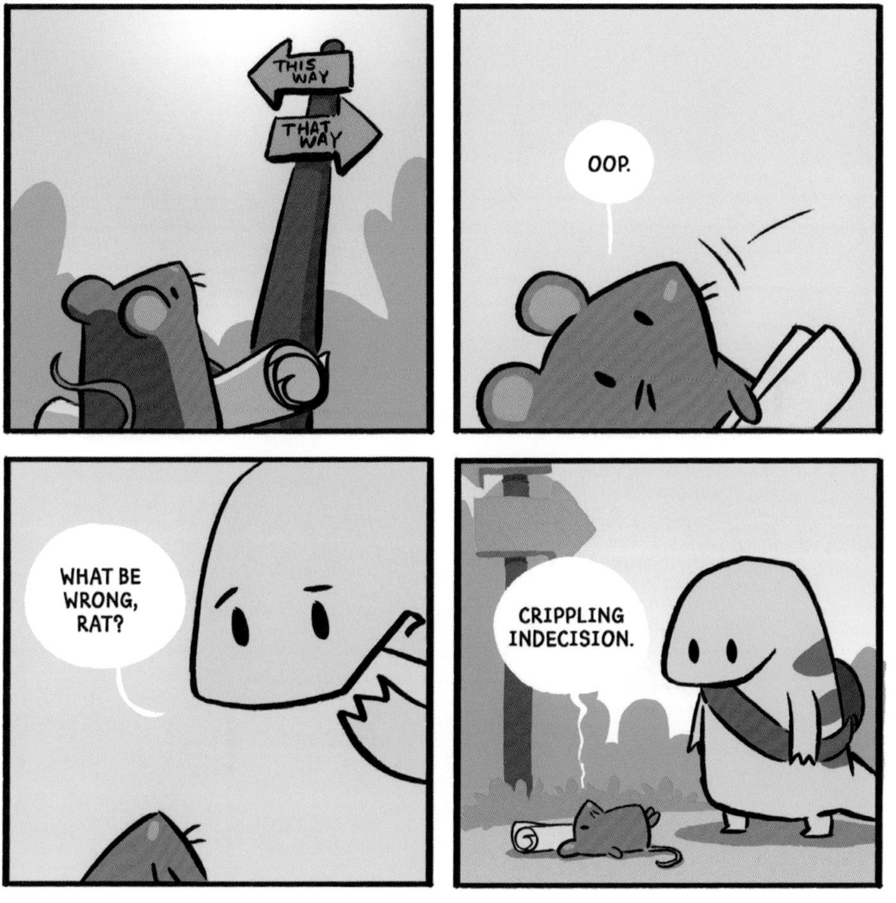
THIS WAY
THAT WAY
OOP.
WHAT BE WRONG, RAT?
CRIPPLING INDECISION.

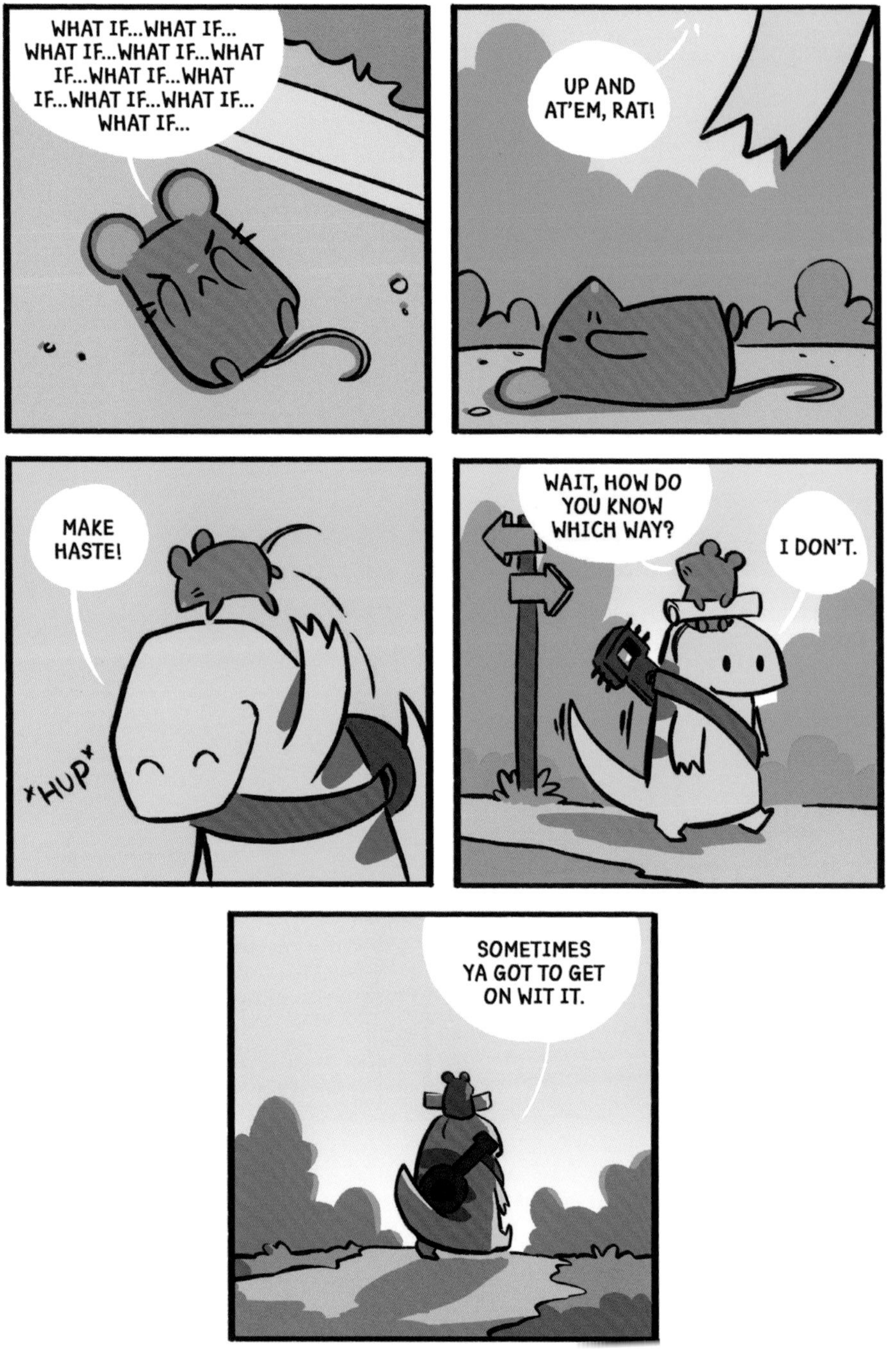
WHAT IF...WHAT IF... WHAT IF...WHAT IF...WHAT IF...WHAT IF...WHAT IF...WHAT IF...WHAT IF... WHAT IF...
UP AND AT'EM, RAT!
MAKE HASTE!
HUP
WAIT, HOW DO YOU KNOW WHICH WAY?
I DON'T.
SOMETIMES YA GOT TO GET ON WIT IT.

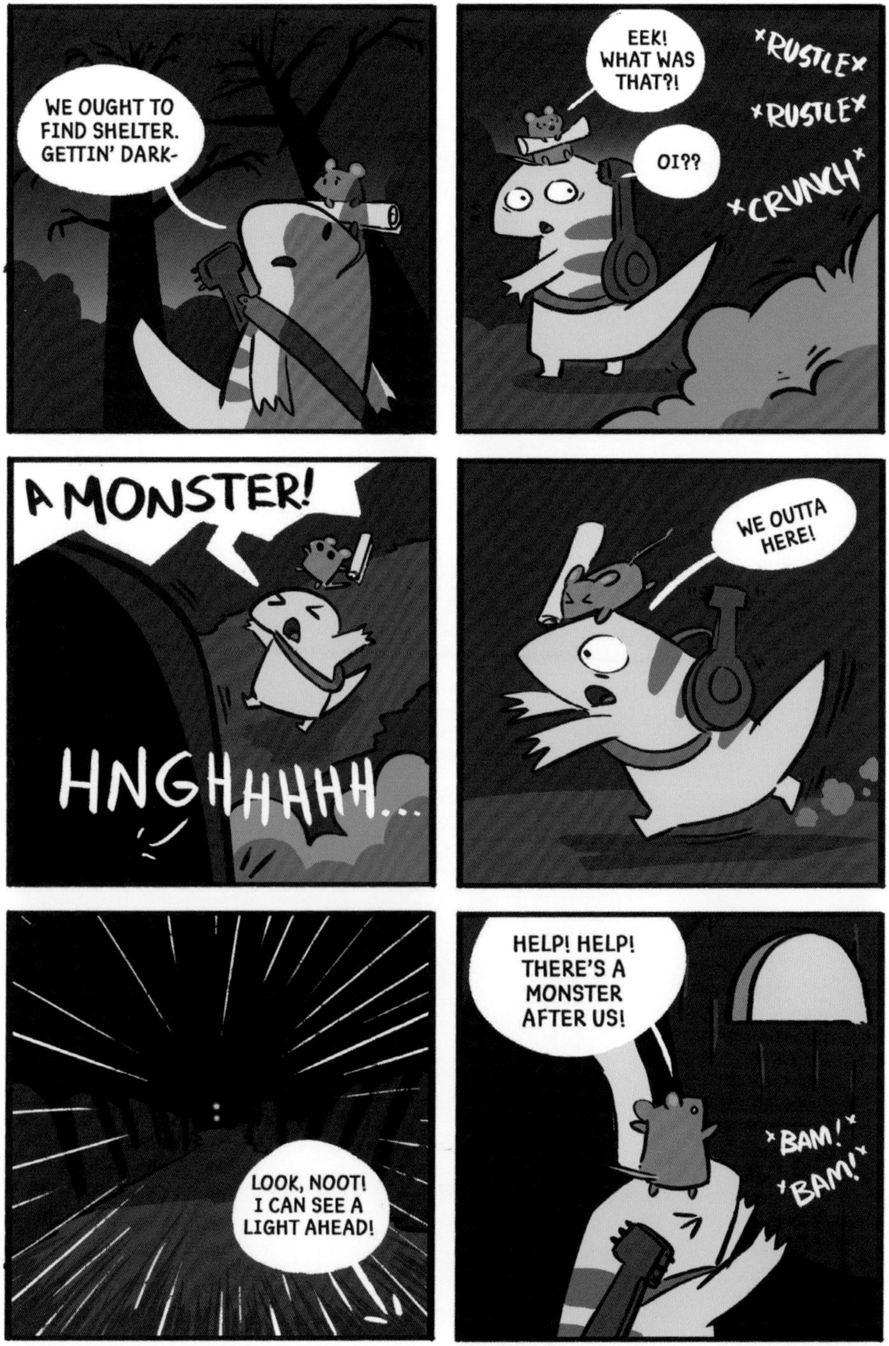
WE OUGHT TO FIND SHELTER. GETTIN' DARK-
EEK! WHAT WAS THAT?!
OI??
RUSTLE
RUSTLE
CRUNCH
A MONSTER!
HNGHHHHH...
WE OUTTA HERE!
LOOK, NOOT! I CAN SEE A LIGHT AHEAD!
HELP! HELP! THERE'S A MONSTER AFTER US!
BAM!
BAM!

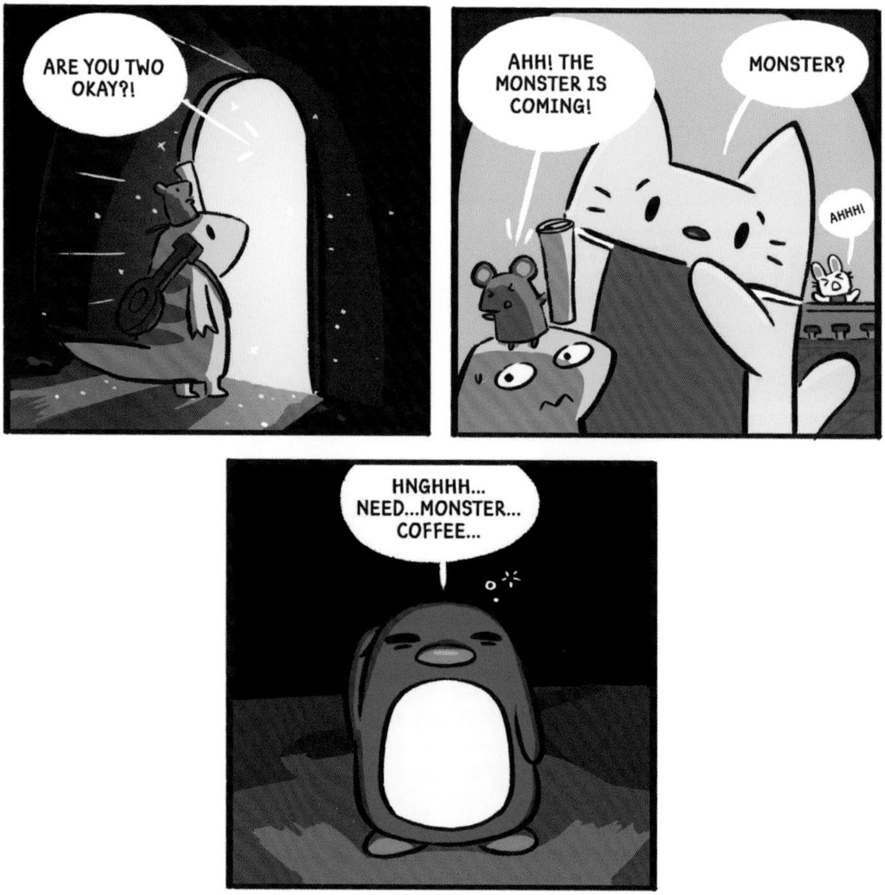
ARE YOU TWO OKAY?!
AHH! THE MONSTER IS COMING!
MONSTER?
AHHH!
HNGHHH... NEED...MONSTER... COFFEE...

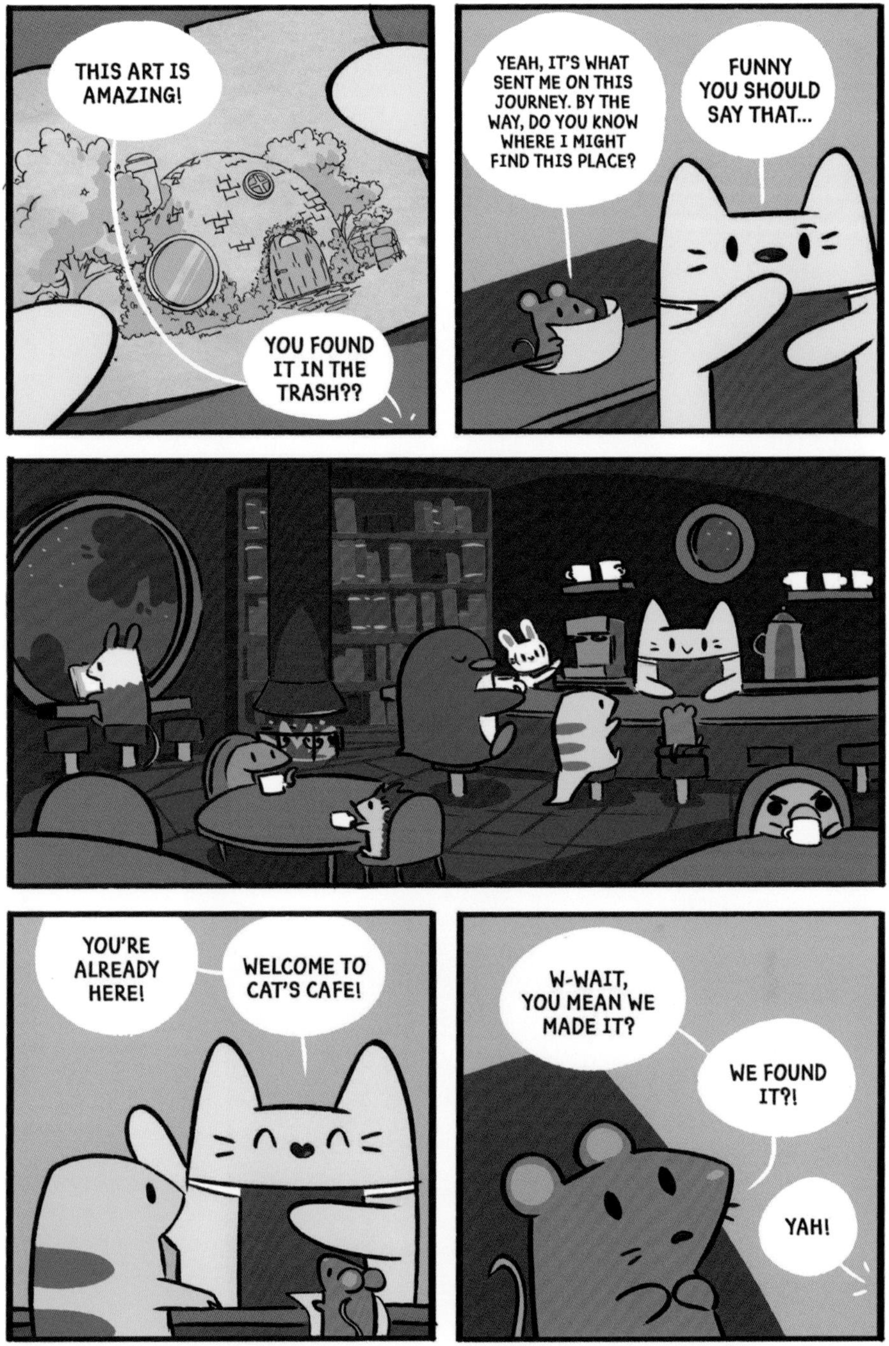
THIS ART IS AMAZING!
YOU FOUND IT IN THE TRASH??
YEAH, IT'S WHAT SENT ME ON THIS JOURNEY. BY THE WAY, DO YOU KNOW WHERE I MIGHT FIND THIS PLACE?
FUNNY YOU SHOULD SAY THAT...
YOU'RE ALREADY HERE!
WELCOME TO CAT'S CAFE!
W-WAIT, YOU MEAN WE MADE IT?
WE FOUND IT?!
YAH!

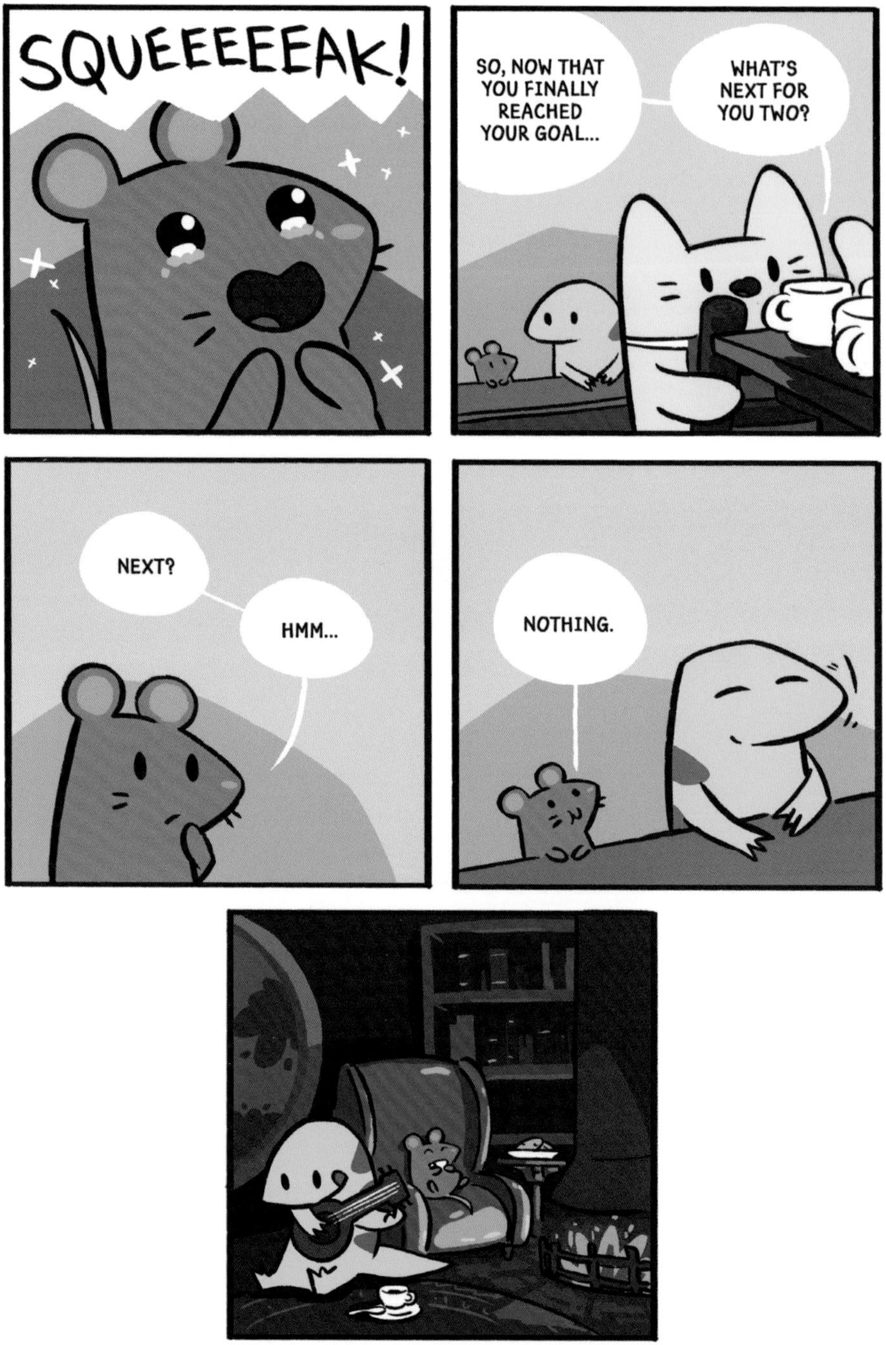
SQUEEEEEAK!
SO, NOW THAT YOU FINALLY REACHED YOUR GOAL...
WHAT'S NEXT FOR YOU TWO?
NEXT?
HMM...
NOTHING.

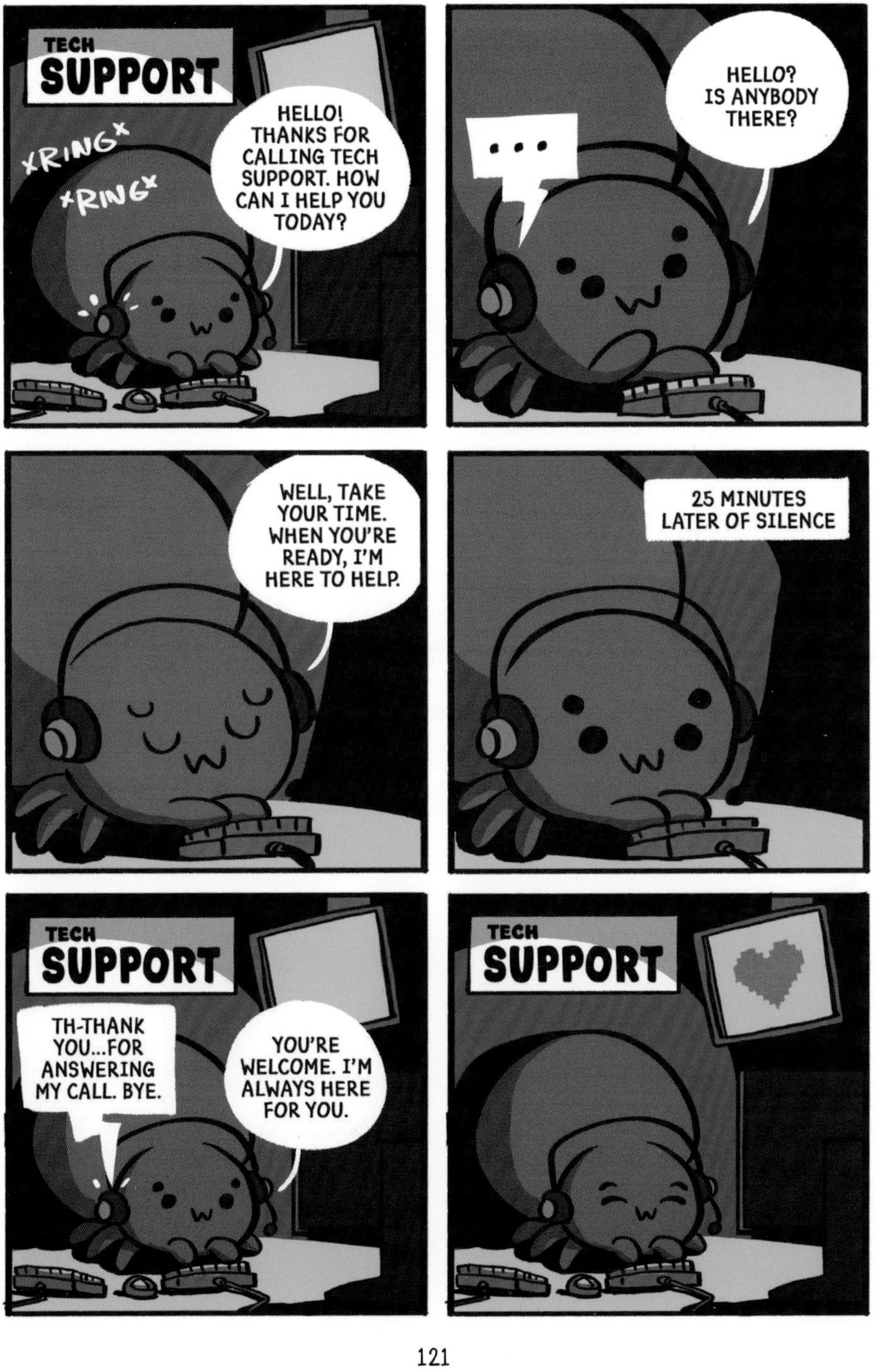
TECH SUPPORT
RING
RING
HELLO! THANKS FOR CALLING TECH SUPPORT. HOW CAN I HELP YOU TODAY?
...
HELLO? IS ANYBODY THERE?
WELL, TAKE YOUR TIME. WHEN YOU'RE READY, I'M HERE TO HELP.
25 MINUTES LATER OF SILENCE
TECH SUPPORT
TH-THANK YOU...FOR ANSWERING MY CALL. BYE.
YOU'RE WELCOME. I'M ALWAYS HERE FOR YOU.
TECH SUPPORT

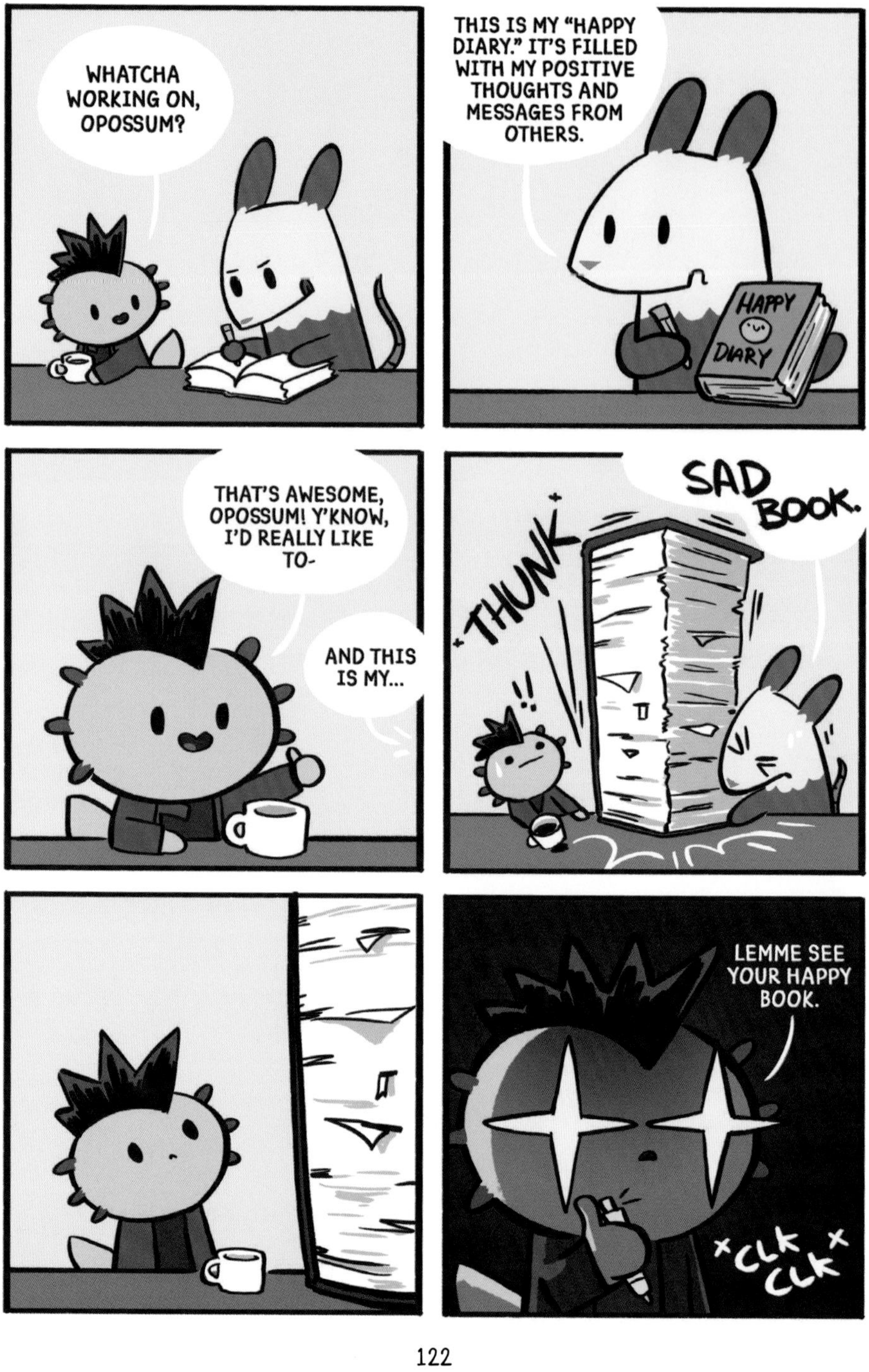
WHATCHA WORKING ON, OPOSSUM?
THIS IS MY "HAPPY DIARY." IT'S FILLED WITH MY POSITIVE THOUGHTS AND MESSAGES FROM OTHERS.
HAPPY DIARY
THAT'S AWESOME, OPOSSUM! Y'KNOW, I'D REALLY LIKE TO-
AND THIS IS MY...
SAD BOOK.
THUNK
LEMME SEE YOUR HAPPY BOOK.
CLK CLK

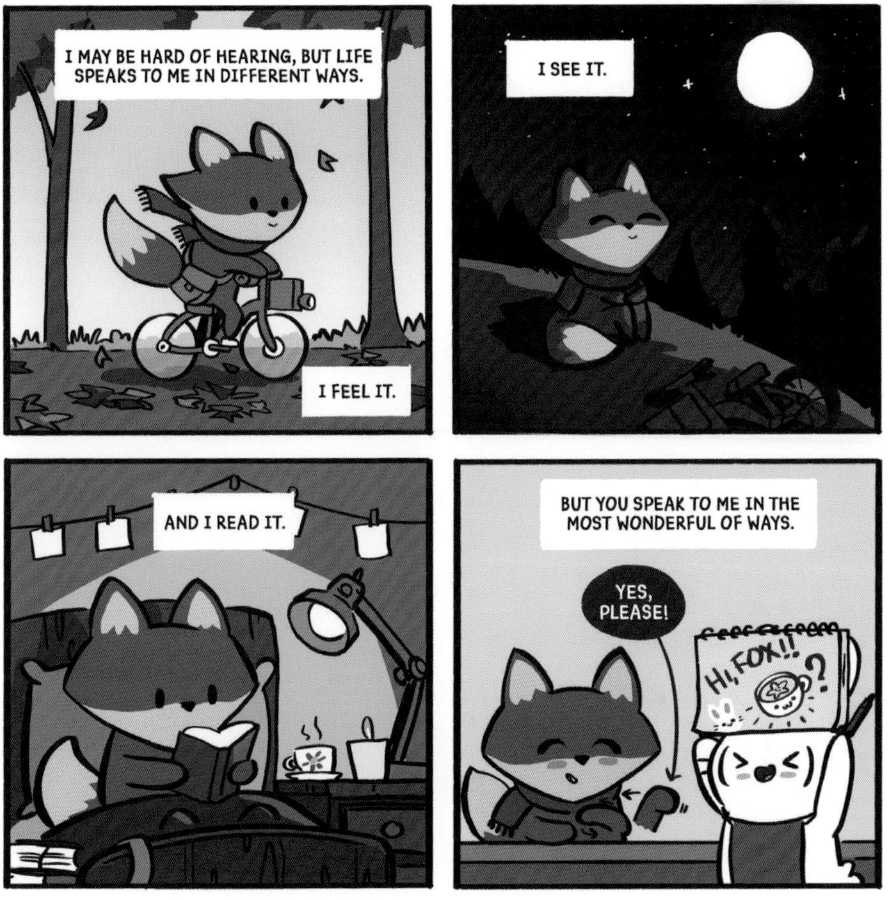
I MAY BE HARD OF HEARING, BUT LIFE SPEAKS TO ME IN DIFFERENT WAYS.
I FEEL IT.
I SEE IT.
AND I READ IT.
BUT YOU SPEAK TO ME IN THE MOST WONDERFUL OF WAYS.
YES, PLEASE!
HI, FOX!!
?

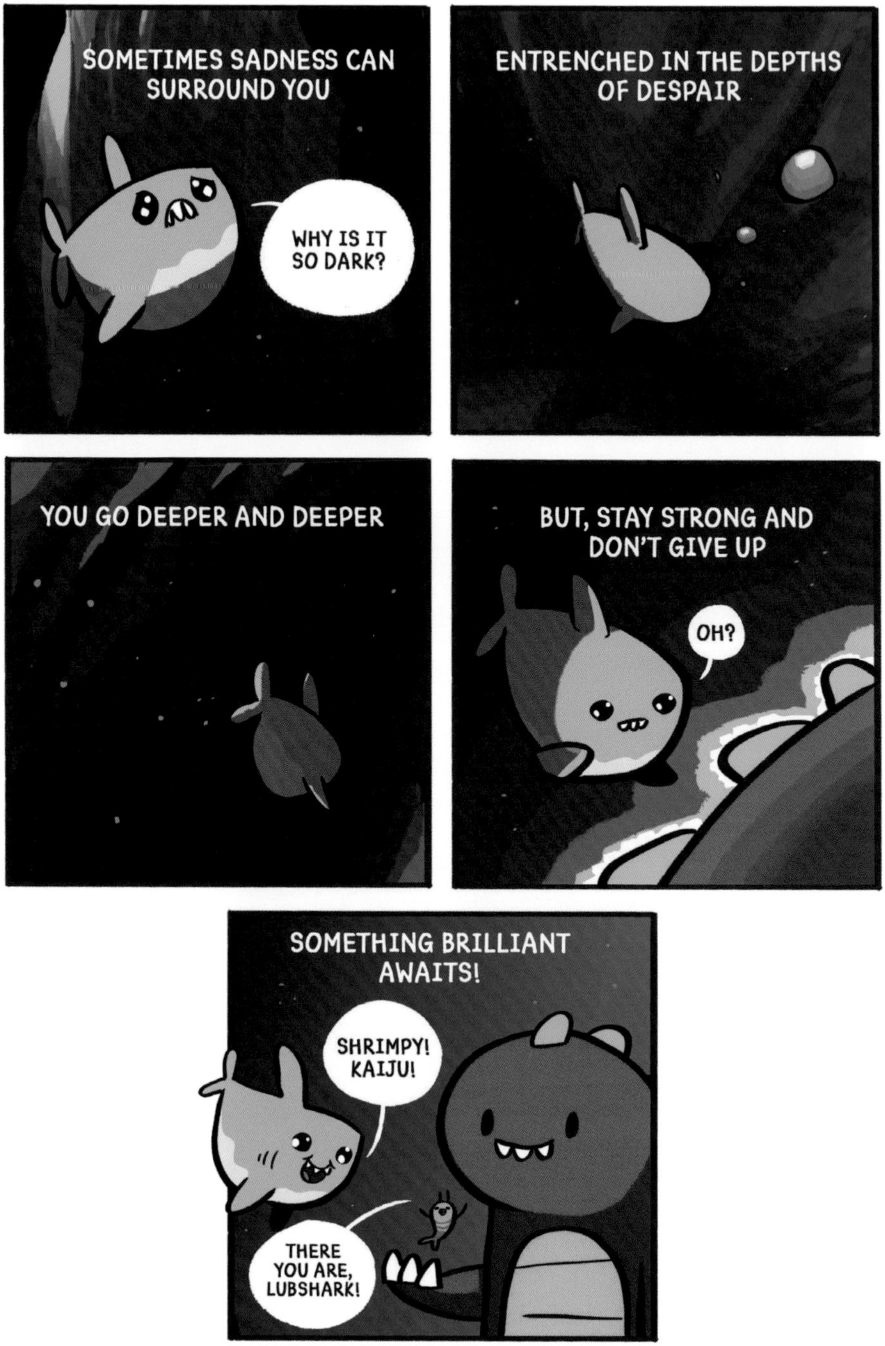

SOMETIMES SADNESS CAN SURROUND YOU
WHY IS IT SO DARK?
ENTRENCHED IN THE DEPTHS OF DESPAIR
YOU GO DEEPER AND DEEPER
BUT, STAY STRONG AND DON'T GIVE UP
OH?
SOMETHING BRILLIANT AWAITS!
SHRIMPY! KAIJU!
THERE YOU ARE, LUBSHARK!

KIWI'S FAVORITE SOUNDS:

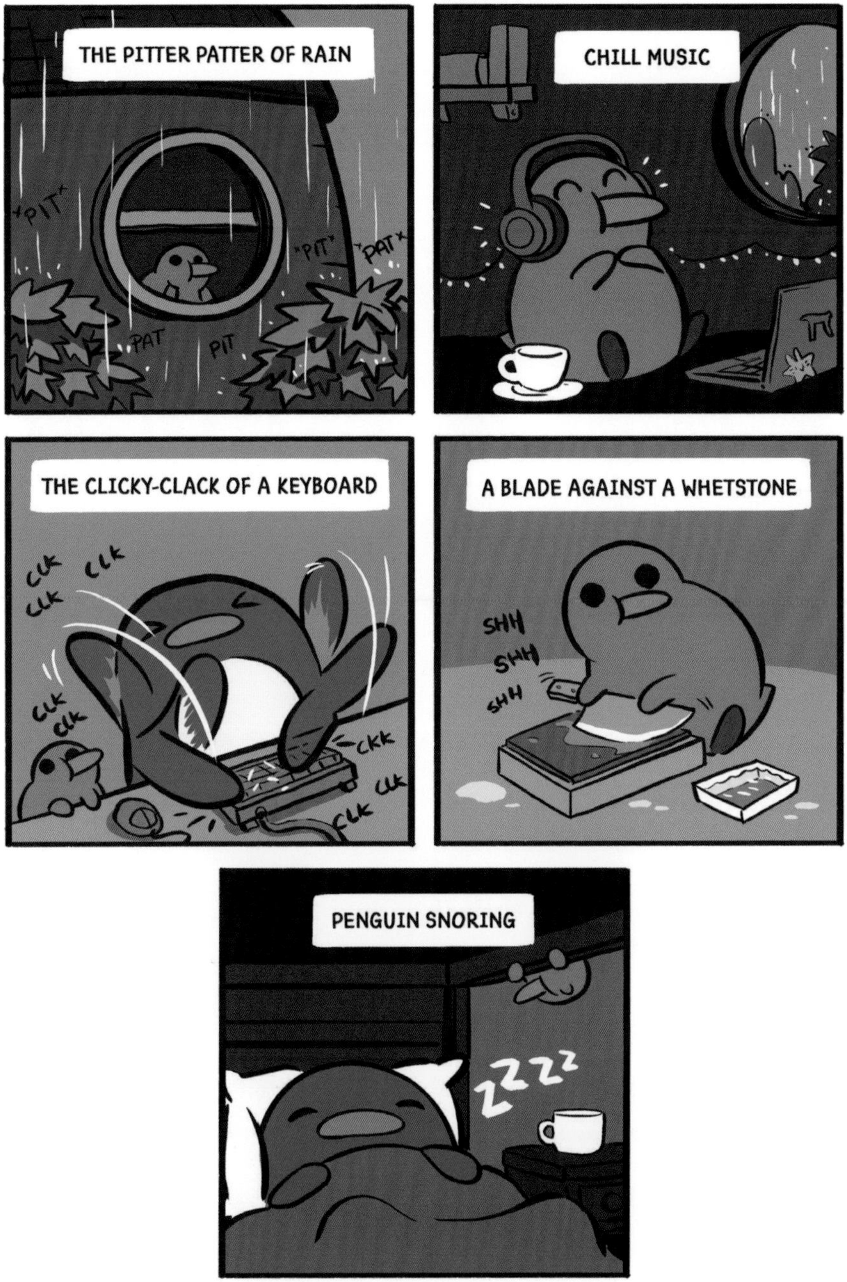
THE PITTER PATTER OF RAIN
PIT
PIT
PAT
PAT
PIT
CHILL MUSIC
THE CLICKY-CLACK OF A KEYBOARD
CLK CLK
CLK
CLK
CLK
CKK
CLK
CLK
A BLADE AGAINST A WHETSTONE
SHH
SHH
SHH
PENGUIN SNORING
ZZZZ

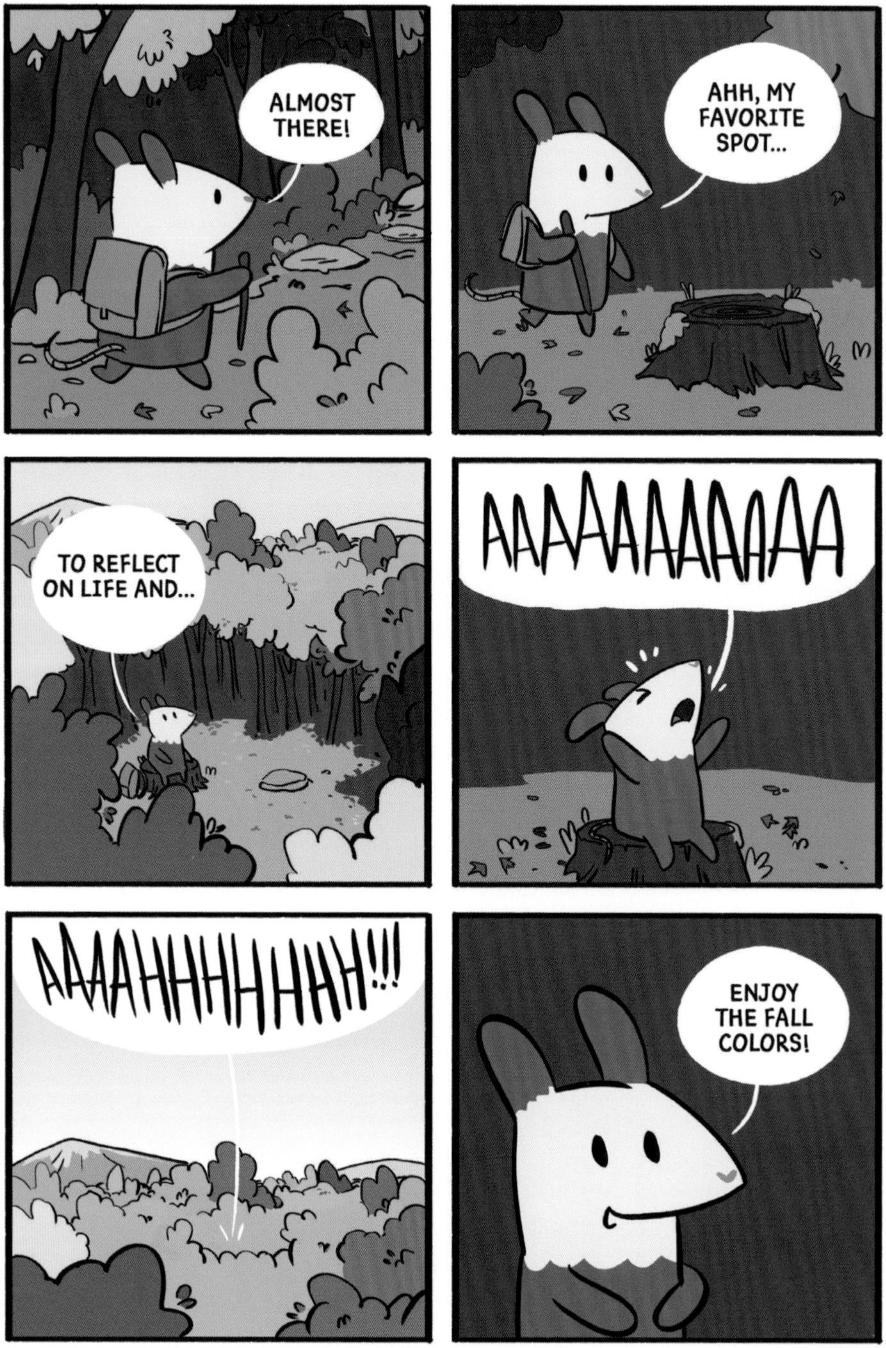
ALMOST THERE!
AHH, MY FAVORITE SPOT...
TO REFLECT ON LIFE AND...
AAAAAAAAAAA
AAAAHHHHHAH!!!
ENJOY THE FALL COLORS!

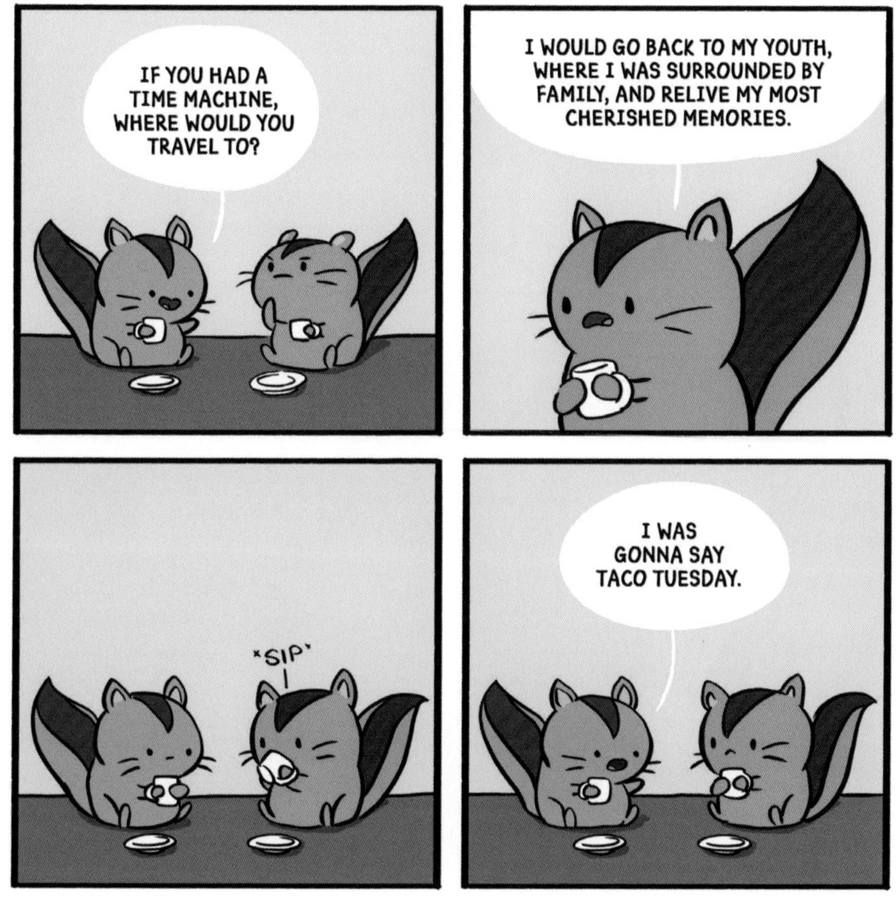
IF YOU HAD A TIME MACHINE, WHERE WOULD YOU TRAVEL TO?
I WOULD GO BACK TO MY YOUTH, WHERE I WAS SURROUNDED BY FAMILY, AND RELIVE MY MOST CHERISHED MEMORIES.
SIP
I WAS GONNA SAY TACO TUESDAY.

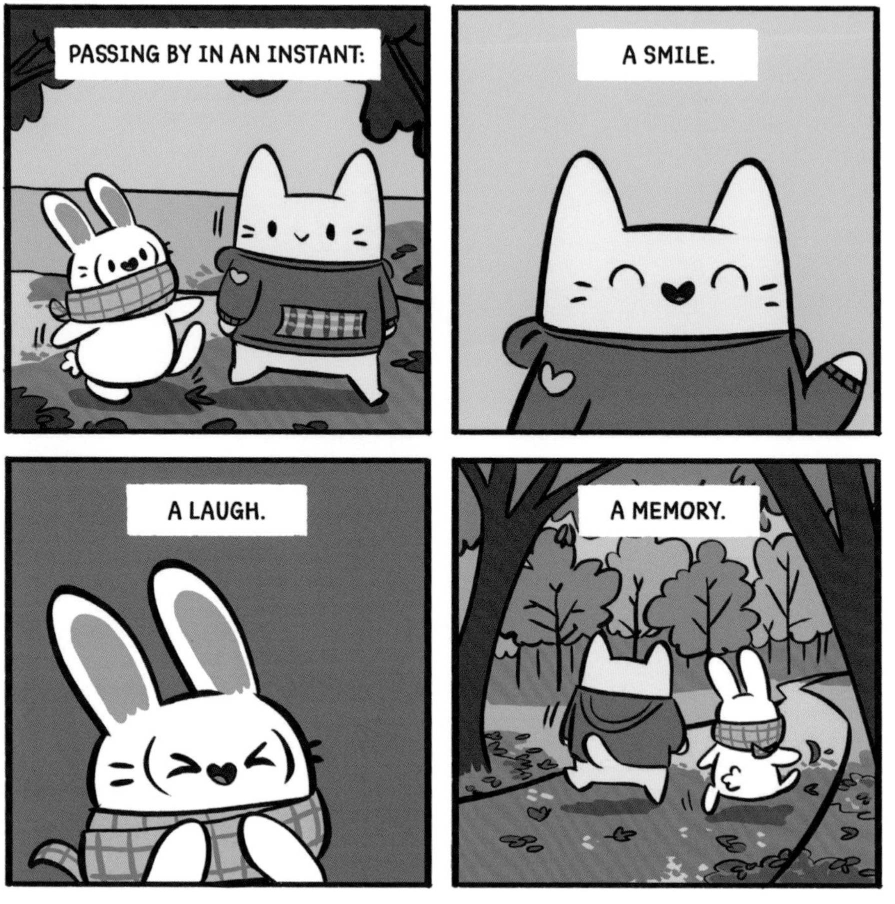
PASSING BY IN AN INSTANT:
A SMILE.
A LAUGH.
A MEMORY.

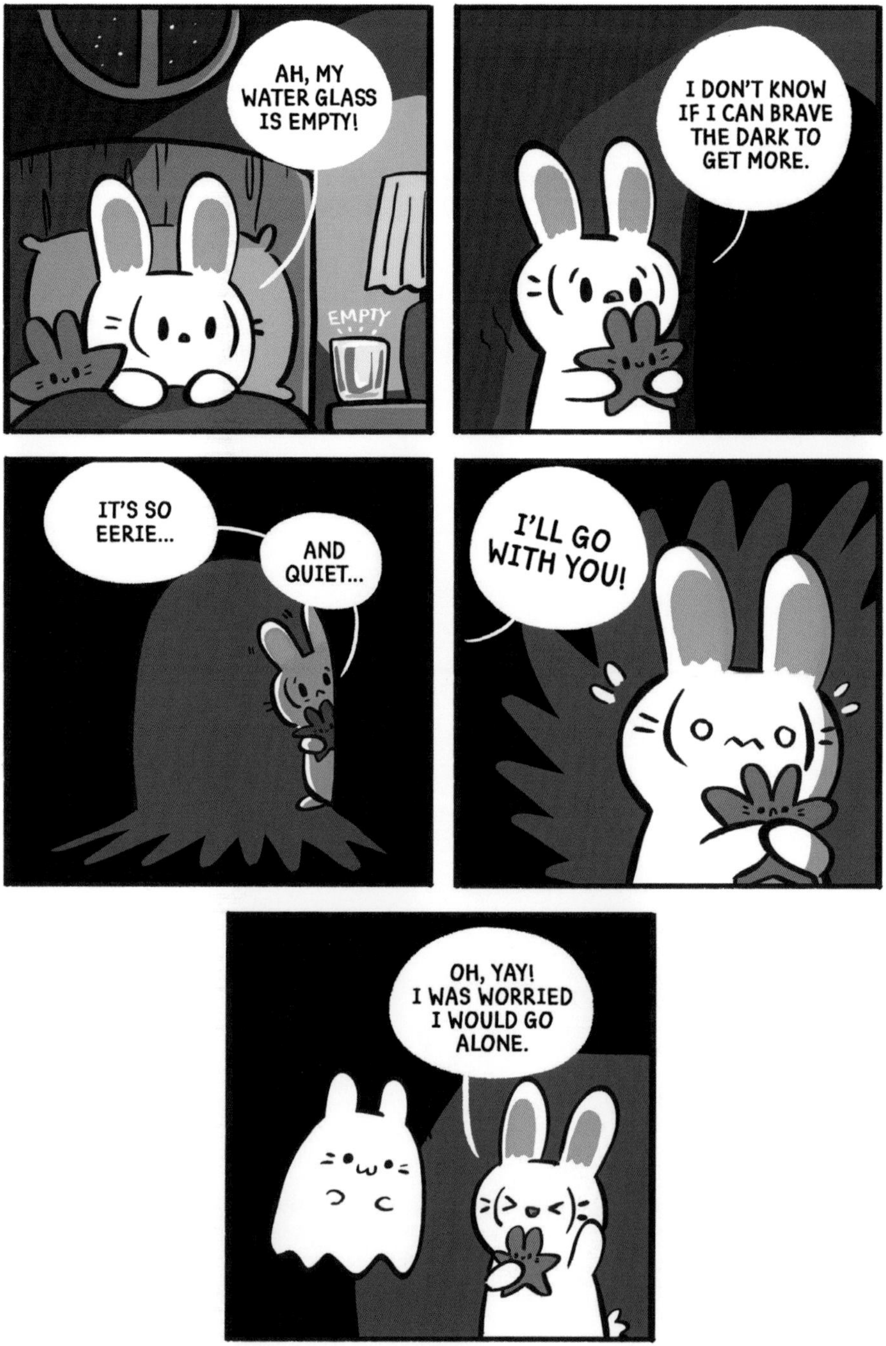
AH, MY WATER GLASS IS EMPTY!
EMPTY
I DON'T KNOW IF I CAN BRAVE THE DARK TO GET MORE.
IT'S SO EERIE...
AND QUIET...
I'LL GO WITH YOU!
OH, YAY! I WAS WORRIED I WOULD GO ALONE.

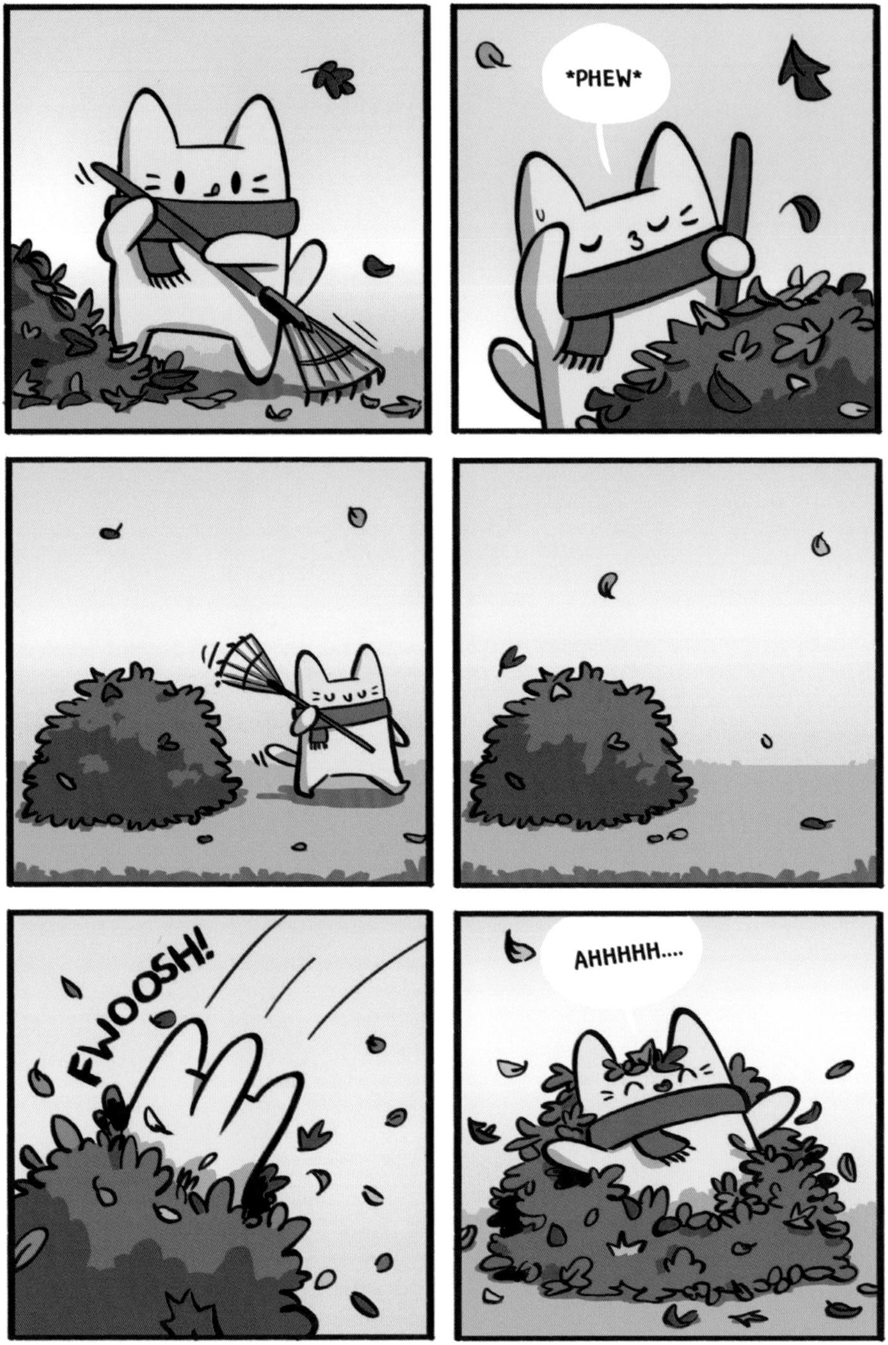
PHEW
FWOOSH!
AHHHHH....

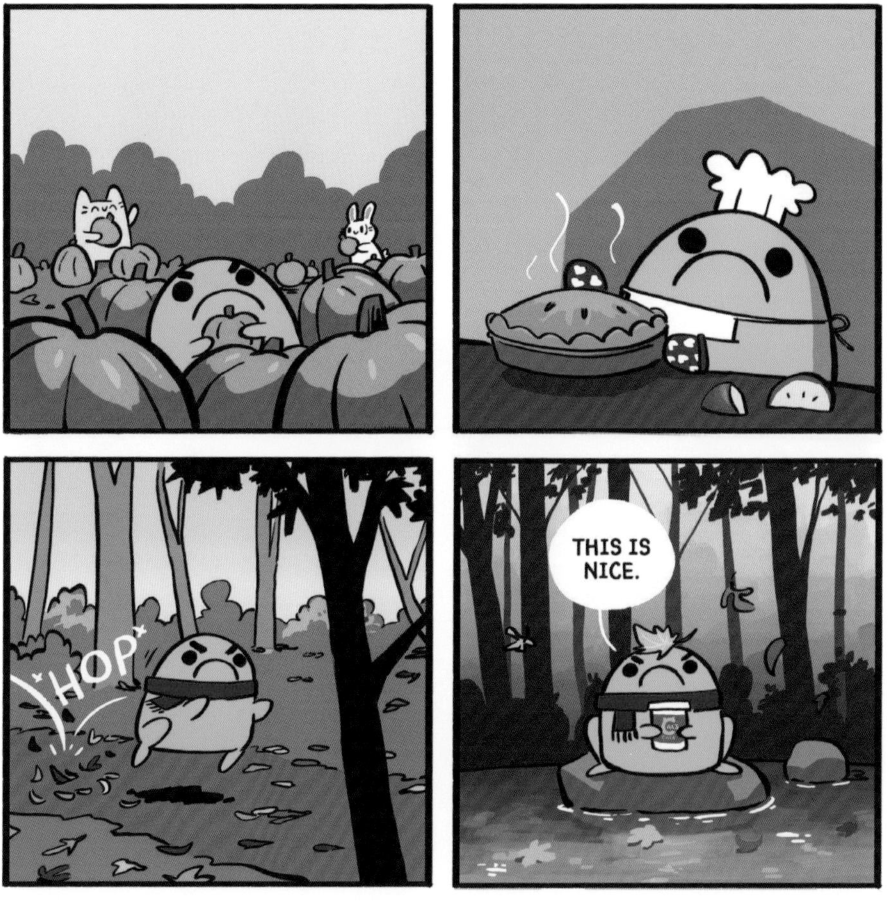
HOP
THIS IS NICE.

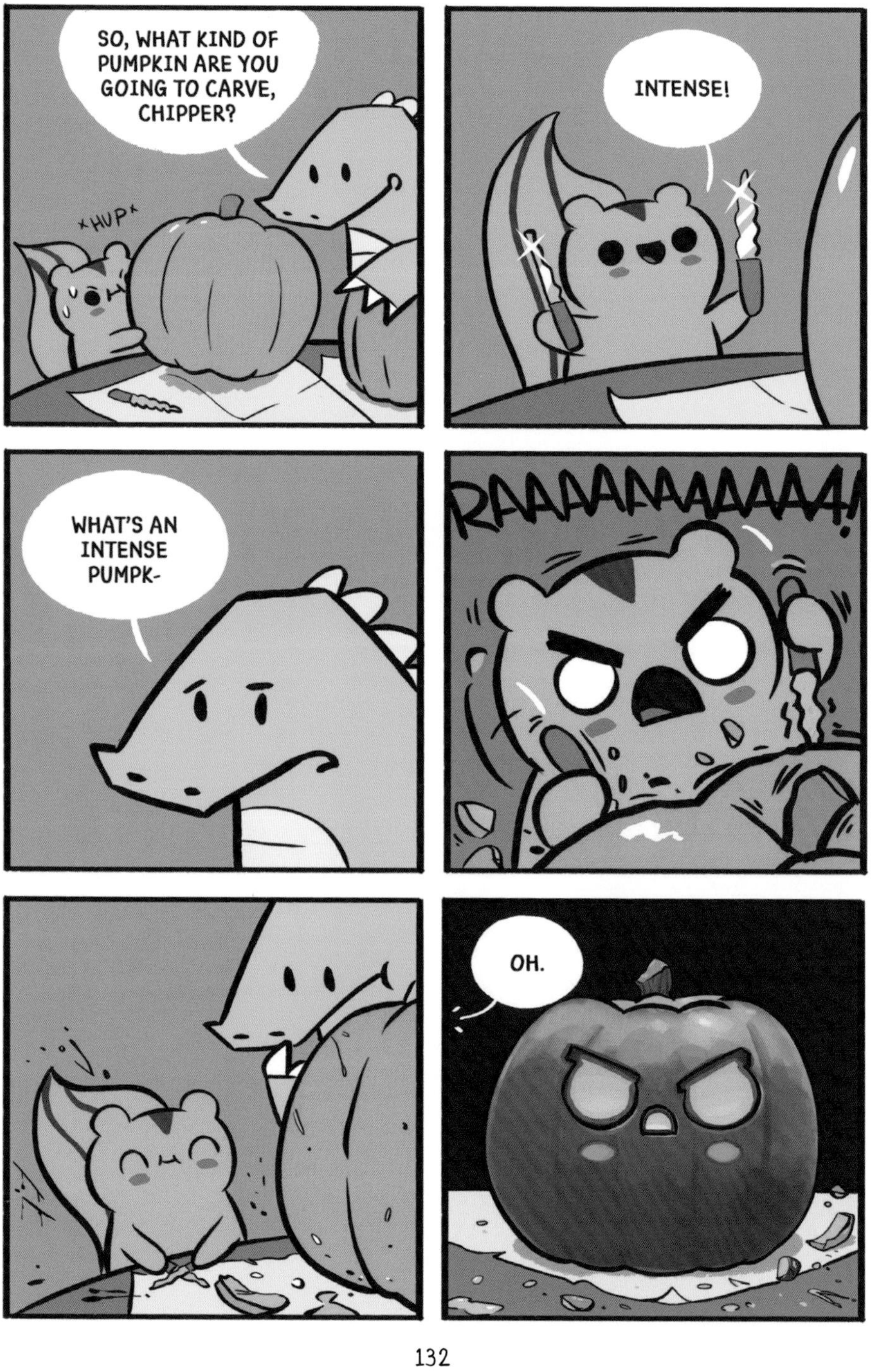
SO, WHAT KIND OF PUMPKIN ARE YOU GOING TO CARVE, CHIPPER?
HUP
INTENSE!
WHAT'S AN INTENSE PUMPK-
RAAAAAAAAAA!
OH.

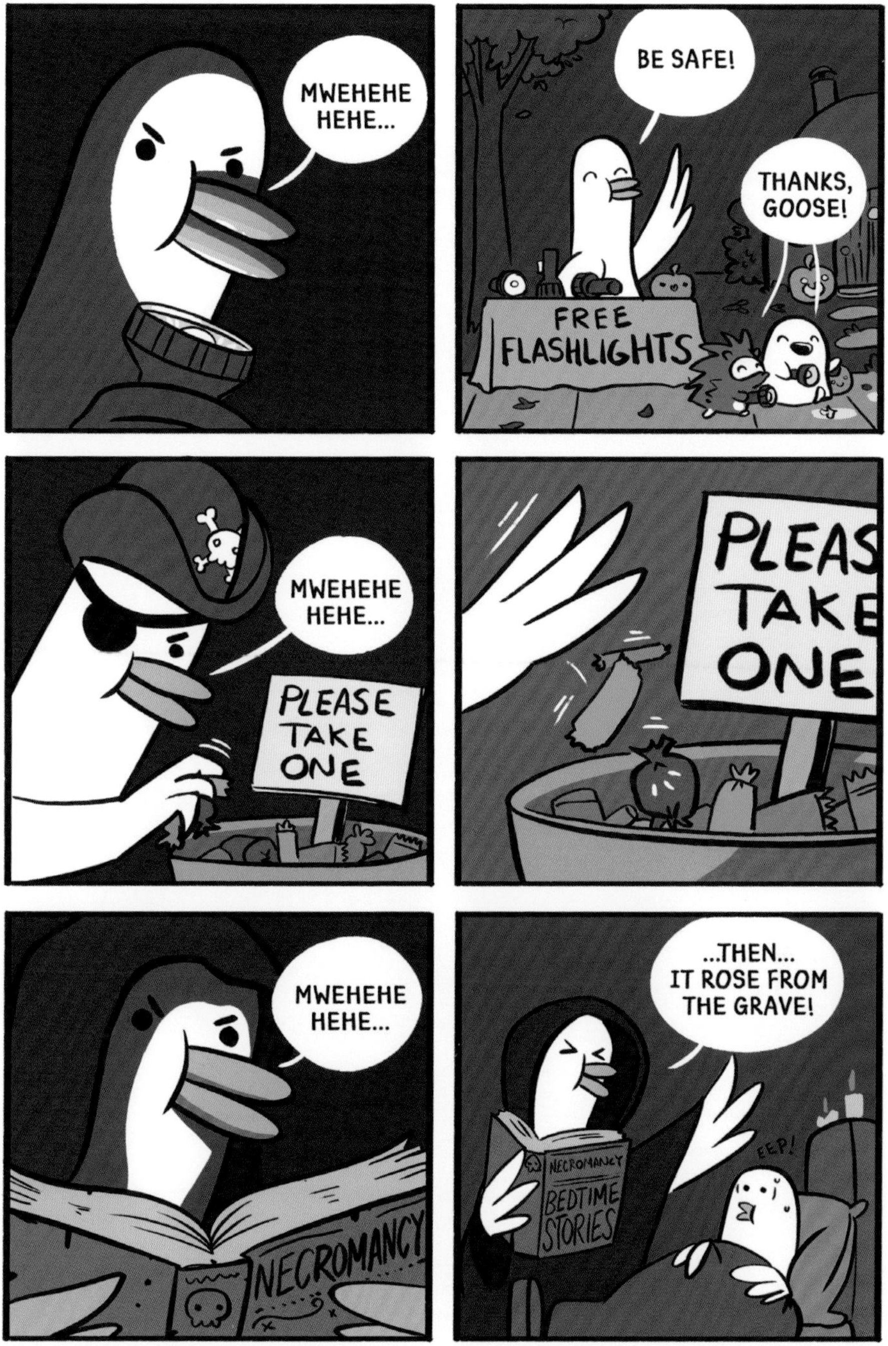
MWEHEHE HEHE...
BE SAFE!
FREE FLASHLIGHTS
THANKS, GOOSE!
MWEHEHE HEHE...
PLEASE TAKE ONE
PLEASE TAKE ONE
MWEHEHE HEHE...
NECROMANCY
...THEN... IT ROSE FROM THE GRAVE!
NECROMANCY
BEDTIME STORIES
EEP!

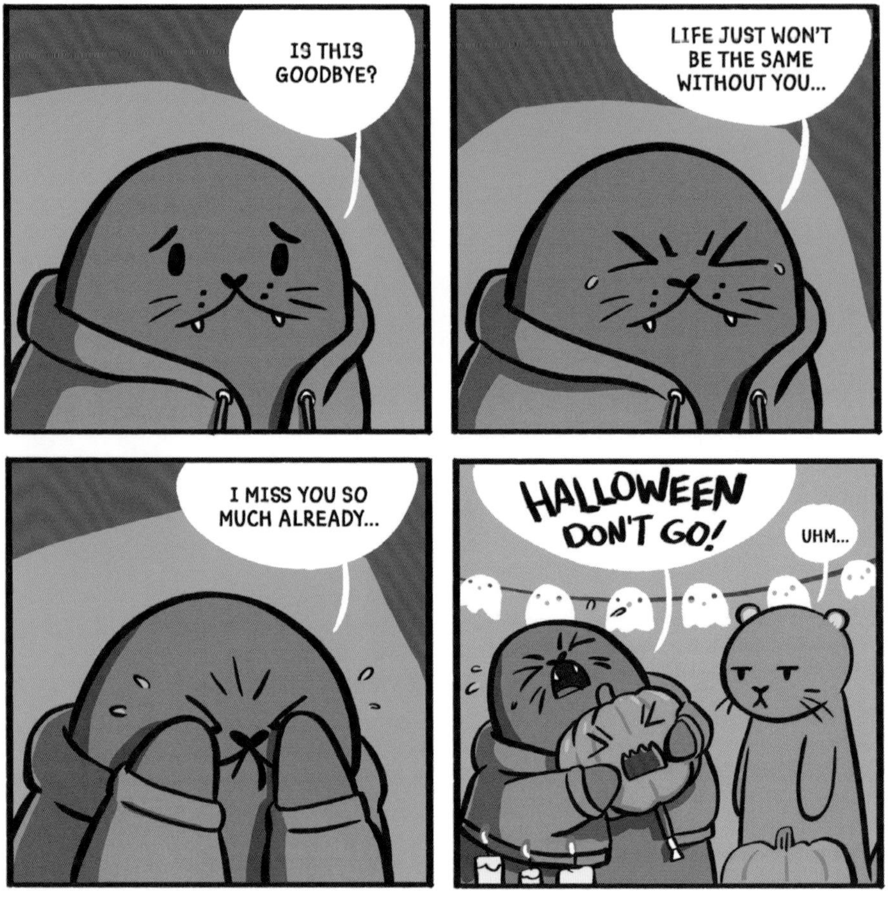
IS THIS GOODBYE?
LIFE JUST WON'T BE THE SAME WITHOUT YOU...
I MISS YOU SO MUCH ALREADY...
HALLOWEEN DON'T GO!
UHM...

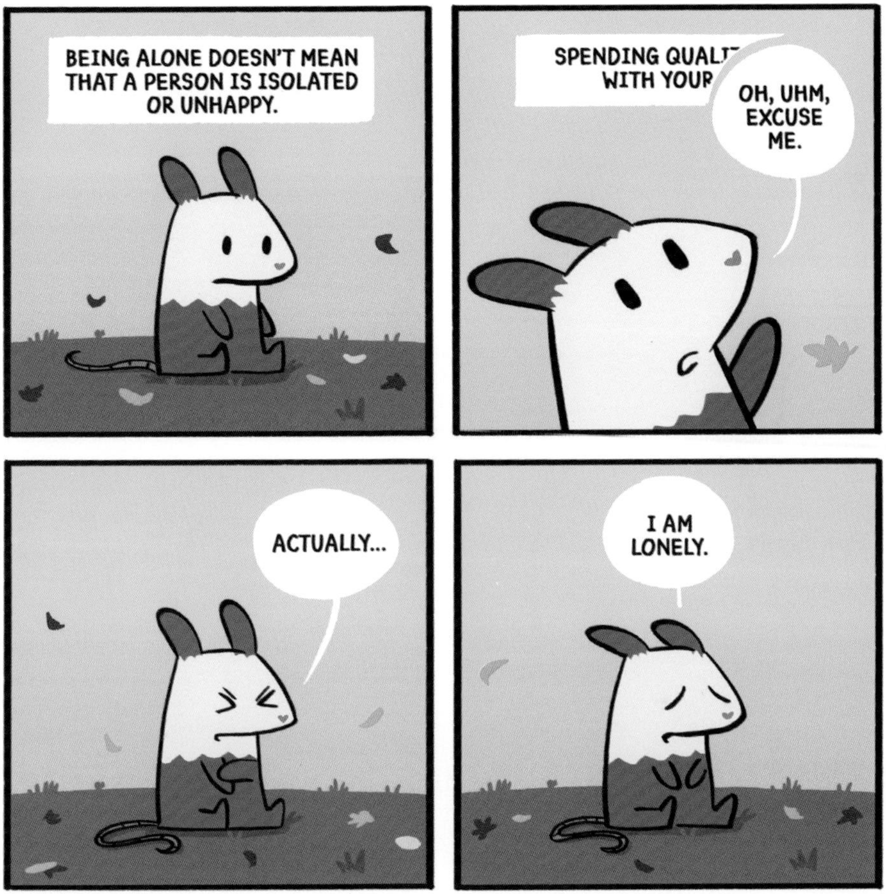
BEING ALONE DOESN'T MEAN THAT A PERSON IS ISOLATED OR UNHAPPY.
SPENDING QUALI
WITH YOUR
OH, UHM, EXCUSE ME.
ACTUALLY...
I AM LONELY.

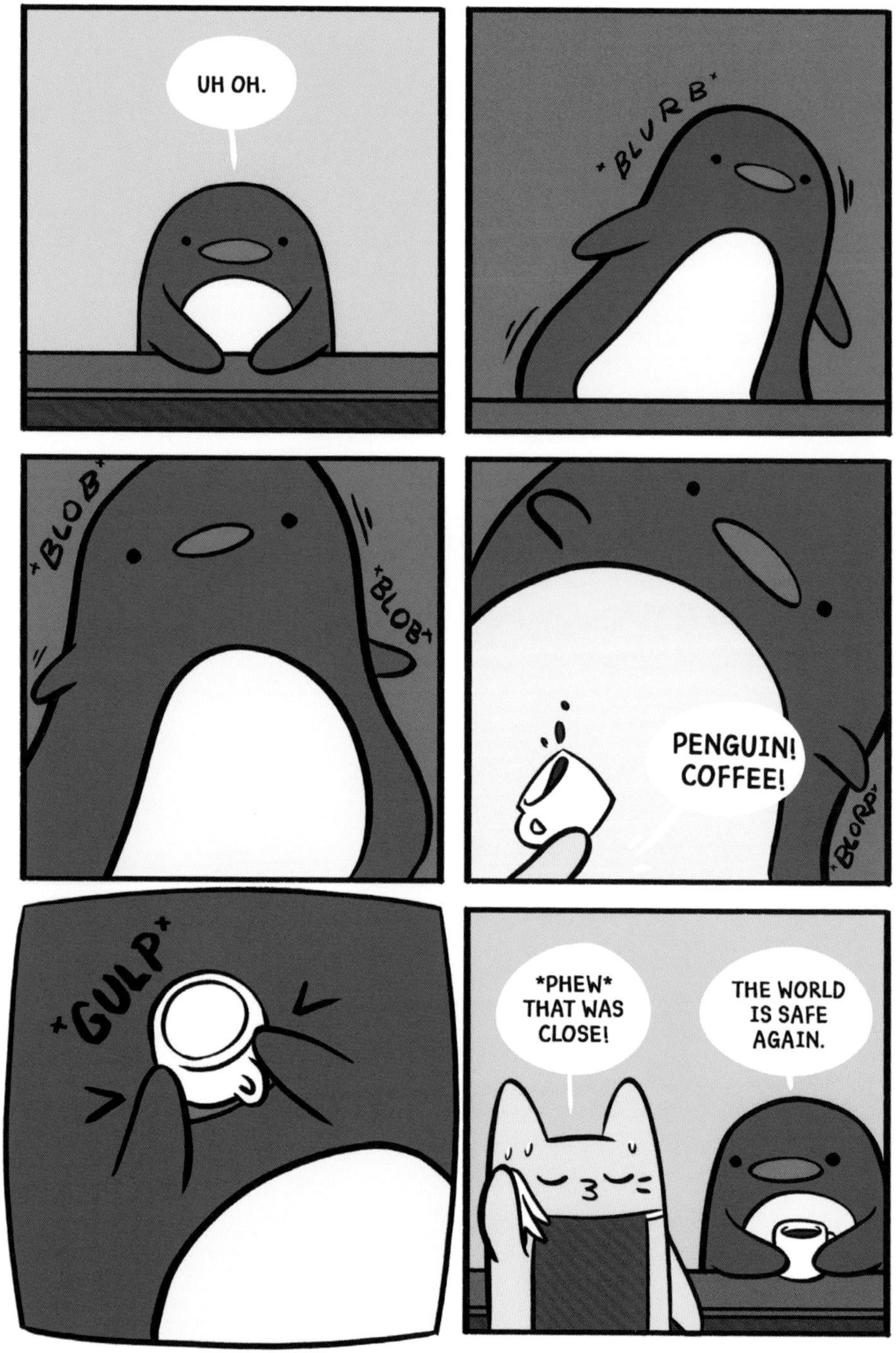
UH OH.
BLURB
BLOB
BLOB
PENGUIN! COFFEE!
BLORP
GULP
PHEW THAT WAS CLOSE!
THE WORLD IS SAFE AGAIN.

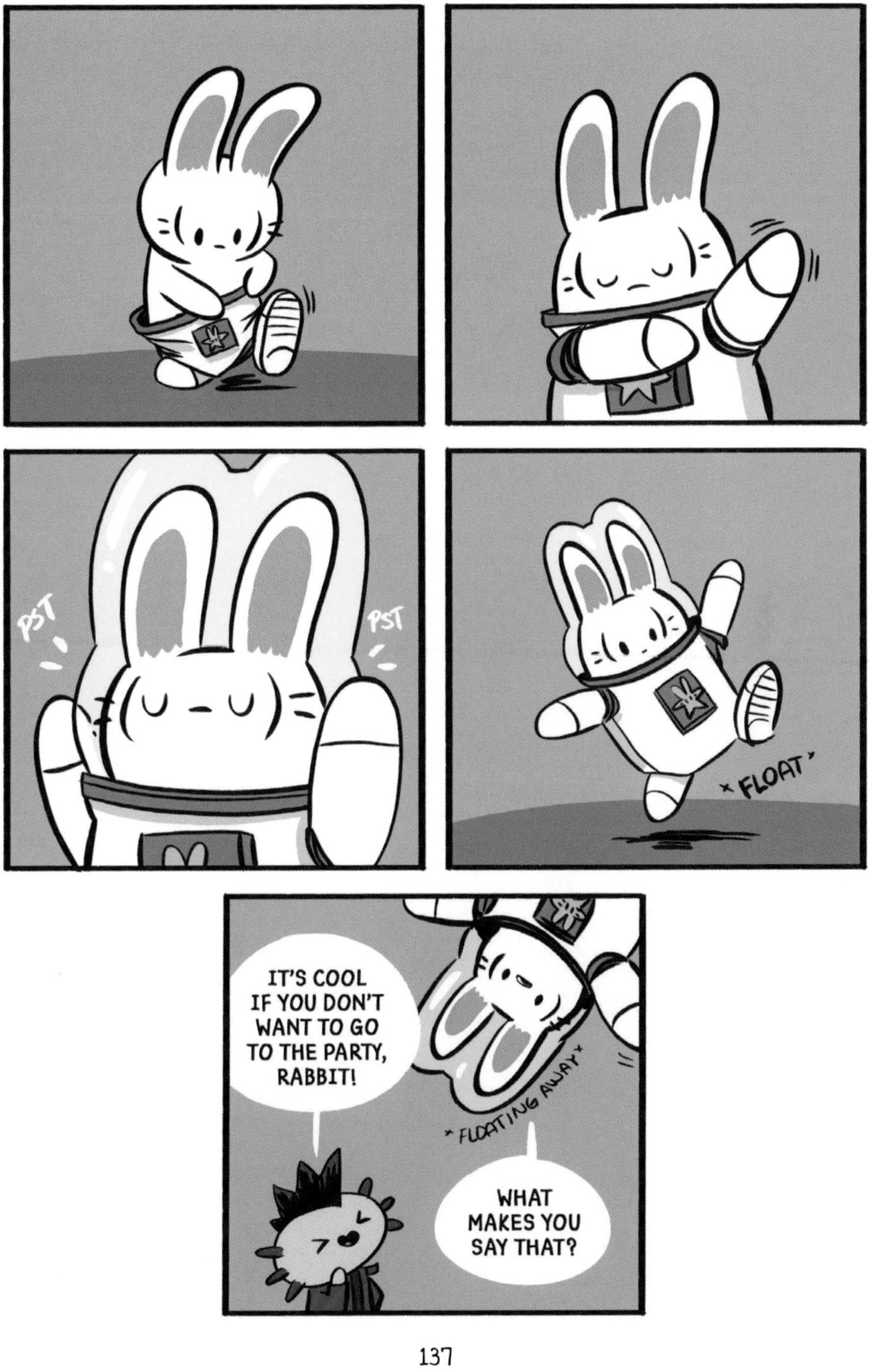
PST
PST
FLOAT
IT'S COOL IF YOU DON'T WANT TO GO TO THE PARTY, RABBIT!
FLOATING AWAY
WHAT MAKES YOU SAY THAT?

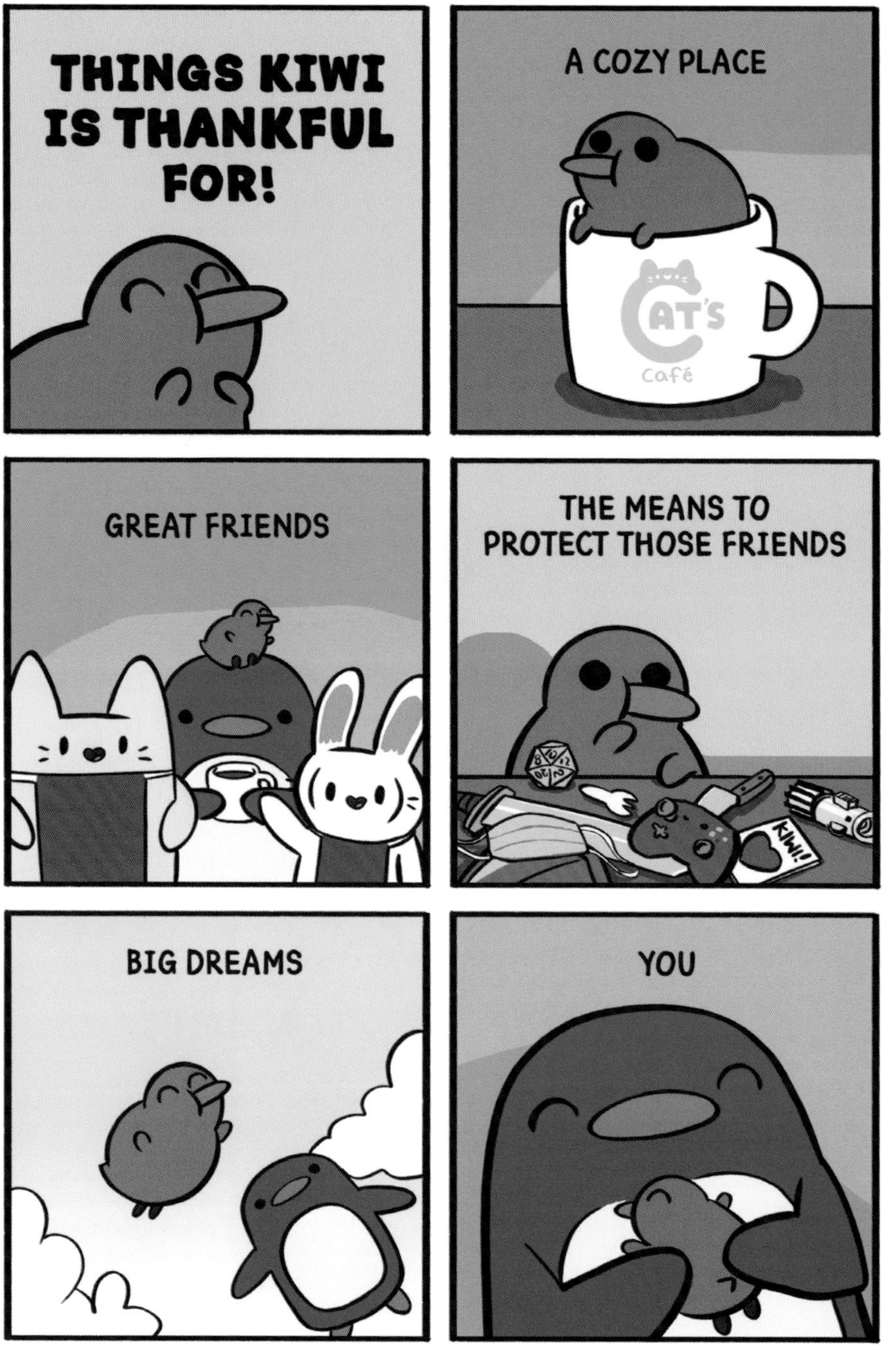
THINGS KIWI IS THANKFUL FOR!
A COZY PLACE
CAT'S
Café
GREAT FRIENDS
THE MEANS TO PROTECT THOSE FRIENDS
KIWI!
BIG DREAMS
YOU

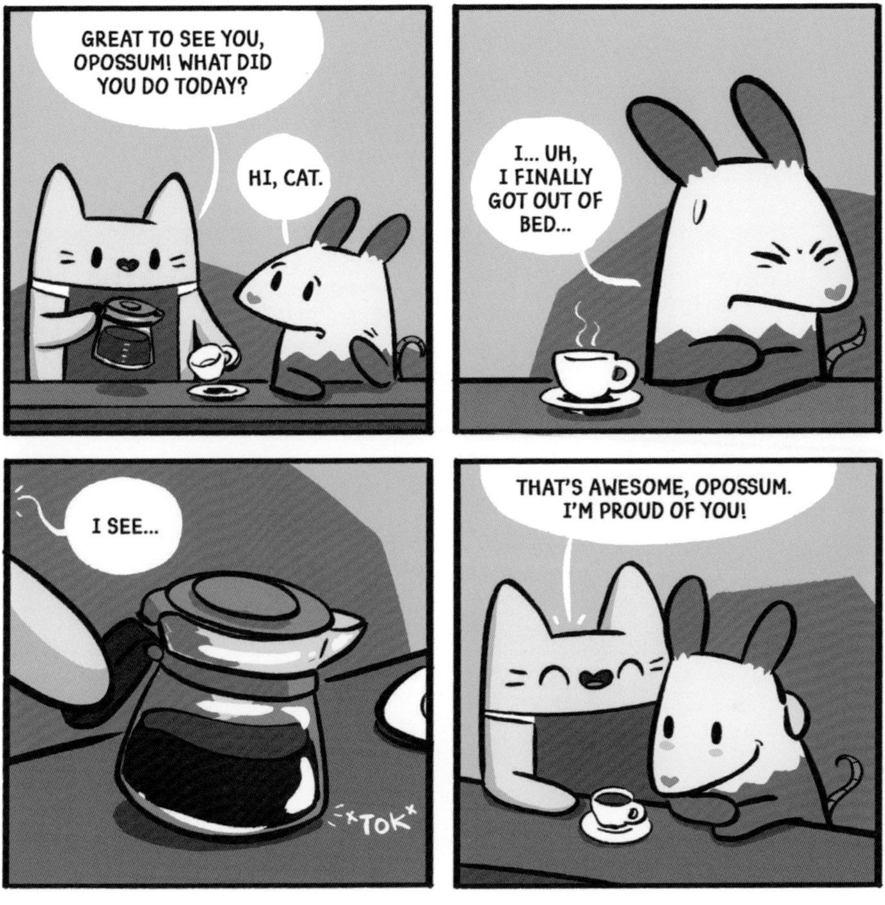
GREAT TO SEE YOU, OPOSSUM! WHAT DID YOU DO TODAY?
HI, CAT.
I... UH, I FINALLY GOT OUT OF BED...
I SEE...
TOK
THAT'S AWESOME, OPOSSUM. I'M PROUD OF YOU!

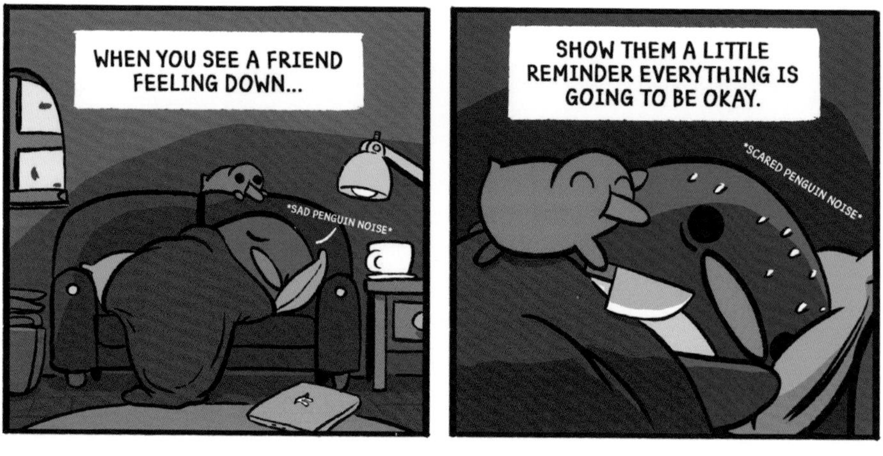
WHEN YOU SEE A FRIEND FEELING DOWN...
SAD PENGUIN NOISE
SHOW THEM A LITTLE REMINDER EVERYTHING IS GOING TO BE OKAY.
SCARED PENGUIN NOISE

HOW TO BLANKET

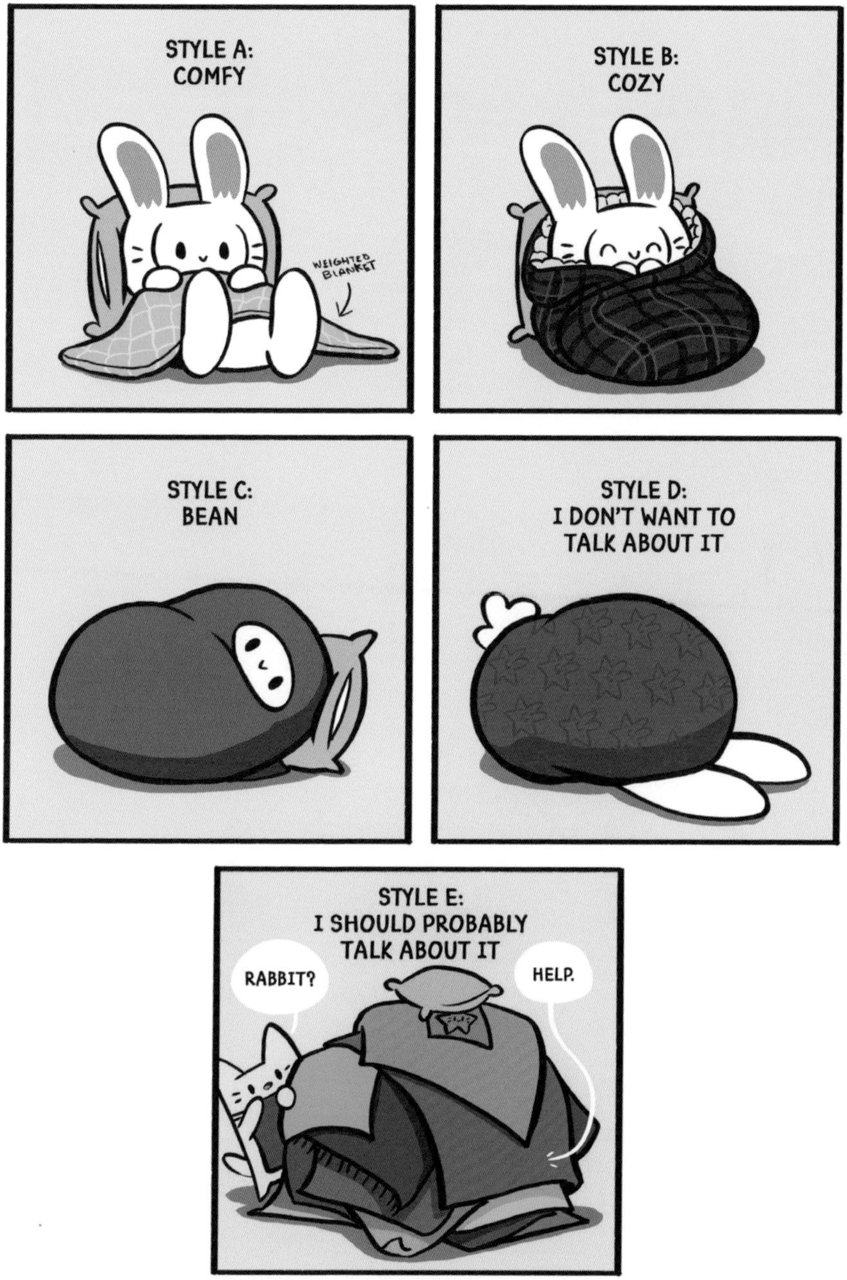
STYLE A:
COMFY
WEIGHTED BLANKET
STYLE B:
COZY
STYLE C:
BEAN
STYLE D:
I DON'T WANT TO
TALK ABOUT IT
STYLE E:
I SHOULD PROBABLY
TALK ABOUT IT
RABBIT?
HELP.

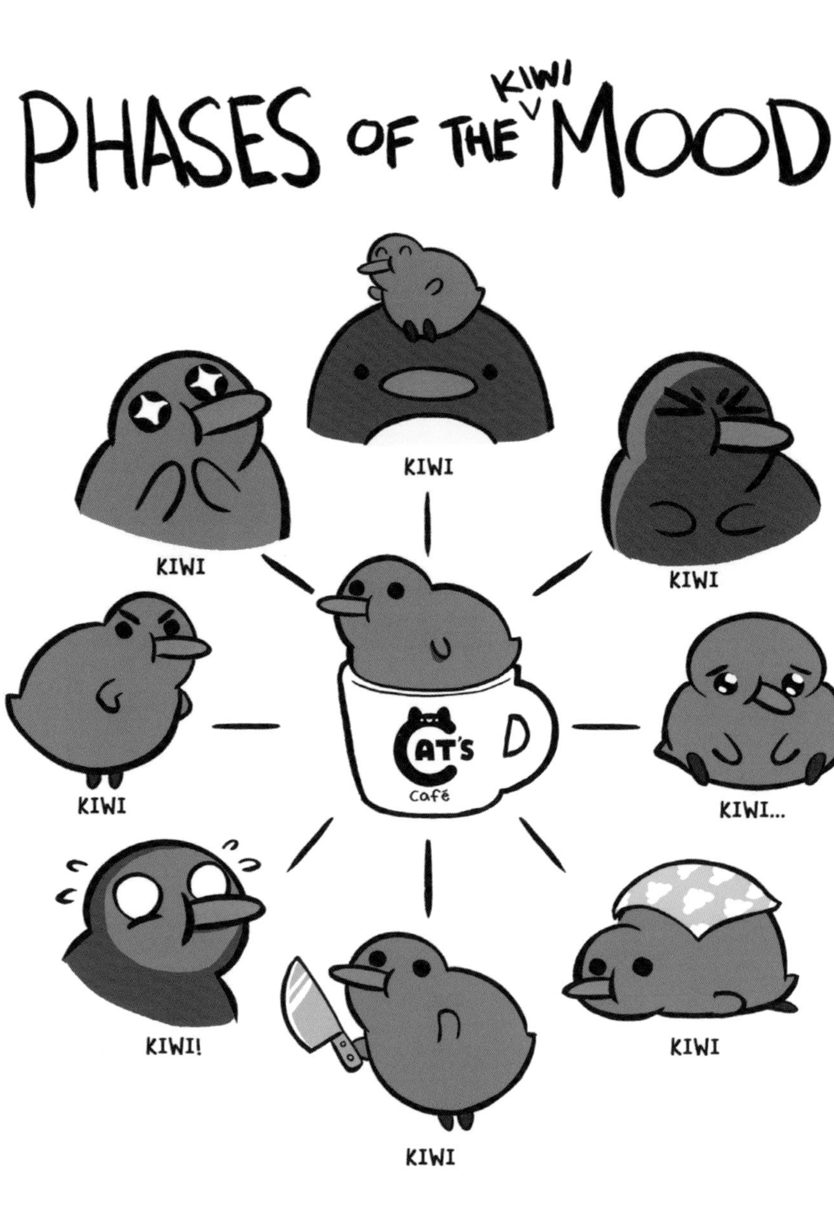
PHASES OF THE KIWI MOOD
KIWI
KIWI
KIWI
KIWI
KIWI...
CAT'S café
KIWI!
KIWI
KIWI

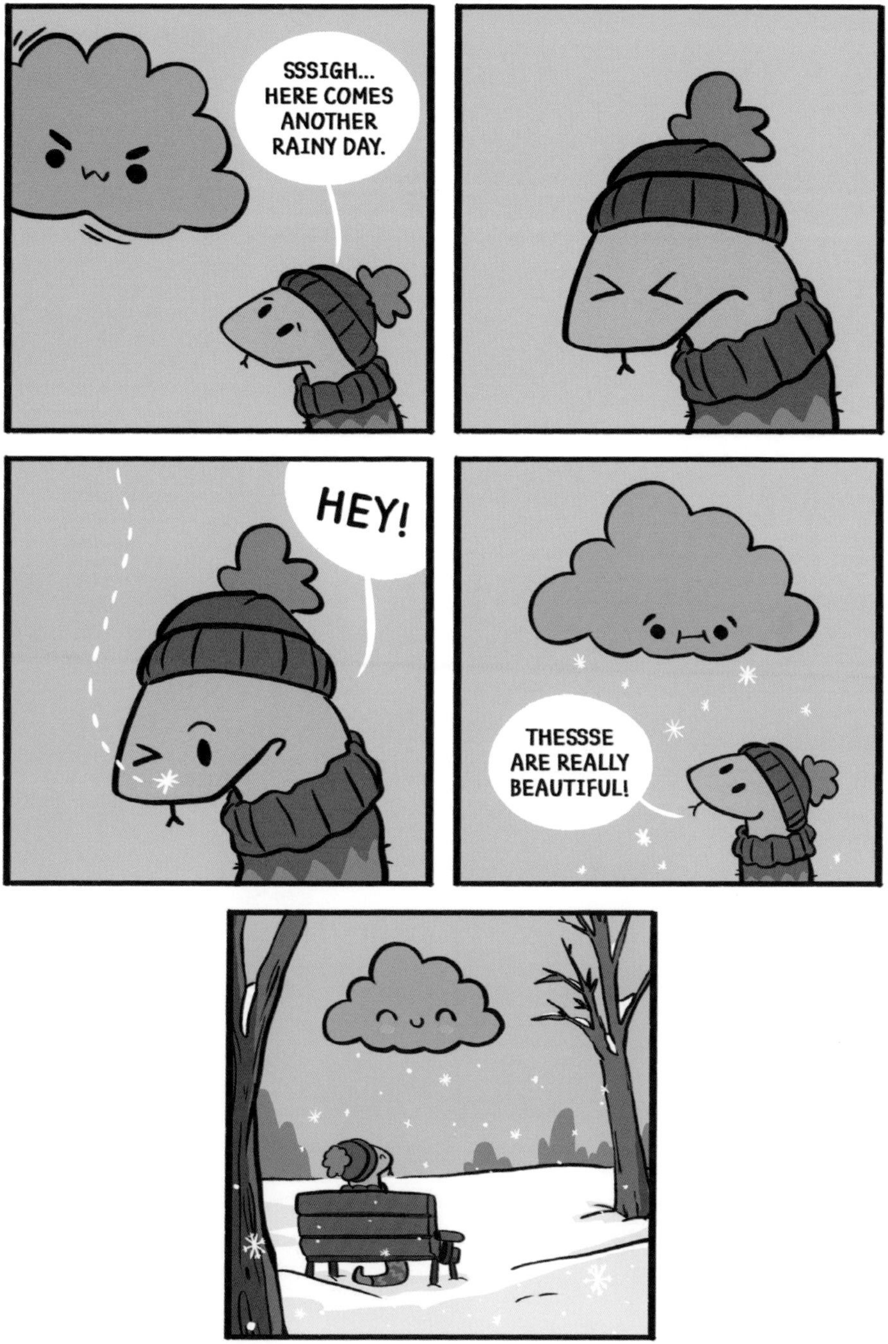
SSSIGH... HERE COMES ANOTHER RAINY DAY.
HEY!
THESSSE ARE REALLY BEAUTIFUL!

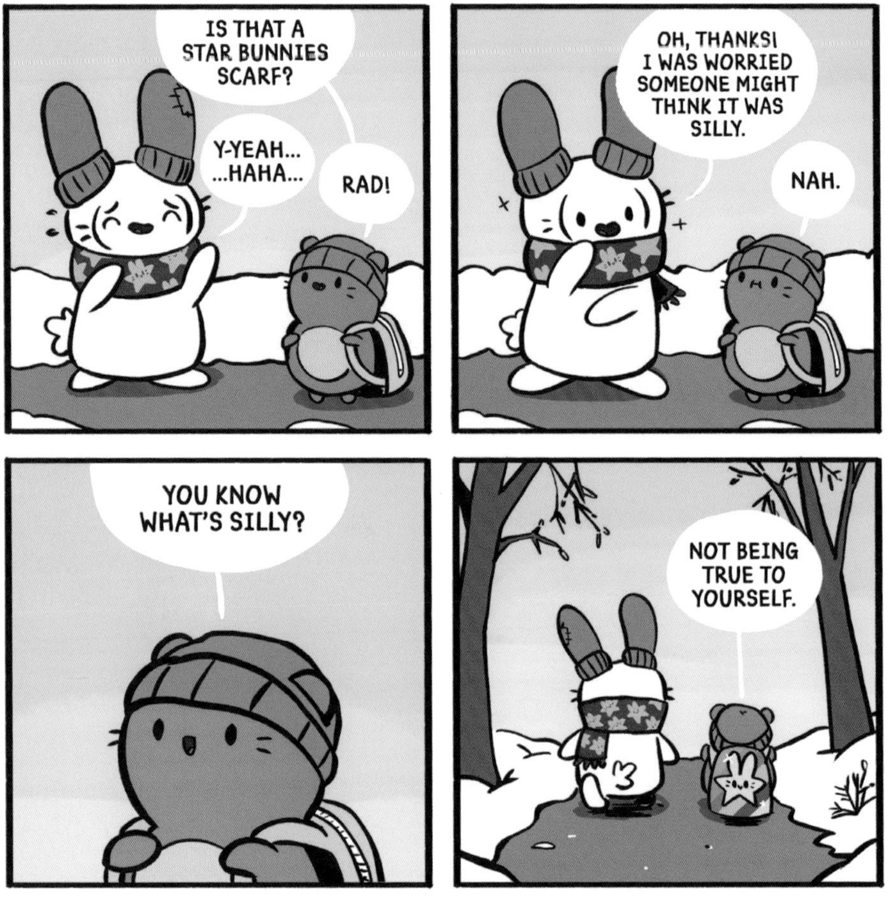
IS THAT A STAR BUNNIES SCARF?
Y-YEAH... ...HAHA...
RAD!
OH, THANKS! I WAS WORRIED SOMEONE MIGHT THINK IT WAS SILLY.
NAH.
YOU KNOW WHAT'S SILLY?
NOT BEING TRUE TO YOURSELF.

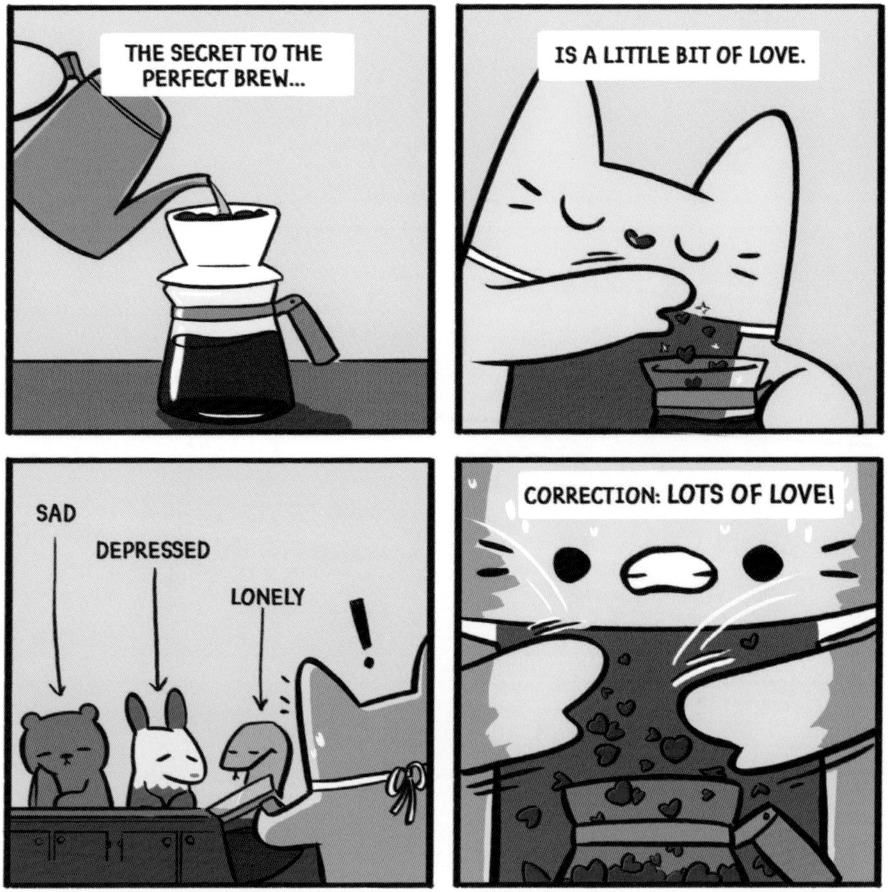
THE SECRET TO THE PERFECT BREW...
IS A LITTLE BIT OF LOVE.
SAD
DEPRESSED
LONELY
!
CORRECTION: LOTS OF LOVE!

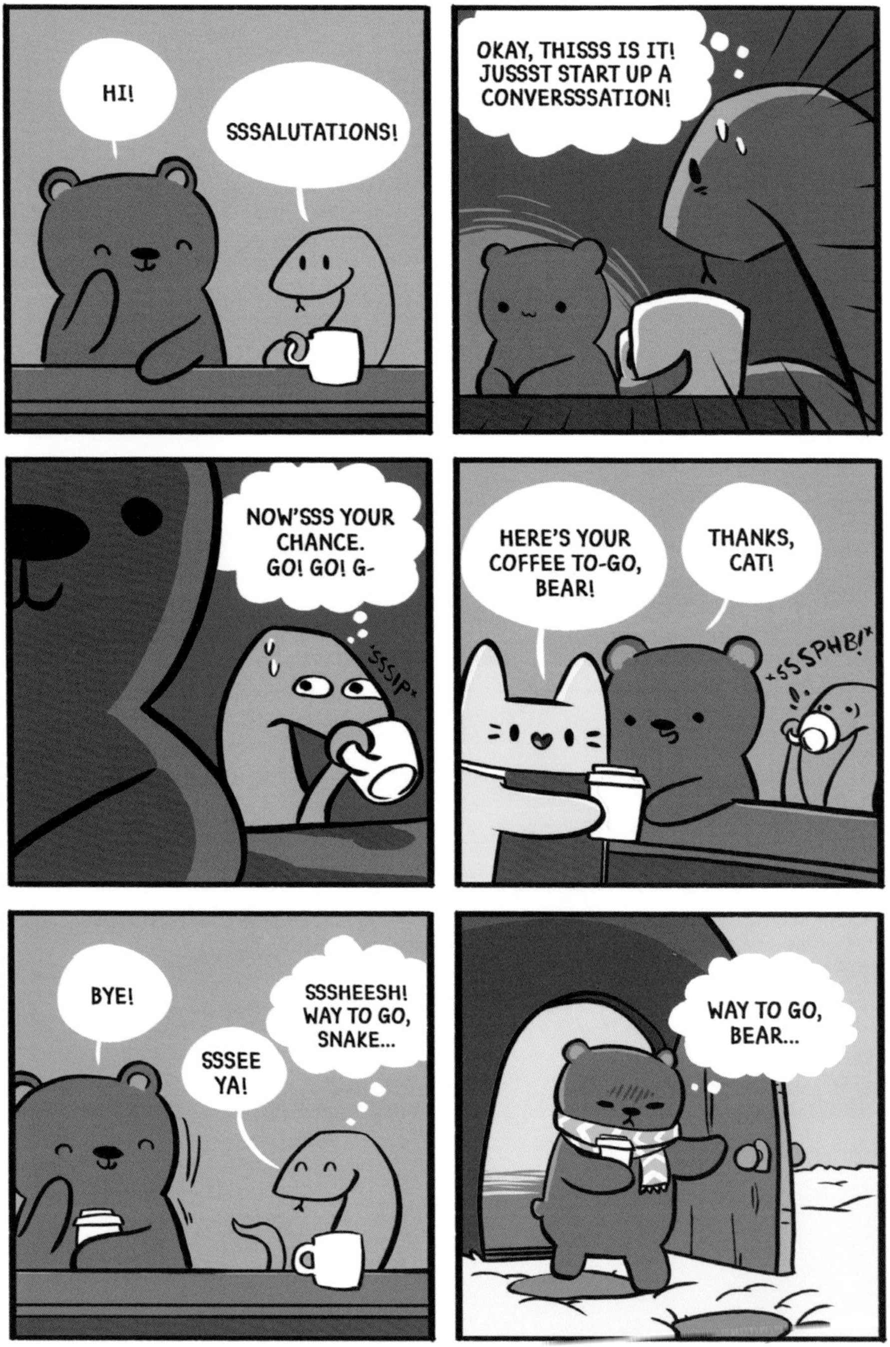
HI!
SSSALUTATIONS!
OKAY, THISSS IS IT! JUSSST START UP A CONVERSSSATION!
NOW'SSS YOUR CHANCE. GO! GO! G-
SSSIP
HERE'S YOUR COFFEE TO-GO, BEAR!
THANKS, CAT!
SSSPHB!
BYE!
SSSEE YA!
SSSHEESH! WAY TO GO, SNAKE...
WAY TO GO, BEAR...

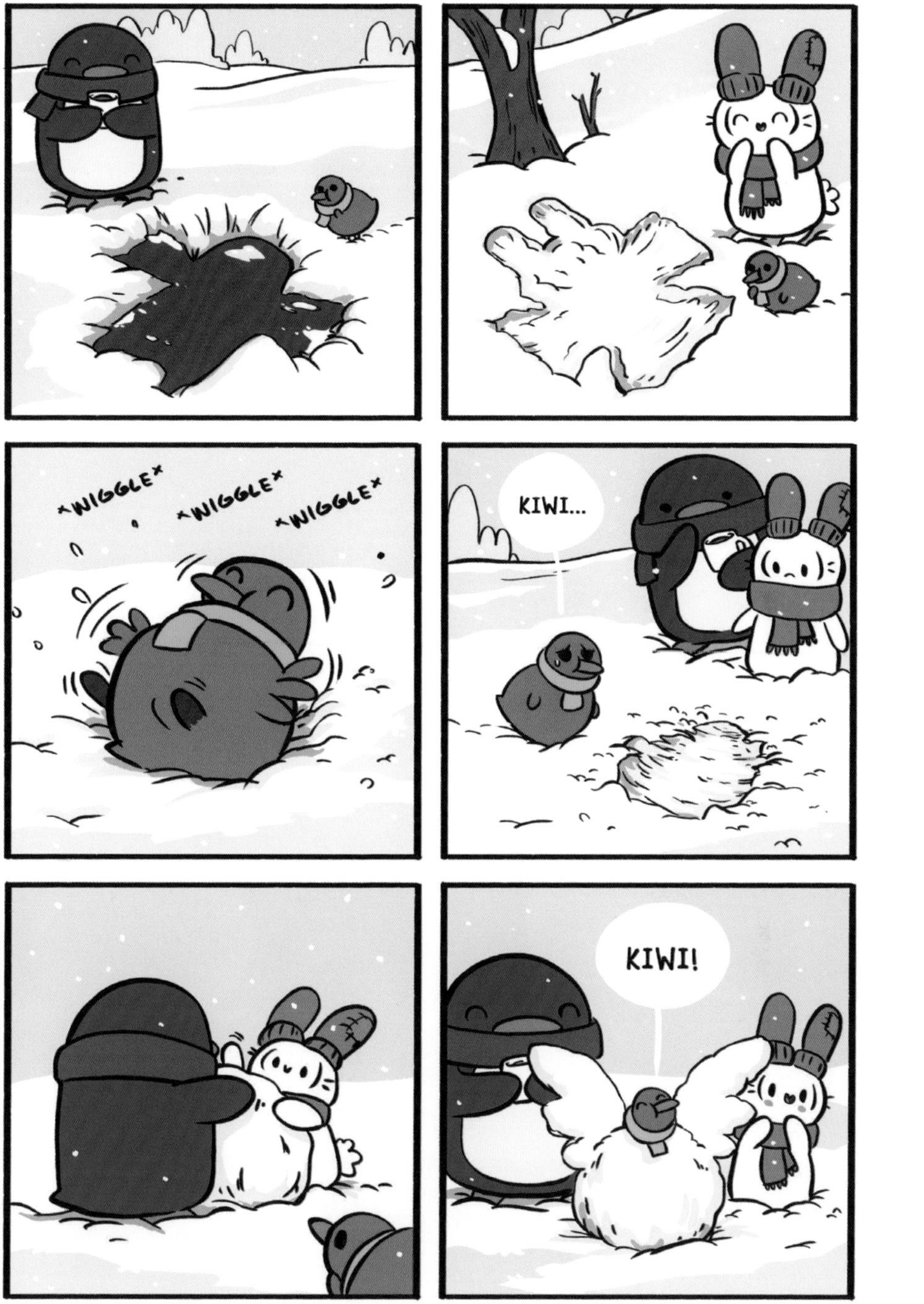
WIGGLE *WIGGLE* *WIGGLE*
KIWI...
KIWI!

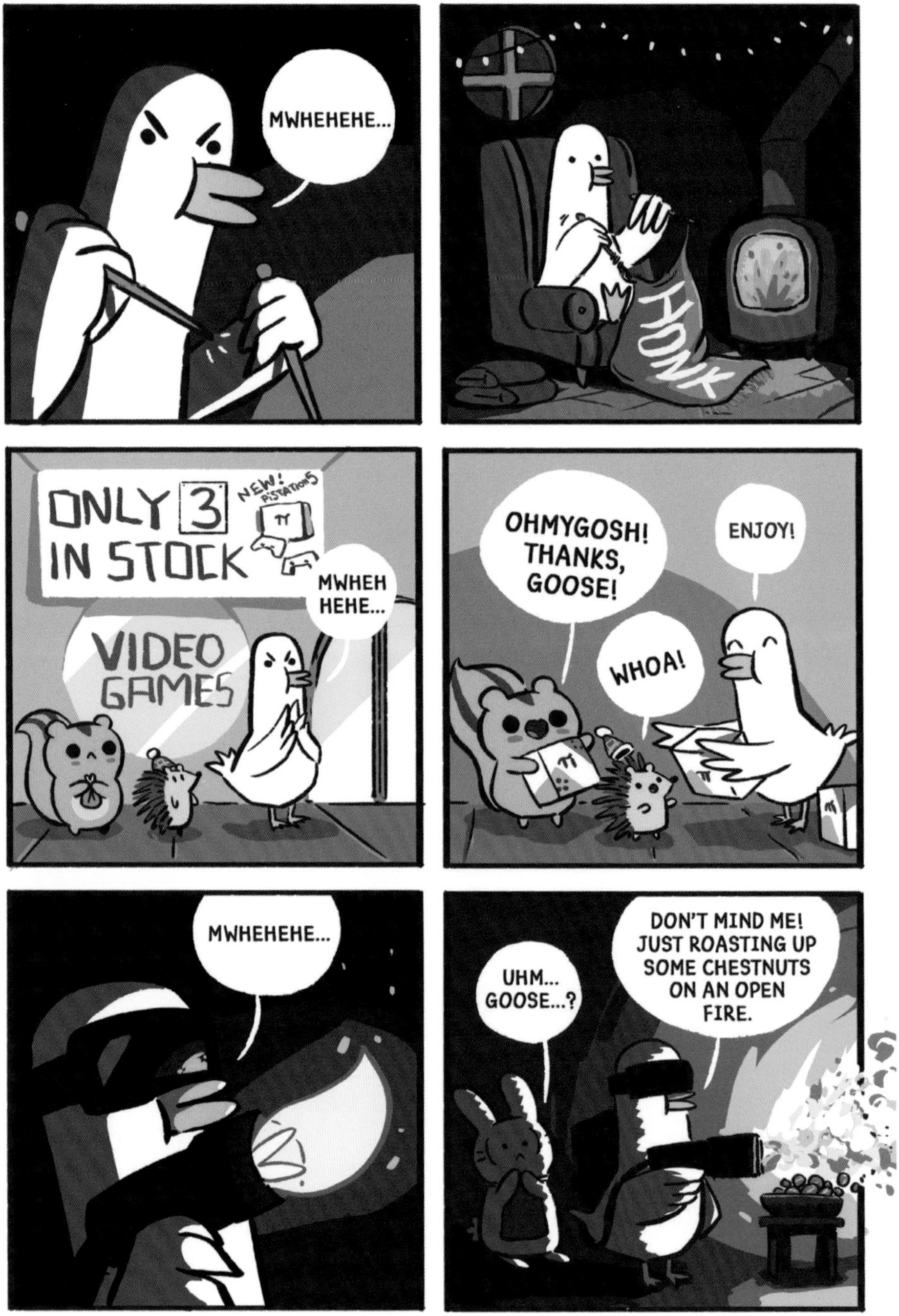
MWHEHEHE...
HONK
ONLY 3 IN STOCK
NEW!
VIDEO GAMES
MWHEH HEHE...
OHMYGOSH! THANKS, GOOSE!
ENJOY!
WHOA!
MWHEHEHE...
UHM... GOOSE...?
DON'T MIND ME! JUST ROASTING UP SOME CHESTNUTS ON AN OPEN FIRE.

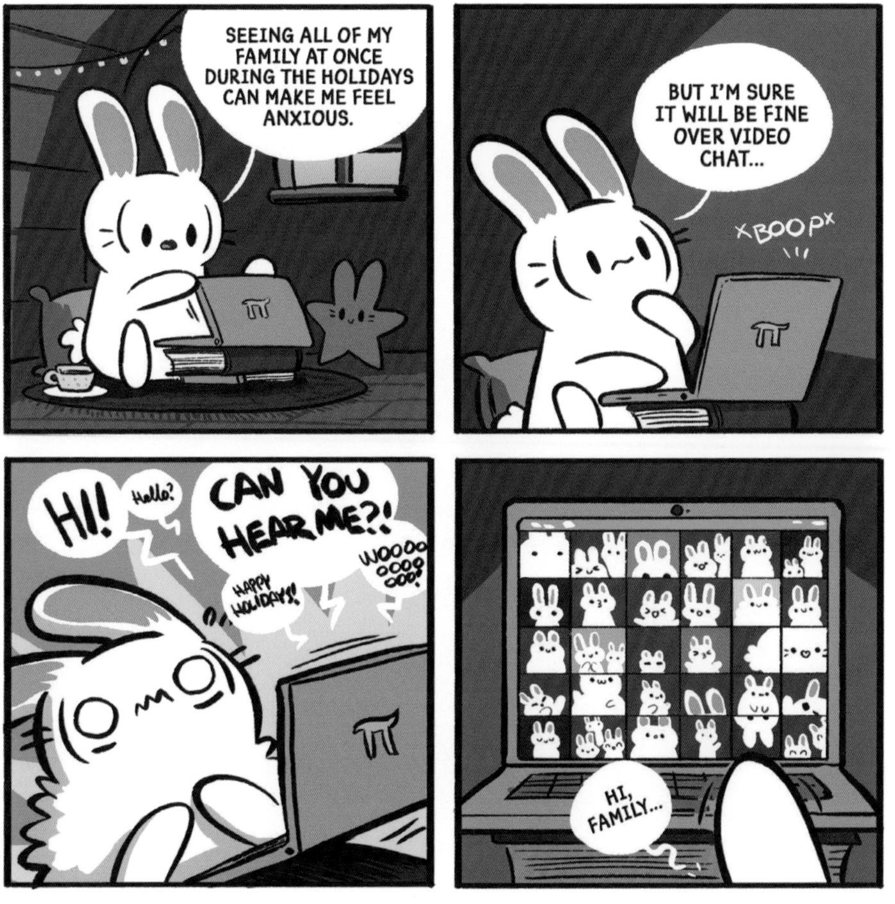
SEEING ALL OF MY FAMILY AT ONCE DURING THE HOLIDAYS CAN MAKE ME FEEL ANXIOUS.
BUT I'M SURE IT WILL BE FINE OVER VIDEO CHAT...
BOOP
HI!
Hello?
CAN YOU HEAR ME?!
HAPPY HOLIDAYS!
WOOOOOOOOOOOO!
HI, FAMILY...

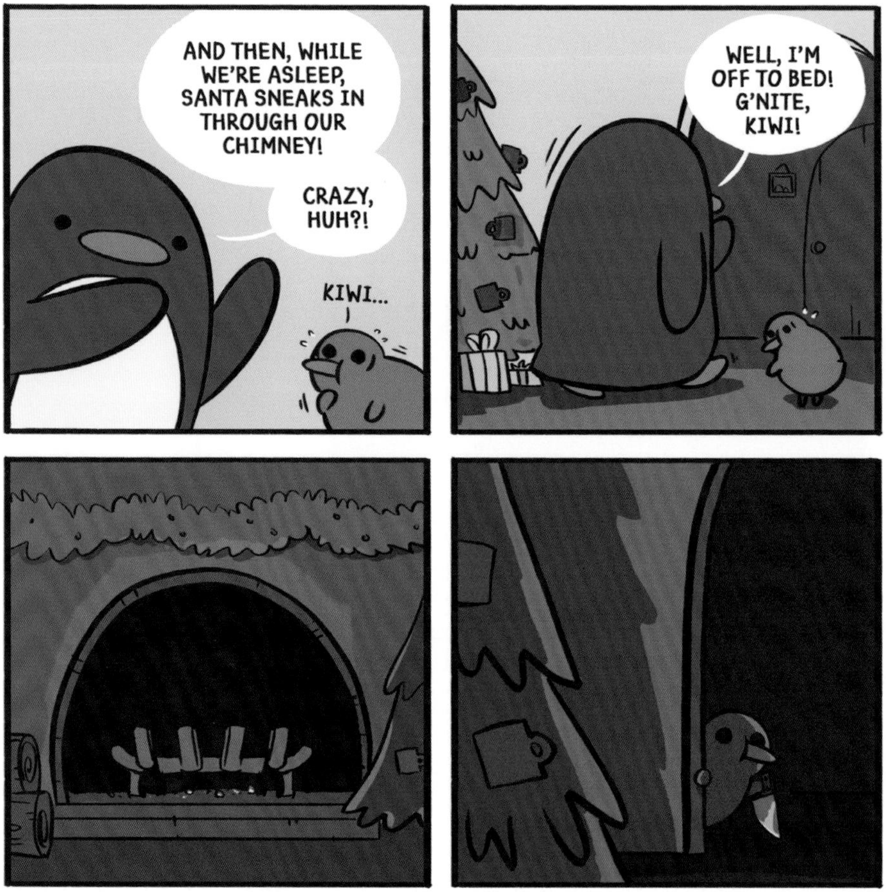
AND THEN, WHILE WE'RE ASLEEP, SANTA SNEAKS IN THROUGH OUR CHIMNEY!
CRAZY, HUH?!
KIWI...
WELL, I'M OFF TO BED! G'NITE, KIWI!

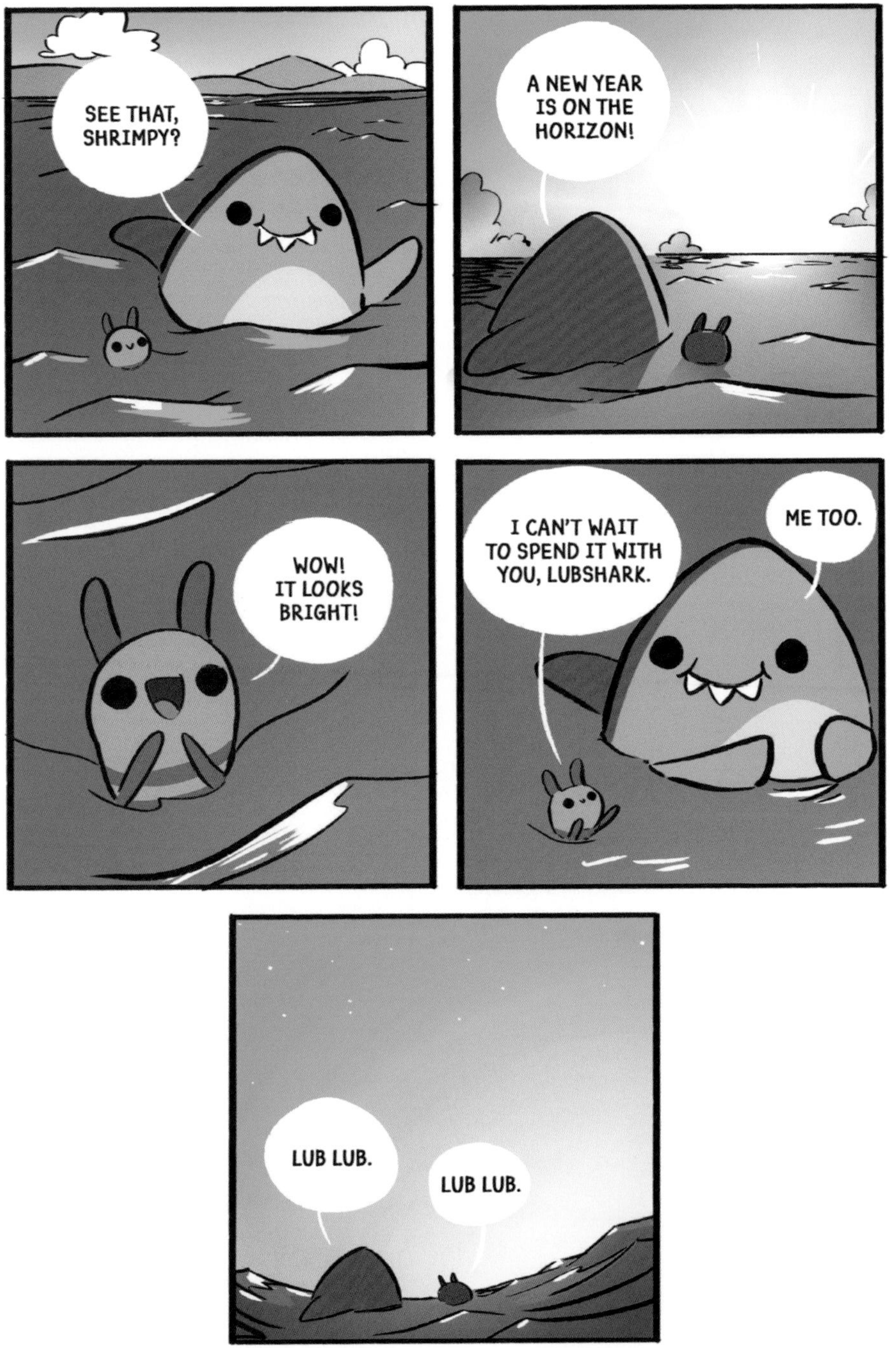
SEE THAT, SHRIMPY?
A NEW YEAR IS ON THE HORIZON!
WOW! IT LOOKS BRIGHT!
I CAN'T WAIT TO SPEND IT WITH YOU, LUBSHARK.
ME TOO.
LUB LUB.
LUB LUB.

THOUGHTS AND FEELINGS

Andrews McMeel Publishing
a division of Andrews McMeel Universal
1130 Walnut Street, Kansas City, Missouri 64106

www.andrewsmcmeel.com

www.catscafecomics.com

22 23 24 25 26 SDB 10 9 8 7 6 5 4 3 2 1

ISBN: 978-1-5248-7218-2

Library of Congress Control Number: 2021951521

Editor: Allison Adler
Art Director: Tiffany Meairs
Production Editor: Elizabeth A. Garcia
Production Manager: Tamara Haus

ATTENTION: SCHOOLS AND BUSINESSES

Andrews McMeel books are available at quantity discounts with bulk purchase for educational, business, or sales promotional use. For information, please e-mail the Andrews McMeel Publishing Special Sales Department: specialsales@amuniversal.com.

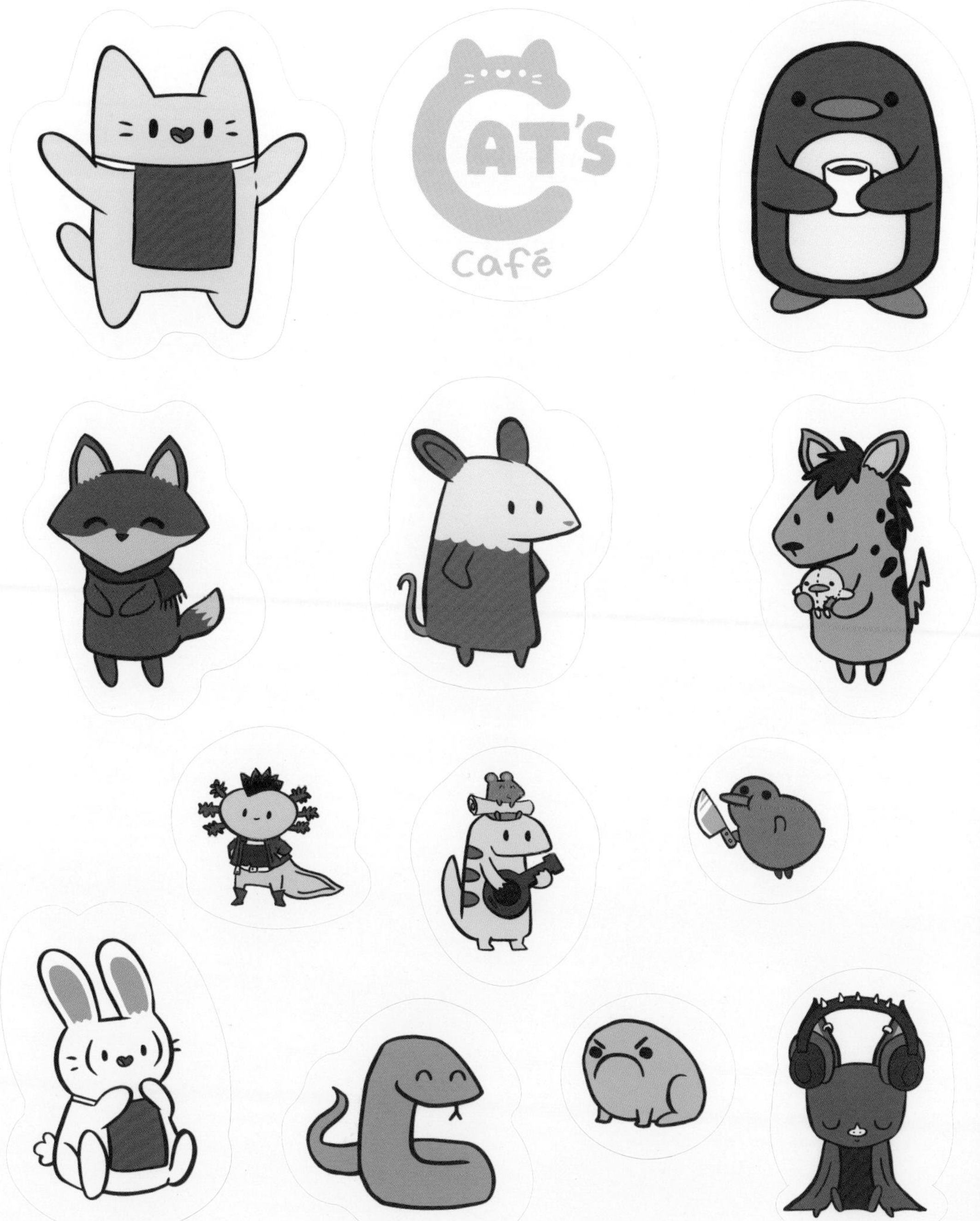
CAT'S
Café

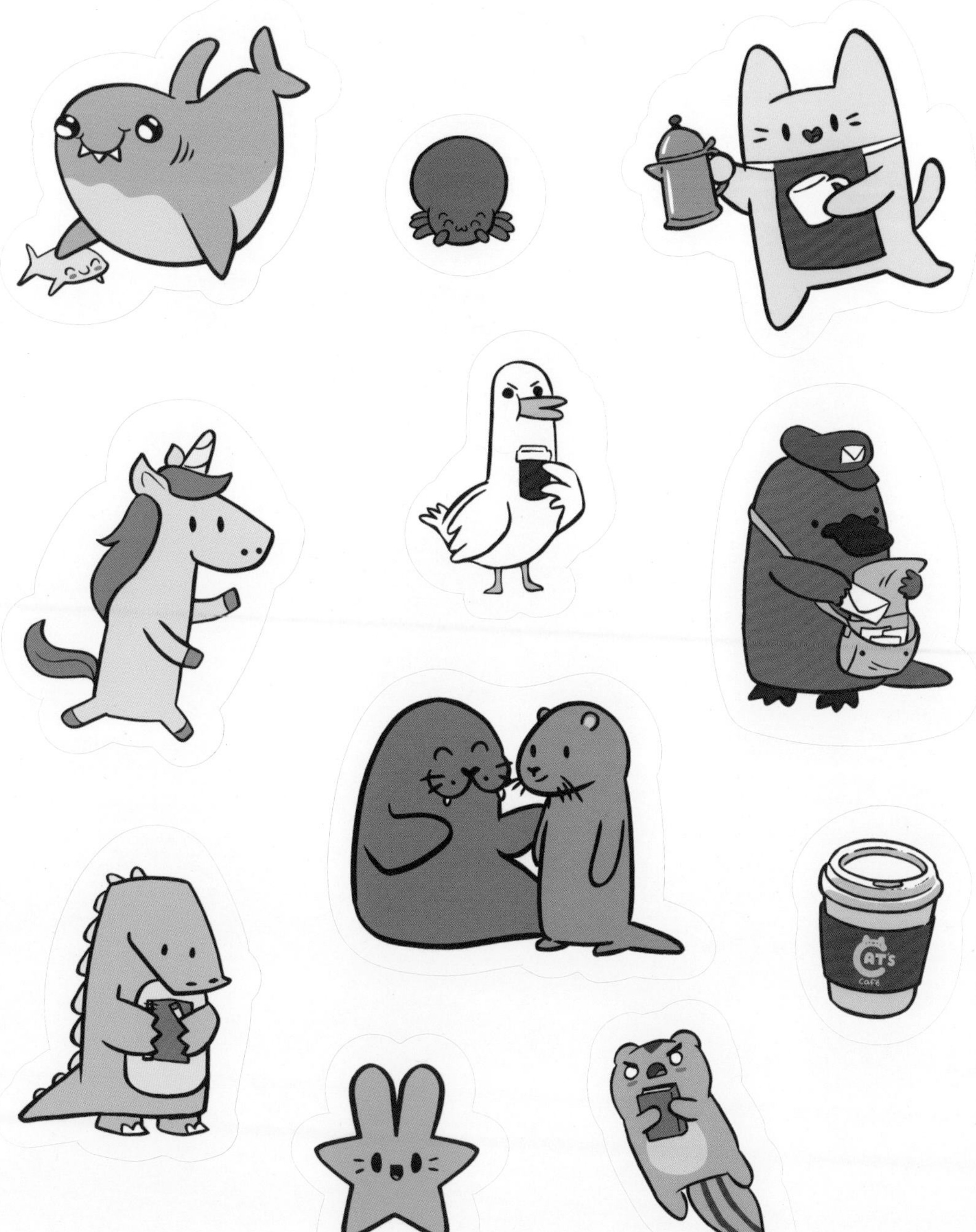
CAT'S
café